SWIFT PRIDE

Alec Merrill

Copyright © 2014 Alec Lindsay Merrill.

www.alecmerrill.com

All rights reserved. No part of this book may be reproduced, stored, or transmitted by any means—whether auditory, graphic, mechanical, or electronic—without written permission of both publisher and author, except in the case of brief excerpts used in critical articles and reviews. Unauthorized reproduction of any part of this work is illegal and is punishable by law.

ISBN: 978-1-4834-2148-3 (sc)
ISBN: 978-1-4834-2147-6 (e)

Because of the dynamic nature of the Internet, any web addresses or links contained in this book may have changed since publication and may no longer be valid. The views expressed in this work are solely those of the author and do not necessarily reflect the views of the publisher, and the publisher hereby disclaims any responsibility for them.

Any people depicted in stock imagery provided by Thinkstock are models, and such images are being used for illustrative purposes only.
Certain stock imagery © Thinkstock.

Lulu Publishing Services rev. date: 11/17/2014

CONTENTS

Chapter 1 1
Chapter 2 7
Chapter 3 13
Chapter 4 19
Chapter 5 23
Chapter 6 31
Chapter 7 37
Chapter 8 41
Chapter 9 47
Chapter 10 55
Chapter 11 69
Chapter 12 79
Chapter 13 83
Chapter 14 89
Chapter 15 93
Chapter 16 101
Chapter 17 109
Chapter 18 113
Chapter 19 119
Chapter 20 123
Chapter 21 129
Chapter 22 139
Chapter 23 145
Chapter 24 149
Chapter 25 155
Chapter 26 163
Chapter 27 169
Chapter 28 175
Chapter 29 187

Chapter 30	191
Chapter 31	197
Chapter 32	203
Chapter 33	211
Chapter 34	217
Chapter 35	229
Chapter 36	235
Chapter 37	241
Chapter 38	245
Chapter 39	251
Chapter 40	257
Chapter 41	267
Chapter 42	273
Chapter 43	279
Chapter 44	285
Chapter 45	289
Chapter 46	297
Chapter 47	301
Chapter 48	311
Chapter 49	321
Chapter 50	331
Chapter 51	335
Chapter 52	341
Chapter 53	345
Chapter 54	353
Chapter 55	359
Chapter 56	367
Author's Notes	375
About the Author	383

CHAPTER 1

CRACK!
He was unsure which registered first, the sound from the crack of the starter, or the stinging sensation felt in his buttocks.

It was the changing of the watch. Lieutenant Rylett, the third lieutenant and incoming officer of the watch, disliked the sail configuration. This was a common occurrence with Rylett. A course or topsail was not drawing properly unless it was set to Rylett's exacting standard. It mattered not whether the men on watch were inconvenienced, or whether the outgoing officer of the watch viewed the current sail configuration as satisfactory. It didn't matter that most adjustment could be completed from the deck. It didn't even matter if the outgoing officer of the watch was senior to Rylett. As officer of the watch, Rylett would have his way. Despite the fact that no one else could find any fault with the set of the sails, Rylett shouted, "Call the watch, topmen aloft". The watch responded accordingly. That response was not fast enough for Rylett, who expected men to launch into action at this command. To spur on the watch, Rylett ordered the bosun's mates to use starters.

Jon Swift, an able seaman and the senior rating for the mizzen, collected the mizzen team and headed to the ratlines. As the last man, he was already across the deck reaching for the ratlines on the larboard side when the starter struck. As a reflex action, the right hand immediately dropped and covered the source of pain, the right buttock. Consequently, he nearly missed grabbing the ratlines and barely avoided falling overboard.

Jon swung outboard over frothy water, controlling the swing with a massive effort of arm and shoulder muscles. As both feet and the other hand contacted the ratlines, he regained physical control of his movement. Mentally, it was more difficult. Despite knowing it might be a mistake, Jon looked through narrowed eyes at the man who had 'started' him -- Mr. Pearson, the bosun's mate. There was no mercy in the man's face -- just a hard, dispassionate return stare. Although neither of them said a word, anyone who saw their faces would have said the communication between the two men was clear and decidedly hostile.

After reaching his post in the tops, Jon cursed himself for letting Rylett and Pearson get to him. Just pausing and staring at 'Prick' Pearson could be grounds for insubordination should the bosun's mate make anything of it. The result would be a striped back, but that wasn't the half of it.

He was caught between a rock and a hard place and knew it. If Pearson decided to make an issue out of this, or Rylett coerced Pearson, and that wouldn't take much, all the efforts expended to keep the position as senior rating on the mizzen would be forfeited. Since being pressed, Jon was proud of the hard work completed to improve and elevate himself above a landsman. As the senior rating for the mizzenmast, he was responsible for all men working the mizzen. He received no extra pay, or any other benefit; yet was expected to train and lead these men up in the tops in any conditions. Everyone knew the most dangerous work on board one of His Majesty's warships was in the tops. In the months he'd been on this ship, he'd never seen a commissioned officer, or any petty officer for that matter, in the tops.

The rash of deaths from yellow jack over the previous few months had decimated the midshipmen and topman ranks alike. There were only two midshipmen left on board. Mr. Elkhorne, who had far more experience, was the acting signals officer. The other, Mr. Farley, was the captain of the tops and Jon's direct superior, but in reality so young and inexperienced, he barely knew what was happening. That left the real load on the shoulders of the senior ratings of each mast. Using a starter on one of them was a breach of lower deck unwritten rules.

A reckoning was coming.

The mizzen topmen were silent and appeared oblivious to the events below. They were waiting for orders to fix a non-existent problem.

Dangling one hundred feet over the deck, Jon wondered for the hundredth time why in hell he was even there. There was no real reason any topmen had to be up in the tops at this time. Any adjustment to the trim of the sails could easily be done from the deck. It was just the dammed officer of the watch, Lieutenant Rylett, exerting his authority. He always had to rub in his superiority.

Jon shuffled out along the yardarm, maintaining a neutral face to mask a seething bitterness. He occasionally rubbed his buttocks with his one free hand to ease the stinging.

"It looks like someone has a sore arse, or maybe something didn't come out right when he was on the jakes," said Mannion jokingly.

"You'd have a sore arse if you had a bruise the size of a fist on it," replied Hale.

"That'll be enough of that. The next time someone opens his mouth, there'd better be a good reason, or you'll regret it," growled Jon.

No one on the yardarm dared say another word, but that didn't stop the snide looks and smirks. It didn't matter whether the men liked it or not, Jon could not afford the risk another run in with Rylett, especially for something as trivial as speaking in the tops.

Jon made an effort to stop rubbing his sore ass.

There was no point taking it out on the men. They weren't responsible, but in a way, they were. If they had hurried to the ratlines, none of this might have happened. None of the men, Jon included, could see any reason why they had to rush aloft. If there was any need to hurry, all Jon had to do was shout. Looking at it from that perspective, it was Jon's fault. Just the same, even with the rush, Rylett hadn't issued any orders yet.

Jon should have seen trouble coming. He knew Lieutenant Rylett was the officer of the watch when the head count occurred, and that bastard had it in for him.

What could anyone do about it? Complaints were about as popular on this ship as rats; about as numerous, and had about the same likelihood of being resolved as eradicating all the rats on the ship. Just at the moment, however, Jon would settle for getting rid of a few rats off the quarterdeck and one rat in particular. Jon vowed not to let Rylett get to him.

Looking to his left, Jon regarded the other men working on the yardarm. Bare feet gripped the rough hemp ropes of the horse, providing some measure of balance, but limited security. The upper chest rested against the yardarm with one arm gripping the sail canvas over the top of the yardarm, and the other hand under the yardarm. This was his world, where one moment's neglect would put more than a crimp in your day -- it would probably result in an abrupt halt to it.

Up the mast, three things ruled -- the sea, the wind, and the dammed officers -- in that order. Each of them was potentially lethal. The sea always caused the masts to sway, sometimes dramatically, making balance critical at all times. Spray could coat the rigging making it slick; or frozen in the northern latitudes. The wind continuously plucked at a man, the sails and the rigging. Wind-chill could freeze hands and feet so much that it was difficult to grip the ropes or sail. All of this he could live with; they were just the normal hazards of the job. It was the dammed officers that you had to watch.

The dammed officers would order you aloft in the worst weather or at night just to adjust a sail that didn't need adjusting. Most of the time it was just to prove they had the power to do so or that they were better at watch duties than the officer they relieved. If their actions caused problems, loss or injury of a man, then they would conveniently dump all the blame on the senior rating for the respective mast.

Jon focused on Beck, the man next to him, and examined his actions carefully. Six months ago, Beck had fallen from the yardarm. They had been learning how to strike the royals on the mainmast, when Lieutenant

Rylett ordered them to hurry up. Rylett was hungry, hung-over, in a vile mood and wished to get below out of the hot sun. Rushing to comply with the order, Beck had failed to maintain a grip. Jon could still vividly remember Beck slowly starting to slide. He had screamed a warning, but it was too late. Beck's slide accelerated into a fall. He dropped a few feet and hammered backwards into the topgallant yard, breaking a few ribs in the process. He was lucky. By hitting and bouncing off the topgallant yard, he was redirected over the side and dropped into the water feet first. Without that re-direction, he would have splattered over the deck. When he hit the water, he broke both of his legs. Again, he was lucky. If he had hit at any other angle, he probably would have had all the air knocked out of his lungs and kept going straight down to the bottom. As it was, there was enough air still in his body to keep him afloat, because Beck couldn't swim.

Despite those injuries, Jon considered Beck luckier than he was. After six months, Beck was back working in the tops and was rapidly approaching the same level of dexterity he had prior to the accident. Jon, on the other hand, had still not fully recovered. Even though Lieutenant Rylett had been detailed as the safety officer for the training, and Midshipman Farley the direct supervisor, all the blame had been dumped on Jon. Facing possible punishment at the inquiry, Jon had stood his ground, thereby incurring the wrath of Lieutenant Rylett. Rylett, as safety officer had been seen as ineffective. A deficiency in his abilities had been exposed, and that was something Rylett couldn't bear. Although Jon was unaware of any repercussions against Rylett, it was enough to set Rylett off. Jon was still paying a price at every opportunity Lieutenant Rylett could find. On top of that, any trust he had with any of the men in the mess had instantly vanished, and it still hadn't fully returned.

Jon generally took position at the extreme end of the yardarm. When initially trained as a topman, it was explained that a good leader never asked another man to do any job he was not prepared to do himself. In other words, you have to be prepared to do the risky jobs before sending someone else to do them. Like a fool, he bought into this hogwash, and now was paying the penalty for it, rather than being safer near the mast, or even better on deck. He sure as hell never saw any commissioned officer do a dirty job before ordering a man to do it.

Directly below him was the side of the ship and water. If he slipped or fell for any reason, he hoped that at least he would clear the side of the ship. Hitting the water from this height was bad enough, but at least the water had more give than the side of the ship. During previous engagements, he had seen small cannon balls bounce off those thick oaken hull walls. If he hit the bulwark or deck, they would probably have to use a shovel to scrape him up and throw the remains overboard. He could just imagine the curses from the poor bastards that would have to holystone the residue, but then he would probably be laughing about it from up on high.

Shuffling further over, he rigorously applied the tried and true maxim 'one hand for His Majesty and one hand for yourself.' This had been repeatedly hammered into his skull during training, and he had just as stringently emphasized it to his team members. After Beck's fall, no one needed to be reminded.

He shook his head, trying to focus on the present and not dwell on the past and things that he couldn't change. It was easier said than done. He had just returned to the ship after a couple of weeks of shore duty with the army where he had been treated with respect by those army officers with whom he had dealt. He had a greater degree of freedom with them than he had ever had in His Majesty's navy. He had never been struck once, and his body had managed to recover from the mass of bruises he always seemed to carry since running afoul of Rylett.

Now that same torment was commencing again if the 'starting' this morning was any indication.

CHAPTER 2

Trying to avoid Lieutenant Rylett's attentions wasn't Jon's only concern, but it bothered him the most day to day.

In any topman's world, there was the ever-present danger of falling. Each time the bow of HMS Mermaid lifted as she crested a swell, the effect one hundred feet higher was more pronounced. The mizzenmast moved rearward of perpendicular a few feet. As the Mermaid shifted position and slid slowly down the reverse side of the wave, the mast was propelled forward of perpendicular a few feet. Depending on the wind a slight lateral motion might also be present. If the ship was rolling, that lateral motion would increase. Luckily today, there was no lateral motion. To an untrained man, the motion was nauseating. To a trained topman, in a gentle sea such as they were sailing at the present, it was like a gentle lullaby. In a storm, it was a terrifying, dangerous place.

That was a topman's lot on any ship. HMS Mermaid, however, wasn't just any ship. She was a naval ship o' the line -- a forty-gun warship. She wasn't as big as the newer ships that mounted fifty and sixty-four guns, but if need be, she was expected to slug it out with ships of that size.

HMS Mermaid was currently positioned to guard the invasion fleet anchored in Gabarus Bay. She also had a secondary responsibility; to engage any Frenchmen whenever and wherever possible. That's because England and France were at war and had been for the past couple of years.

Some called it King George's war, but the name really didn't matter, so long as it lasted, no one on this ship was going home.

Home was something dear to Jon, but as time passed since being pressed, the allure of returning home decreased. Just the same, family meant everything.

The Mermaid had left the expedition fleet anchorage two days before to patrol off the coast of Ile Royale near the entrance to the Gulf of St. Lawrence. The patrol was routine. They had been patrolling at different stations off Ile Royale since April when the invasion fleet arrived to end the French rule at Louisbourg. Jon, as well as the majority of the Mermaid crew, had found the blockade duties boring.

The Mermaid's size had been her undoing. She was one of the larger warships within the British and colonial invasion fleet. In case a French line-of-battle ship appeared, the Mermaid would fight, as the smaller sloops could not be expected to survive an engagement with such large enemy warships. The Mermaid, therefore, maintained a constant state of readiness.

The constant tacking back and forth on the various stations was no different than what the 'lobster-backs' did in front of the gates to a fort. The only excitement for the Mermaid's crew occurred when they investigated a strange sail on the outer station. Those sails had belonged to the French sixty-four gun Le Vigilante en-route to reinforce Louisbourg.

Slogging it out with the Vigilante would have been akin to a five foot five, twelve stone lightweight boxing against a six foot, eighteen stone bruiser. The Vigilante had larger guns and more of them. Her broadside could fire nearly double the weight of the Mermaid. The previous captain, Captain Douglas, had turned in front of the Vigilante. Using the Mermaid as a target, he had drawn the Vigilante back to the main fleet, where British weight of numbers would overwhelm the Frenchman.

Throughout the withdrawal, Jon had a prime seat. He had been standing on the topsail yard when the first ball had whipped past. He was so surprised that it took several more balls for him to realize the danger he was in. He had foolishly considered hiding behind the mast. That idea was abandoned when he realized there would be more danger from wood splinters than just the ball. All of this had lasted mere minutes. After that, he was too busy making repairs to severed ropes to notice the balls passing.

When they broke through a fog bank in front of the main fleet, the Vigilante realized her predicament. She turned tail and ran. That's when the real excitement started.

The Mermaid closed and let loose a broadside. After a lengthy chase, the Mermaid was able to get in two additional broadsides before finally boarding her. It had been Jon's first ship to ship engagement and he remembered every second of it. He still had the scars from being wounded during the boarding to prove he'd been there.

As for the rest of the time on blockade, Jon was just bored, when he wasn't incurring the wrath of Rylett in one form or another. The feeling of boredom was hard to break. The food was monotonous, and the water got progressively worse the longer they were at sea. Combine that with poor pay received months in arrears, close-quarters, and harsh discipline, it wasn't surprising that a main topic of conversation was desertion, or running, as the men called it.

This early July morning they were steering back towards land. No one forward of the mast was ever told where they were heading, but all they had to do was look at the sky. The sun was in the east and on the aft larboard quarter. They were currently heading south on a starboard tack as the winds were from the west.

Although the mizzenmast was at the aft of the ship, with both the main and foremast obscuring any forward view, the entrance to the bay and harbour at Louisbourg was clearly visible on their starboard side. The Mermaid had maintained this heading so many times while on blockade duties during the recent siege, that everyone had lost count.

The distance between the harbour entrance and the Mermaid's current position was hard to estimate. It was obvious they were closing -- well within range of the French guns located on Battery Island. Jon said a silent prayer of thanks that those guns were no longer hostile since Louisbourg had capitulated on June 26th. He would gladly forgo the experience of having metal orbs from those French guns flying all around him.

"Furl the topgallants," ordered the officer of the watch, breaking into Jon's wandering thoughts. The mizzen topmen rushed to comply with the order.

"Quartermaster, course west southwest. Make for the entrance to the harbour," ordered Lieutenant Rylett, the officer of the watch. The quartermaster on the wheel repeated the order out loud, as he complied.

Jon thought, that's odd; it looks like we're heading into the harbour. I wonder why?

"Course sheets, topsail sheets, take the strain," called the bosun. "Heave! Come on; put your backs into it."

The course and topsails were pulled even further aft on the larboard side.

"Belay - Make fast those sheets," shouted the bosun.

The Mermaid adjusted to her new course. Jon knew it was only temporary, as they needed to be on a reaching larboard tack to move up the entrance channel into the harbour.

About two thirds of the watch on deck repositioned themselves to the starboard side in preparation for the next series of commands to heave on the lines. The other third remained in place to loosen the lines on the larboard side.

"Come about to starboard," ordered Lieutenant Rylett. Again, the quartermaster on the wheel repeated the order as he swung the wheel.

The bosun was watching and timing the manoeuvre so the ship did not hang in stays.

"On the starboard course sheets and topsail sheets take up the slack," shouted the bosun. When he calculated the timing was right, he shouted, "Heave."

There was frantic action, and the deck crew pulled the courses and topsails around to a larboard reaching tack, which was as far aft starboard as the yards would move. Jon and his men clung tightly as the yards swung around. He was now positioned directly over the quarterdeck. He was almost directly over Lieutenant Rylett's head.

What a tempting opportunity; but no matter what happens they'd blame me and that means a striped back or dangling from the yardarm. It ain't worth it, thought Jon.

The Mermaid continued sedately up to and through the Louisbourg harbour entrance channel. Jon glanced down to the quarterdeck and noticed the captain was present. Jon had been otherwise occupied and hadn't noticed when the captain had arrived on deck.

"Prepare to anchor," ordered the captain after the Mermaid cleared the channel into the harbour. "Take in the topsails."

"Furl the topsail," ordered Jon to his mizzen team. The well-trained topmen streamed out along the topsail yard and began furling the sail. Single gaskets were strategically placed around the sail to keep it from catching the wind.

With only the courses on her, the Mermaid slowed as she entered the harbour proper. Finally, as she nosed into an anchorage location, orders were again shouted and signalled.

"Let go," shouted the first lieutenant. The anchor splashed into the water. It was the first time their hook had been dropped in a port since early March.

"Furl fore-courses and mizzen lateen."

The mizzen lateen and foremast course were furled in response to the order. Jon and his team relaxed once their work was done. The main course was allowed to hang loose. All yards were squared by the bosun and the deck crew. The wind then caught the loose main course and gently pushed the Mermaid sternwards over the anchor, where she swung at anchor so her bow was pointed toward the direction of the wind. Once in position, the officer of the watch ordered the main course to be furled.

The Mermaid had anchored away from all other ships. Whether that was to keep the men from swimming to other vessels, it was unclear. What was clear was that the Mermaid was the only large warship in the harbour. Even the Superb, the flagship was absent.

What did that mean for the Mermaid?

CHAPTER 3

A new harbour always invites the inquisitive. The crew of the Mermaid was no exception. They stood gawking at the place, but only momentarily. His Majesty's naval officers never like to see a seaman idle. Lest the crew get any ideas, they were put to work.

Jon remained idling with his topmen up on the mizzen platform. The only top-related work needed while the ship was at anchor and all the sails were furled, was the inspection of ropes and pulleys. However, with his men up in the tops, they tended to be out-of-sight and out-of-mind of the officers below. They were, therefore, less likely to be tasked with other jobs most topmen felt were below their station.

Jon Swift was an agile, lithe, muscular young man approaching eighteen years of age. His dark hair was kept reasonably short compared to the braided queues adorning other crew members. Known as Jon Smith on the Mermaid, he was rated as an able seaman. While normally working the larboard watch as the senior rating for the mizzen, he also had duties as the second gun captain on a 24-pounder on the lower gun deck when the ship was cleared for action.

Jon surveyed his surroundings, as did the other men on the top. The harbour of Louisbourg was crowded. A large portion of the invasion fleet had moved into the harbour to avail themselves of the docks and other 'advantages' offered in a port. There was an absence of warships though. All the ships visible were merchantmen.

To the southwest was the fortress of Louisbourg. The fortress looked as impressive from this angle as it had from every other angle from which he had observed it. It had strong stone walls. One glance at the shore in any direction could attest to the availability of stone and timber.

The size of the settlement surprised him. Louisbourg was supposedly the biggest, strongest fortification the French had in North America. If this small settlement was the Frenchmen's largest, it baffled him why all of New France had not already fallen. Even Rye, which was near where he was born, was as large as or larger than this place. After Portsmouth and other places he had been, he didn't consider Rye that large.

Just this side of the fortress were the docks used by the entire settlement. These docks were a beehive of activity. Every berth space was occupied. Every ship present appeared to be hoisting cargo.

To the east was Battery Island, aptly named as it was the home of a large stone emplacement where batteries of cannon guarded the entrance to the harbour. Less than a week ago, Jon had been ashore bombarding this position. Two weeks before that, he had participated in an assault on the battery itself. They had been badly mauled by the French guns and troops.

"The docks seem unusually active. You were ashore Jon. Why so much activity, and why does it appear that there are women on the docks?" asked Cecil West.

West was one of the mizzen topmen who reminded Jon of a young cocker spaniel, even though he didn't look like one. He was a young, fit man of average size and height. He always seemed to have a sunny disposition and had been an admirer of Jon's since Jon had come aboard the Mermaid. It just seemed to Jon, that Cecil was always nearby, looking for attention, and wagging his tongue instead of his tail to show that he was friendly. One didn't wag his tail on one of His Majesty's vessels -- it was too likely to attract the wrong type of attention.

"Why do you think the women are on the dock Cecil? Same reason women in any port are on the docks when the ships come in, and you can bet they ain't stevedores," quipped another topman named Mannion.

Mannion's comment garnered some hushed chuckles from most of the topmen. None of the topmen wanted to call attention to them from the officers on the deck below.

Mannion was an older version of West, being in his late twenties. In Jon's opinion Mannion was a good man, although he differed from West in that he was a bulldog. Once Mannion got his teeth into something, he rarely let go until he accomplished what he set out to do.

"It's been a long time since I saw a white woman," remarked George Hale, another young muscular topman with wiry dark hair. Jon considered Hale a terrier. He even looked a little like a terrier with his wiry hair. Hale kept nipping at a job until he accomplished it.

"I venture that you'd rather do more than just look at one," snickered West.

"You got that right, mate," replied Hale. "I wonder if they are going to place the ship 'Out of Discipline' while we're here."

"What difference would it make to you?" asked Mannion. "You, me and almost every other man aboard don't have two pennies to rub together even if they did place the ship out of discipline. You know we haven't been paid for nigh on a year. You know that Jon is the only one with any money. Maybe he'll lend some to us?"

"You can forget any of that," said Jon sombrely.

"Why?" asked more than one man.

"Take a good look at the ship on the near side of the closest pier. Watch the hoists. They aren't unloading - they're loading," said Jon.

After closer examination, Hale replied, "You're right, but what are they loading?"

"You weren't ashore, so you probably aren't aware of the overall situation. I'll try and explain it to you," replied Jon.

"Most of the men that landed with the army are colonials from New England. They are something like us, but with one major difference -- they all volunteered for the expedition against Louisbourg. None of them was pressed. They are only paid a pittance for joining this expedition; but were promised a portion of the loot captured at Louisbourg -- their prize money so to speak. When Louisbourg surrendered, they were happy as all get out. They didn't have to storm the walls and take the fortress, and they would still get a portion of the loot. What they didn't know was that under the Articles of Capitulation all French residents of Louisbourg, military and civilian were to be provided 'unmolested' transport in British vessels back to France. This 'unmolested' transport meant the Frenchmen can take their personal possessions with them. In other words, the colonial soldiers get no prize money, even though they won and now hold the fortress."

"That must have pissed them off," said Hale.

"You have no idea," replied Jon. "I thought I was going to be beaten or killed, they were that pissed."

"So what did you do?" asked West.

"Made myself scarce," replied Jon. "It was a pretty tense night after they were given the word."

"Why would the admiral accept such a condition in the surrender? Didn't he know the effect it would have on the men?" asked West. His astonishment and that of the others was evident.

"I expect he did," replied Jon. "I guess in his position, you have to look at it from all sides. First let's set things straight, there is no admiral here. Commodore Warren in the Superb commands the naval forces. Some colonial general named Pepperell commands the army. This General Pepperell made the decision to accept the surrender. Since he's a colonial, I guess he would know the terms of recruitment for his men."

"If I were in his shoes, I would have to ask myself what was more important. If I could get Louisbourg without storming the walls, but it meant giving up some of the loot, would I do it? How many men do you think he would lose if he had to storm those walls? I do know that the British regulars were not happy with him when he fired heated shot into Louisbourg. If he decided to reject the surrender in order to get more loot for his men, do you think Commodore Warren, or the officer commanding the British regulars, would continue to support him? I don't know the answer to that, but if I were him, I sure wouldn't want to find out the hard way. Pepperell accepted the surrender. I think he was kind of stuck between a rock and a hard place."

"The end result was that he got both Louisbourg and a lot of pissed-off troops. You can understand the troops' feelings. They got little pay and had to put up with primitive conditions and poor rations; then all their anticipated loot was taken away from them. They considered that a betrayal. They were hostile, and ready to vent their anger on anyone that was not one of 'them'. By the next day, they had calmed down some, but they effectively quit. They just wanted to get home as fast as possible and put this whole expedition behind them."

"That's what you see at the docks. The powers-that-be want to get rid of the French as fast as possible. They want to set up Louisbourg under British control and ensure it is defensible against any French attack. They can't do that with the French here. I would also imagine that there are plenty of colonial troops willing to relieve the French of anything that they fancy. That would pose problems -- it might violate the terms of the capitulation, and the colonials would likely have to hang some of their men. So the authorities want to get the French out as fast as possible to prevent that. That's why the urgency in loading. The women are loading to go back to France."

"You figure the fleet is going to sail soon?" asked George.

"Yeah. Most will head south -- back to New England. A ship or two will escort the French back to France. The rest of us will likely go back to the Indies just in time for the heat of summer," replied Jon.

"Well that explains why the docks are so busy," said Mannion. "But what I'd really like to know is why you're back here and getting 'started' instead of running when you had the chance? I know I sure as hell would have run."

Before Jon could provide a response, the pipe for 'Up Spirits' was heard and everyone made haste to get back down on deck.

Nothing interferes with a sailor getting his grog.

CHAPTER 4

The daily issue of the spirit ration was the happiest time aboard any of His Majesty's warships. That was even before the spirits were consumed.

The crew of the Mermaid milled around in the waist eagerly awaiting their respective turn to collect the spirit ration. Mannion had rushed below and gathered the mugs for each member of the mess. The mugs were distributed to his mess mates as they queued for their grog. To make sure that each man received his ration and not a drop more, each man was responsible to collect it. The master-at-arms issued the ration under the close scrutiny of the purser who annotated each drop issued. With over two hundred men aboard, the process was slow. No one complained.

With his spirit ration in hand, Jon headed below for the hot noon meal. The first men down dropped the mess table into position and set up the table. Each man's mess items were placed in his regular place around the table. On merchant vessels, men forward of the mast sometimes had sea chests which were used as seats. On most navy vessels without a berthing deck, there was no space for sea chests. Men had to make do with ditty bags and benches to sit on. The benches were positioned and men plopped themselves down waiting for the designated 'cook' of the day to bring their rations.

The noon meal was the only hot meal of the day. Daily, each man was entitled to sixteen ounces of bread minus the purser's cut, which in reality meant he only received fourteen ounces. The average man saved this for supper and to break his fast the next morning. The hot meal was the real daily ration.

Today's ration was twenty-eight ounces of boiled beef, or what the purser and cooks claimed was beef. It was the same every fourth day. On other days, it was pork, and to be honest, there was little difference between the two in taste as far as Jon was concerned.

There were no illusions about the meal. The beef would be barely edible. The beef was stored in the hold in huge barrels. It was heavily salted and by the time it was used, it had the same consistency as a block of wood. After a few months, some of the meat was so tough that some men had been observed using it for carving as it was harder than some wood.

The so-called 'cooks' tossed the meat into a huge copper cauldron to boil. This softened the meat somewhat and got rid of as much salt as possible. By the time it reached Jon and the men in the mess, they could at least gnaw away at it. The spirit ration helped immensely, as the rum deadened the taste buds.

There was always limited conversation during the first part of the meal as every member of the mess concentrated on consuming his rations. Once that was completed and the rum had some time to work, tongues generally loosened, so the conversation became more animated.

"Before we came down, you were going to explain why you didn't run," said Mannion.

"You asked the question. I didn't say anything."

"Well are you going to tell us why you didn't run?" asked Hale. "Just about everyone here, with maybe the exception of Langtry would run given half a chance."

"What about you Langtry? Would you have run if you had been put ashore like I was?" Jon had been ordered ashore to assist the colonial army handle boats during the assault against Battery Island.

Langtry stared hard at Jon, determining if Jon was baiting him or not. Langtry was a much older man, had spent over twenty years in His Majesty's service, and was highly respected within the mess. Jon wasn't sure of him. There was a bit of coyote in him. Langtry appeared to be like any other topmen in the mess, but his actions appeared territorial, at least in respect to the mainmast where he was the senior rating. Langtry was also elusive in his responses and liable to snap at anything or anyone he considered threatening. Jon really didn't trust him. It was as if Langtry harboured some form of resentment towards him. Just the same, Jon had to live with him.

"I'm happy where I am," replied Langtry after some hesitation.

"Come on Jon, you keep dancin' around the question. Why didn't you run?" asked Hale.

"I always fancied myself a dancer."

"I've seen you on deck when the hornpipe was being played. You had a hard enough time just tappin' your foot in beat with the music, let alone dancin'," said Young, another member of the mess. "Just answer the bleedin' question."

"Pretty hard to run when there's an army officer standing beside you to make sure you get in the boat," said Jon. "Even though I'll readily admit, I was thinking about it."

"If the officer wasn't present, would you have run?" asked Hale.

"Running is one thing. Getting caught is another. Given the situation, I figure running would have been easy. I figured getting caught would be just as easy. The only way out of here is by ship, and I reckoned that they'd be checking for runners both at loading time and when unloading back in New England. There's also the problem of what to do once you get to New England. I spoke to some of the colonials about life there. Without money, it's just as hard to make a living there as any place."

"You got money," said Hale.

Everyman on board the Mermaid knew that Jon was the richest man forward of the mast. No one knew how much Jon had, but most knew where some of that money came from. There had been an auction of dead man's effects after the yellow jack. Jon had purchased over sixty dead man's belongings. These effects had later been sold to a purser on another ship. The word was a considerable profit had been made. Not one man aboard begrudged Jon making a profit at a purser's expense.

"Not enough, and the only skills I got are as a seaman. I reckon I could get a job on some merchantman, but I figure it wouldn't be long until some man o' war boarded and I'd be pressed again."

"Same position most of us are in," stated Mannion.

"Besides ….. I still got ties in England."

"You mean your family?" said West.

"Yeah. When I was pressed it left them in a lurch, or at least I reckon it did."

"After all of this time, don't you think they would have given up on you, or at least the possibility of your coming back? I mean at your age, you would have been leaving home anyway to make your own way," said Mannion.

"I don't know, and that's always in the back of my head."

CHAPTER 5

A good seaman is always aware of his surroundings. He is aware of the state of the sea, the force and direction of the wind. A seaman on one of His Majesty's warships was also sensitive to any tension around him. It was sometimes a matter of survival.

As Jon was discussing running with the other members of his mess, he became increasingly aware of the raised voices at the mess behind him. The endless tacking back and forth across the entrance to Louisbourg harbour had been monotonous. Men were bored and easily aggravated. A careless word or a bump on a rolling deck had led to numerous heated arguments. Since the Mermaid was at anchor and the deck was stable, Jon figured the cause of this little ruckus behind him was something more personal in nature. He kept his ears tuned, in case it escalated.

The little ruckus didn't escalate - it exploded. He heard a distinct thump like a fist striking flesh, which was instantly followed by a heavy object falling on his back. He was rammed forward into his mess table, which in turn caused the table to thump into the three men sitting on the opposite side.

Instantly the entire mess, less Jon, rose. Since they were still eating dinner, many had knives already in hand. Jon was delayed in rising as he was too busy crawling out from under the man who had fallen on him. The man who had thrown the punch was now in grave danger. The danger was not from the punched man, as that man was in no condition to retaliate, but from the entire mizzen mess angry at having their meal interrupted.

Jon rolled the unconscious fallen man aside. Standing, Jon noticed his mug containing the daily grog ration had been knocked over, as had several cups of his mess mates. That in itself was enough for an all out brawl. No one messed with another man's spirit ration.

The man who had thrown the punch was Mullen. He was standing in the aisle tensed and waiting -- for what Jon was not sure. Mullen was a brute, a bull of a man, and not a very smart one. He would make two of Jon, or most other members of Jon's mess. It was obvious that Mullen had no friends or at least anyone that was willing to back him, as everyone in the area was backing away from him. Most were more concerned about protecting their meals and drinks. Dumb as he was, Mullen wasn't backing down. One-on-one he would likely crush any man from Jon's mess; but he wasn't going to be fighting them one-on-one, it would be all at once.

In everyone's current state, it would be a short and vicious fight. Mullen would go down. The question was how many topmen would he take with him? Jon didn't want to get hurt, and he didn't want any of his team to get hurt either. He wasn't overly protective of his team; he just didn't want to have to do their work in addition to his own while they healed.

Not a sound was heard on the deck.

Fighting was a chargeable offence. There had already been a number of floggings for fighting. Jon was in no rush to fight. No one won in a fight. Even if you were the victor, you lost because you would likely end up strapped to the grate with a cat-o-nine-tails being laid across your back.

Jon took a step toward Mullen and spoke for all of the mess, as he was the closest man to Mullen.

"Mullen, you interrupted our meal. Your actions caused our grog ration to be wasted. You owe each man in this mess a drink. You can pay us using your grog ration over the next week and we'll forget the whole thing."

"And if I don't?" growled Mullen.

"Then you're stupid," replied Jon. "At the very least you're looking at a striped shirt. If you decide to take us on, we'll drop you where you stand."

"I could break you in two," growled Mullen.

"No doubt," said Jon. "But while you're busy with me, how are you going to defend yourself from the other five men whose drinks you spilled?"

Mullen considered that for awhile.

"What the hell is going on down here?" bawled Mr. Sinclair, one of the bosun's mates. He was standing on the stairwell. The silence of the lower messing deck had probably alerted him that trouble was brewing. When two hundred men stop talking, there is an ominous silence. Such a silence on a man o' war, tends to send cold shivers up the spine of the officers.

"We'll expect your grog ration for the next six days," said Jon to Mullen.

Jon motioned from behind his back for his messmates to go back to their seats.

"Stand fast," shouted Mr. Sinclair. Jon and Mullen, still standing, were caught by that order.

The bosun's mate approached and noticed the man lying on the deck.

"Who's that?" asked the bosun's mate. "And why is he there?"

"Rogers, Mr. Sinclair," said Jon. "He slipped and fell on the 24-pounder and then crashed into my back. I was just getting up to assist him."

"You were fighting," said Mr. Sinclair. It was a statement not a question.

"Mr. Sinclair, I was sitting with my back to Rogers, when he crashed into me. If you will look at my mess table, you will notice that I spilled my spirit ration, as did others at the table. I did not throw a single punch and everyone on this deck can verify that," said Jon quietly.

"Mullen, what were you doing?" inquired Mr. Sinclair.

Mullen just stood there. Mullen's silence as he pondered what to say was incriminating.

"Mullen was just getting up to aid Rogers, Mr. Sinclair," said Jon hastily. "He's from the same mess as Rogers and just going to help his mate down to the surgeon. Isn't that right Mullen?"

"That's right, Mr. Sinclair. I was just going to help me mate. If you'll excuse me and with your permission, Mr. Sinclair, I'll take Rogers down to see the surgeon," said Mullen.

"Take him," said Mr. Sinclair. "The rest of you finish your meal and get ready for the watch change." With that, an unhappy Mr. Sinclair stormed away.

Jon sat back down. He was eyed by every member of his mess and many men from other messes.

"Why did you save Mullen?" asked Mannion. "You should have let him swing in the wind."

Every man in the mess was wondering the same thing, as were men from other messes.

"What happens before the mast stays before the mast."

"Everyone understands that," replied Mannion. "You didn't say anything that violated that; but you went further, when you provided an excuse for Mullen. He's too dumb to think of something like that himself. Why?"

"What do you think would have happened, if I hadn't said anything?"

"The bastard would have got what he deserved, a striped shirt," said West.

"More' n' likely, but just how does that help me or you?"

Everyone considered that for a few moments, but no one responded.

"Okay, look at it a different way. If Mullen were flogged, what do you think the chances are that he would forgo his spirit ration to pay us for what was spilt?"

The consensus was 'none'. Mullen would keep his ration for himself, if for no other reason than to ease the pain of the flogging.

"So now he owes us. He got away without a flogging because we covered for him. So what do you think the odds are now that we will get his spirit ration to cover for what was spilt?"

"He doesn't owe us - he owes you," said Langtry. "So I figure that you at least will get his ration for at least one day."

"As far as I'm concerned, the deal was to cover each man in the mess."

"Let's say he provides you his ration for a day, and then doesn't bother with the rest of us. What do we do then?" asked Langtry.

"I think that we all made a point when we were prepared to have a go at Mullen together. The other messes will see that we aren't to be fooled with. As far as whether we all get a day's spirit ration, that we'll have to wait and see about. If Mullen doesn't honour it, everyone before the mast will know about it. He'll never be trusted again. I think the price of six days without a grog ration is a small price to pay for that."

"I'll believe it when I see it," said Langtry. Jon shrugged.

"Alright, you've explained why you covered for Mullen. What I don't understand is how is it that you thought of all of this when Mr. Sinclair asked?" inquired Mannion. "I sure as hell didn't think of it. In fact, I wouldn't have even considered it. I was more worried about making sure that I wasn't going to get a striped shirt myself."

"Believe me, that was on my mind; but I figured that since none of us had thrown a punch and there were enough witnesses to that fact, we might be alright," said Jon. "The big question on my mind was whether or not the bosun's mate had seen the rest of you with your knives drawn. If he had, there would be more to it, so I had to think of an explanation. What you heard was all that I could come up with at the time."

"Well you sure saved Mullen's ass," said Hale. "He was destined for a flogging for sure."

"Honestly, I don't give a rat's ass about Mullen. Just the same, I'm glad I didn't have to go up against him."

The mess conversation shifted and Jon lost interest. His disinterest was noted.

"Whatcha thinkin' about Jon?" inquired Hale.

"Something you said triggered an old memory George. You said I saved Mullen's ass. In effect, I changed his destiny. That got me thinking of other discussions I had with my mates about a man's destiny on the Winchester."

"Go on," said Hale.

"We used to have discussions on whether a man controlled his own destiny or our destiny is preordained."

"What was the verdict?" asked Hale.

"I'm not sure if we really came to any conclusion. I've given it some thought from time to time, and the only thing that I realize is that the decisions you make control your destiny. Either you control that destiny or someone will control it for you."

"That's bullshit," said Langtry.

"Why do you say that?"

"The destiny of every man here is controlled by the captain of this ship," replied Langtry.

"I agree in general. The captain controls most things while we are on board this ship, but he does not control everything. He will never control my mind - the way I think. I admit he might have some influence on it, but I make the decision whether I'm happy or miserable. Take a simple example. When any one of you first was brought aboard one of His Majesty's ships, you were probably a landsman. The captain of the ship didn't make the decision that you were going to be a topman - you did. Even you did Langtry. What happens when the captain is not around? He certainly didn't control things while I was onshore at Louisbourg. What happens when this ship is paid off, whenever that might be? Who controls your destiny at that time? That's why I say that you control your destiny to some extent."

"Just keep your bullshit to yourself, and stop trying to poison the minds of these men," said Langtry before he stormed off.

"Langtry's got a pretty strong argument Jon," said Mannion. "I mean everything we do - when we work, when we eat or sleep, even what we eat is controlled by the captain."

"You're missing the point. Sure, the captain controls those things, and they presently control much of your life, but is that your destiny? I think it's the decisions that you make that control your destiny. Let's say you run. The captain won't have any say in that decision. Your life will change. You could get caught, or you could get away. If you get away, then you will have to make decisions so you aren't caught. You will also have to make decisions about what you are going to do to put food in your stomach and a roof over your head. Those decisions will ultimately shape you. There will always be things that happen that are beyond your control. It's the decisions that you make when they happen that change your destiny."

"What you're saying makes some sense, Jon, but we're all stuck here," said Beck. "I agree with Mannion, and Langtry. We got no say in what happens."

Jon tossed his hands up in surrender. There was no point in arguing, if there was nothing to gain. It was so simple -- every time you make a decision, you change your destiny. The bigger the decision, the bigger the change; they just didn't get it.

CHAPTER 6

Anchored in harbour, or sailing, the officers sure hated to see an idle crew.

The routine for change of watch started with a head count on deck to ensure all members of the watch were present. When sailing, topmen could expect to be sent aloft to adjust the sails, which had been satisfactory, in most cases, up until the change of watch. It was the normal way the incoming officer of the watch exerted his control over the watch. They were currently anchored so no topmen functions were necessary. At anchor, the topmen could expect duties totally unrelated to their normal functions.

"Smith, get your ass and your crew over here, NOW," shouted a voice from behind him. Although Jon could not see who was shouting at him, the authority in the voice was enough to get him moving.

"Let's go," said Jon, as he rapidly led the mizzen topmen across the deck.

"Smith, take your people to the cooper. Help him get the water barrels ready for filling. Once they're ready, load them in the longboat and take them and fill them," ordered Mr. Mason, the bosun.

"Aye, Mr. Mason," said Jon. The men had heard the orders as well as he had, so Jon simply motioned them to follow him.

The cooper was in the waist near the open hatch. Empty barrels were hoisted from the hold as they approached.

"Mr. Grayson, I was told to report to you with my men and assist you in getting water."

"Load the longboat with those clean barrels," said Mr Grayson, as he pointed out a row of barrels on the starboard side. "Once loaded, take the boat over to the west shore. There's a stream over there that I am reliably informed has been used for watering for years. Fill the barrels there, and then return."

Grayson pointed out the stream on the western shore of the harbour and left Jon to it.

"Aye, Mr. Grayson," said Jon to Mr. Grayson's back as the cooper walked away.

"West, you and Hale get a cargo net. Move those barrels onto the net. Mannion go see about the longboat. See if it already has a crew. Move it to the starboard side. If it doesn't have a crew, let me know and I'll get one," ordered Jon.

There was something odd happening here; but Jon, at the present, didn't have time to sit back and consider it. Why was he being ordered to take the watering party ashore? Taking men ashore was always a touchy situation and always reserved for trusted men. To his knowledge, he wasn't trusted.

In short order the barrels were prepared for hoisting, a crew was obtained for the longboat and the longboat positioned on the starboard side for receiving the empty barrels. Once the barrels were loaded, Jon and the remainder of the hoisting crew descended into the longboat. The boat cast off for shore. Mr. Mason or one of the officers had thoughtfully added a Corporal and three Marines to the longboat crew.

As they rowed toward the western shore, Jon considered how the watering crew would respond once ashore. Everyone in the boat, himself included, with possibly the exception of the marines, would likely run given the right opportunity. Jon had no deep desire to be in the navy, but concurrently he had charge of the watering detail. It was his responsibility to ensure all members of the watering party returned. If anyone ran, he would pay the penalty.

Was this a test of his leadership skills? Was it a setup, knowing how the men felt? Who had decided to place him in charge of the watering detail? Normally a bosun's mate was responsible for the watering detail. Something was not adding up. This morning he had been 'started'; yet this afternoon he was in charge of men heading ashore -- a position normally held only by senior trusted men.

Stroke after stroke as they neared shore Jon realized he had to make a choice on how to handle the men. He was sure that whatever decision he made, it would change him. Time ran out as they entered the mouth of the stream.

Jon cleared his throat and gave everyone a little speech. "Listen up. I know that for most of you, this will be the first time you are on shore in the better part of a year. If you're thinking of running, let me explain what you will be up against. First, you'll have to get past our 'lobster-back' friends here. If you succeed in that, there may still be Frenchmen that didn't surrender hanging around, or their Indian allies. If they catch you, they'll most likely kill you. According to the New Englanders that I was working with during the siege, the savages can be right nasty, torturing a man for hours until he dies. If the French or savages don't get you, then the only other people on the island are British. They will identify you as deserters, and treat you accordingly. If you manage to avoid everyone, then all you have to worry about are the animals and starvation. The mosquitoes and black flies will probably drive you mad. There are bears and wild cats bigger than dogs. There are also wolves, which run in packs. All of these will see you as a meal on two legs. Food wise, you could probably survive for the next two or three months. After that, it gets cold, and in winter everything freezes solid. The snow is measured in feet. So if you want to try to run, that's your decision, but even the Royal Navy is a far better life than you will find here if you run."

No one responded, but then again he hadn't thought that anyone would.

The longboat grounded. Jon assigned duties to each man and the watering process commenced. The watering process was simple. The stream was shallow, so the barrels were off-loaded from the longboat. They were then rolled inland. A path had been beaten down in the past from the shoreline to a good watering spot. At that point the barrels were turned on their ends, and the bungs removed. Buckets of water were pulled from the stream, passed from man to man, with the last man pouring the water into the barrel.

As the water barrels were filled, the mosquitoes descended upon them. The bugs weren't bad as it was early afternoon, but they were sufficient to indicate what a runner would be up against. Most of the crew had familiarity with mosquitoes from the West Indies. No one liked them.

Filled barrels were rolled back down to the harbour's edge and left. Once the last barrel was filled, all the barrels were rolled into the water, where they floated. Ropes were used to secure them to the longboat. The longboat was manned and they began towing the barrels back out to the Mermaid. Despite the challenges of towing the barrels, the men appeared happy, mainly because they were shed of the bugs.

Once alongside the Mermaid the process was just as laborious. Cargo nets were dropped over the side into the water. A barrel at a time, the barrels were wrestled into the net and hoisted aboard. After the last hoist, the watering party returned aboard.

No one had run. Maybe the Marines had some influence.

Filling the water casks was just one more indication that they would sail soon. Given the amount of water taken aboard, it was also likely that the trip would be a long one. Heading back to the Indies seemed a reasonable bet.

By the time the watering party returned, it was late in the afternoon and the end of watch. As they filed below, Jon wondered yet again what was behind his selection to lead the watering party.

He attempted to determine who had ordered him ashore, and got nowhere. The bosun had ordered him to lead the watering party. He could have tasked one of his mate's. Why him? If the mates were busy, then why not task Langtry, who was a more trusted seaman? Why had the bosun even done the ordering and not an officer? What had changed between the morning and the afternoon? Was there any significance that he had returned with all of the men?

What was going on?

CHAPTER 7

Night harbour watch always posed challenges.

Since they were still under discipline, there were no problems with strangers on board. There were the usual issues with space. Since both watches were off at the same time, hammock space was limited to fourteen inches. Smelly bodies were that much closer to your nose all night. The only way to fit into the allotted space was to rig hammocks nose to tail. This resulted in someone's feet generally being a foot or so from your nose on either side. Just getting into or out of the hammock without disturbing your neighbour was a challenge. Disturbing your neighbour could result in retaliation. Sometimes it was simple like a fart in the face, sometimes it came to blows. Given the irritation felt by most of the crew after months of blockade duty, it was prudent to tread very carefully.

Harbour watch posed additional challenges for all -- what to do. While everyone liked a night off, they rarely had anything to do. No one had money and they had nowhere to go as they were not allowed beyond their normal confines. That meant they had to make their own entertainment. Talking was generally out, as most men had long since exhausted their stories. That left music, dancing or extra time for crafts such as carving if one was so inclined.

Secreted rum generally flowed. It was an offense to hoard your spirit ration, but generally someone in each mess did. What a man did with his spirit ration was his business. Jon had hoarded his and others had remained silent. Any man that ratted out his mates would pay a heavy price. He would be an outcast from his mess and no other mess would take him. What happened before the mast, stayed before the mast. If someone got drunk, and the officers noticed, that was his problem.

Jon was not tagged for any overnight harbour watch duties, so he knew he would have plenty of time for sleep. With plenty of light until well into the first watch, it was an appropriate time to practise reading. The more practice the better, as it was the only way to improve skill in this area. Removing a borrowed book from the ditty bag, he sought a comfortable spot on the upper deck. Other men sat in proximity, but politely avoided any disturbances. Privacy was non-existent forward of the mast, so an individual's attempt at solitude was respected wherever possible. Just the same, no member of the mess would hesitant to razz him from time to time about reading.

As the light deteriorated to such an extent that he could no longer read, Jon deposited his book back into his ditty bag and returned to the deck to listen to the music and watch those men that danced. Someone had hoisted a lantern over the forward portion of the waist. Men circled the light from lantern, perched in the ratlines, and on the forecastle. All were watching the hornpipe and fiddle players and the dancers. The tunes were jaunty and the dance was lively. Occasionally all the men would clap to the tune, but it was a rare song when more than one or two men sang.

After about an hour of watching, Jon drifted below to get some sleep. There was hushed activity on the gun deck. One wondered if men would run under the present conditions.

During the first dog watch, a boat from HMS Superb, the flagship of Commodore Warren, arrived alongside bearing a package for the captain. Speculation amongst the crew was rife and the ship's bookmakers were doing a thriving business.

Within an hour of the departure of the Superb's boat, a procession of merchant captains from other ships started to arrive. Everyone could tell that these were merchantmen because no naval side-party was called. Each captain was escorted directly to Captain Montague's cabin upon arrival. While Jon, or any other member of the crew, didn't know for sure what was said in the captain's cabin, it was possible to make a calculated guess.

The fact that merchant captains were arriving meant that a convoy was being formed. Since the merchant captains presented themselves to Captain Montague, it meant that he was going to command the senior escort, which would be the Mermaid. As the number of merchantmen captains arriving continued to increase, it was apparent that the size of the convoy was getting bigger. That meant there would likely be other escorts, but smaller than the Mermaid. That only left the destination of the convoy in doubt, and it was on this point that the ship's bookmakers were laying odds.

Bets were placed that the Mermaid was heading to New England, back to Antigua, or France. Given the number of merchant captains that had repaired onboard, the convoy was going to be a reasonable size. From what he had heard ashore, Jon figured the convoy was too big for just the Frenchmen that were supposed to be carried back to France. It was also likely that Antigua was out, simply because of the number of merchantmen. That only left New England. Even with this deduction, Jon didn't place any bets -- he worked hard for his money, and wasn't going to gamble it away.

The size of the convoy continued to grow as more merchantmen captains continued to appear the next morning. Given the number of merchantmen, there was no way that a single escort could provide adequate protection. The men speculated on how many additional escorts would be added to the convoy. That too was confirmed when navy honours were given to two captains who came aboard the next afternoon.

With all the activity in officer's country, Jon figured they would be leaving the next day. In this he was disappointed, as was the entire crew.

The small number of docking spaces in Louisbourg was proving to be a bigger obstacle than anyone expected. Docking space within Louisbourg harbour was required to off-load needed supplies for the new garrison. Ships from the invasion fleet sitting idle in Gabarus Bay for the past six weeks were keen to unload the stores and cargo they had carried for the occupying forces and depart. Any early departure meant money in their pockets, hence the urgency. Ships were needed to load the Frenchmen and their possessions to send them back to France. There was an urgency to get these people into the ships and offshore where there was better security. That security ensured the French prisoners were confined, and kept the New Englanders from 'liberating' the Frenchmen's possessions.

A further requirement was to embark the colonial troops and their associated equipment to get them out of Louisbourg and back home. It was much simpler to load at a dock than attempt to load the men and their associated supplies in a longboat, navigate through the surf, and hoist the men and stores from the longboat.

Day after day was consumed by higher authorities attempting to resolve these issues and bring order in the harbour.

Finally, the crew got the word. The Mermaid was heading to France.

CHAPTER 8

HMS Mermaid raised her anchor from the Louisbourg harbour bottom on a warm, foggy July morning. The anchor's sluggish rise did not match the crews' nature. The crew was enthusiastic.

The reasons for the enthusiasm of the Mermaid's crew varied. Most men, Jon included, were happy to finish the monotonous and boring blockade duty. Although the ship had been doing blockade duty for less than three months, it had ceased to be a novelty after the first week. By the end of the first month it had become boring. After two months, tempers had grown short.

Other men were happy to be heading to England. Although every man on board knew the ship was heading to France to escort the French prisoners, it was a near certainty that the Mermaid would stop in an English port. Supplies and maintenance were necessary before the ship headed back to her assigned station in the West Indies.

Putting in to any English port would be the closest many men had been to their previous life and families in years. There was the prospect of finally being paid. Since they took the Vigilant, there was also the possibility of receiving their prize money. The prospect of going 'out of discipline' was attractive to many. For some the opportunity to run would be the best they were likely to see for some time. Putting all these reasons together, the crew of the Mermaid was anticipating the voyage.

As the anchor broke clear, Jon was in the tops awaiting orders from the quarterdeck.

"Take the gaskets off those sails."

"Let fall," he shouted after hearing the order from below. The wind caught the sails, the ship slowly started moving, the rudder bit, and the Mermaid was underway.

Jon kept his team in place. In order to get out of the Louisbourg harbour it was necessary to tack at least once. With all the traffic moving through a narrow passageway leading out of the harbour, it was likely that additional manoeuvring would be required. This was nothing out of the ordinary, so Jon and his team were content to remain in the tops for further orders and of course out-of-sight of the officers.

There was lots of time to think while waiting in the tops. Jon speculated on which English port the Mermaid would visit. He was reasonably sure it would be a major naval port, as the ship could only draw supplies from naval stores. His best guess was Portsmouth.

Of all naval bases that he could think of, Portsmouth was the closest to his home. It was a long distance over land, but by ship to Rye, relatively close.

Whatever port they anchored at, it was likely to be the closest Jon would get to home in the foreseeable future. The likelihood of his getting off the ship and traveling home was zero. To get home he would have to run. Jon was still uncertain whether he would run. This trip would help him make a decision. If Rylett kept up his tricks, then he would desert in a heartbeat.

At every opportunity Lieutenant Rylett ordered Jon to complete tasks, which all saw as punishment. When undertaking boarding drill practise, Jon was subjected to blows when others weren't watching. Rylett was sneaky and vindictive. Since he was an officer, Jon really couldn't fight back. If he did, he risked punishment. Jon knew one thing; Rylett was never going to beat him. He wouldn't let it happen, but that didn't mean he wouldn't run.

That posed another question -- what would he do if he ran? He would first head home and see his folks. He couldn't be seen there, because the squire's men would just turn him back over to the navy. He had run afoul of the squire's men once before. That resulted in a severe beating which nearly killed him and being pressed into the navy. He certainly didn't want that to happen again. If he was caught when running and turned back over to the navy it would result in a flogging for sure. On board a new ship he would likely be worse off than he was on this one with the possible exception of Rylett. It would be a certainty he would never get shore leave, ever.

If he managed to avoid the squire's men, what would he do to survive? Although he had money, conservation of that was prudent. All his current skills related to sailing. With some ability with his letters and numbers, perhaps a position as a clerk in a store might be possible, but not necessarily palatable. Farming was an option, but after watching his father struggle with that over the years, it was a path to avoid, unless forced into it.

Thinking about the farm and family initiated further speculation. What would he say to the family once he returned? They would remember a boy who was a crafty poacher, but he was no longer that person. He was a skilled, experienced sailor able to take hardship. He had learned to kill and had done so during the boarding of the Vigilant. He was able to make his own decisions. In fact, he supervised more men on the mizzen than his father had ever supervised. To his knowledge, his father had only supervised him.

Even though he hadn't seen a cent of pay since being pressed, according to other men the pay as an able seaman, even a navy able seaman, was better than a farm labourer. Between what he would receive when he was finally paid, and what he had made with all of his trading, he'd probably have more money than his father had ever seen in his life.

Trading had accounted for all of that money. First he had accumulated five pounds from the wagon load of farm produce sold in the Rye market before getting pressed. Some of that had been used to buy dead man's kit during the auction. Of that kit, a portion had been sold to a purser from another ship, some had been kept, and other kit had been bartered for other goods. He had further bartered hoarded rum at Louisbourg. Since being aboard he had bartered other rum for reading and writing lessons. No coin was ever spent except to make more coin. In his eyes, he had amassed a fortune.

Not having any expectations other than visiting his parents was troubling.

Slowly each ship of the convoy emerged from the harbour channel into the Atlantic. Besides HMS Mermaid, the colonial armed sloop Abigail and colonial sloop Hampshire were detailed for escort duties. HMS Mermaid was the senior escort.

There were fourteen cargo ships. The primary mission of the convoy was to escort five vessels carrying the French 'prisoners' back to France. All the additional ships were bound directly for Britain, taking the opportunity to join the convoy and reap the protection benefits of the accompanying escort. They had been advised that the escort's first duty was to ensure the safety of those five vessels carrying the Frenchmen.

Despite the patchy morning fog, the merchant ships of the convoy were finally shepherded into formation and the two sloops positioned. One sloop, the Abigail, was positioned in front of the convoy to spot any trouble advancing toward the convoy. The second sloop, the Hampshire, was positioned aft of the convoy and given freedom to run down any stragglers or unidentified sail. HMS Mermaid positioned herself on the north, windward side, toward the rear of the convoy so she could move directly to any threatened area. Mermaid was like a mother duck shepherding her swimming goslings, the goslings being the merchantmen.

It didn't take long to find out that convoy escort duties could be frustrating. Errant ships had to be shepherded into position, in some cases numerous times. A 12-pounder cannon, charge-only, was fired repeatedly for signalling throughout the morning. Still up in the mizzen, Jon quietly chuckled at the frustration of the officers on the quarterdeck.

It took until the end of the forenoon watch to straighten things out. The convoy was sailing smoothly at a five knot pace to the northeast. This was the fastest speed of the slowest vessel, but in reality, most merchantmen couldn't travel all that much faster. The wind was steady from the west resulting in a larboard tack. The swell was low, so the ship pitched at a regular gentle frequency.

For the North Atlantic, you could not ask for better sailing conditions in July.

CHAPTER 9

If anyone had doubts as to what the afternoon watch would bring, they were quickly dispelled when the drums started to beat and the shout "Clear for Action" was heard.

It was not immediately clear whether this was for real or just another exercise. Assuming it was for real the men launched into their work with zeal. They cleared for action in eight minutes, which was good time. The only faster time that Jon could remember was when they cleared for action against the Vigilant, but there had been added incentives then.

When cleared for action, Jon was the number two captain on the number three 24-pounder. There were seven other men on that gun. There were ten guns on each side, but the Mermaid currently only had enough men to man the guns on one side at a time. If they were called to fight on both sides concurrently, Jon would take half the men and shift to the number three gun on the opposite side.

Lieutenant Caharty, the second lieutenant and Jon's division commander, commanded the guns on the forward half of the gun deck. Lieutenant Rylett, the third lieutenant, commanded the guns on the rear half of the gun deck.

Lieutenant Caharty was an average sized and average looking man. As he paced back and forth along the centre line behind the guns, he continuously had to stoop so he wouldn't hit his head on the beams. As the men prepared the guns, he rarely spoke.

In direct contrast was Lieutenant Rylett. Rylett was a very good-looking man who was only about five foot four in height. Everyone on the gun deck could hear him bellowing at some poor soul or other to hurry up. If Rylett removed his hat, he wouldn't even have to bend over when walking on the gun deck. To remove one's hat was a breach of dress etiquette and Rylett would never succumb to such measures -- it would set the wrong example. Rylett was better than that. He would never open himself up to the ridicule of his fellow officers.

Virtually every sailor on the guns in the forward half of the gun deck was thankful that Lieutenant Caharty and not Rylett commanded them. That's not to say that Lieutenant Caharty didn't have a sharp tongue, it was just that he only used it when needed, and not to impress those around him of his importance.

As the guns captains lifted one fist in the air, signalling their gun was ready, word came down from the quarterdeck that the guns would exercise using mock procedures. Obviously, the captain didn't want to scare the merchantmen by firing a broadside.

The next three hours were brutal. It was no fun heaving the 24-pounder up to the gun port, saying 'bang', and then having to haul the gun inboard again, only to repeat the mock loading again.

When the order came to "Secure guns" there was a collective sigh of relief from the entire crew. As the guns were secured, the work commenced on restoring the ship to normal sailing stations. When complete, there was a collective rush to the water butts by heavily sweating men attempting to grab a drink before the next watch started.

There was little rest for Jon, as he went immediately on watch. This was life on board His Majesty's ships. It did have one benefit. If the men were always busy, then they didn't have much time to reflect on their lot in life.

Finally, on the last dog watch, Jon had the opportunity to relax. The dog watches were generally the only time Jon had to himself. On most nights, he practiced with his throwing knife for a few minutes. It was essential as far as he was concerned. He carried money on his person and every member of the crew knew it. He was considered the richest man forward of the mast, although that was not saying much as virtually every other man was broke. Few men realized how much money he had and Jon certainly didn't broadcast it. His fear was that some night a group of men would attempt to steal his valuables.

Practicing with his throwing knife sharpened his skill and concurrently broadcast to others that he would resist any attempt against him with lethal force. Just the difficulty in throwing bolstered men's opinion of the threat. Jon could not throw the knife on the upper deck. A man throwing a knife up there might be construed as a threat against an officer -- an offence punishable by hanging. Throwing had to be accomplished on the gun deck. The height wouldn't allow a standing man to throw overhead. Jon therefore practiced throwing overhead from a kneeling position, from a sitting position, and occasionally from a lying position. He also practiced underhand throwing.

Throwing a knife into a mast or bulkhead repeatedly would be considered damaging to His Majesty's vessel. He had instead scrounged some wood and made a target, which he hung at different locations. One of the most common locations was between two cannon. He would toss the entire width of the ship.

Over time his skill had improved remarkably. He had the capability to hit a sideways plank at twenty-five feet. As he had started practicing the occasional man would challenge him. Now no one even attempted. He was just so much better.

Another thing he attempted most nights was to spend an hour reading. On a typical evening, he would grab a ship's biscuit from the bread barge and drop it into a pocket. A place to sit near some light was sought after extracting the only book he possessed from the ditty bag. He would then attempt to read as many pages in the book as possible. That was easier said than done. Jon had his ABCs, but had no skill in reading. An older pastor had initially taught him the rudimentary skills back home. Further lessons had been acquired at a cost on this ship. Those ceased when it was determined the man teaching him was more interested in the rum payment than if Jon could read or write.

The only reason he persisted was that in order to progress any further at sea, he would need to read and write. Jon did not want to spend the next few years as a topman, and certainly not a topman in the navy. The result was his nightly attempts to read while sucking on a ship's biscuit trying to soften it enough to chew and swallow.

Before first light as they did every day at sea, the crew was rousted and stood by the guns. When no strange sails were sighted, the crew was stood down and the daily routine commenced. The captain dictated that the forenoon watch would be spent exercising the great guns and the afternoon watch spent doing boarding drills. There was a collective groan when they received word about working the great guns. It would be a repeat of the previous afternoon.

In contrast, the crew welcomed boarding drills. It was fun for the crew to attempt to best their mates in skill at arms. Jon welcomed the boarding drills so long as he didn't have to do cutlass drill. Lieutenant Rylett always chose him as a sparring partner --read target.

Rylett was considered the best cutlass man on the ship, as he had proved repeatedly. After a period of practice, they generally played a game called "King of the Hill". The king would stand on the hatch cover with a wooden sword or cutlass and take on all challengers, one at a time. The winner of the challenge would remain on the hatch cover until someone ousted him. When Rylett took the hatch cover, there were no challengers and he always remained king.

Over the previous months, Jon had been used repeatedly as a training dummy to show other crewmembers the correct position and what not to do. This invariably meant that the dummy was struck forcibly. Jon was covered in bruises. It was all perfectly legal and there was little Jon could do about it. In order to protect himself, Jon had developed skills that he might not have acquired so rapidly or effectively. One of these was the ability to read a man's moves. This had helped him enormously in all combat. It had even allowed him to best Rylett on one occasion.

Even when he had been bested at a skill of arms, Rylett continued his vendetta against Jon. Since Jon had struck an officer, an offence punishable by death, Rylett played it up. Not to be outdone by Rylett, Jon had removed his shirt so all could see the numerous inflicted bruises. Captain Douglas, the previous captain, had called Rylett into his cabin. No one heard the conversation, although there were plenty of ears attempting to listen. What was known was Captain Douglas, had put a stop to further body strikes before the injuries became serious.

Captain Douglas had since assumed command of the larger Vigilant in recognition of the Mermaid's actions in taking her. Captain Montague had replaced him on the Mermaid. It appeared that Lieutenant Rylett was using this transition to resume his old practices. If that was correct, Jon could expect to be the recipient of bruises and ill treatment without any recourse.

The afternoon boarding drills started as dismally as Jon expected. He was assigned cutlass drill with Lieutenant Rylett. Rylett immediately picked him out to be his sparring partner. Rylett seemed to take delight in inflicting irritating minor hits on Jon's arms and torso. It was all that Jon could do to contain his anger. The worst part about it was Rylett's smile. Every time he scored a hit on Jon, Rylett had this infuriating little smile. Jon wanted desperately to wipe that smile off his face, but Rylett was too good.

Captain Montague remained on the quarterdeck through all of the boarding drill practice. He observed all of the practice. Toward the end of the afternoon, he appeared satisfied. All practice stopped. Everyone thought the orders would be to stand down, but the captain surprised everyone and called for "King of the Hill", and pointed at a man on the starboard watch.

"You there, you're the first king of the hill. Take your position," ordered Captain Montague.

There were a dozen challengers. The king pointed at the first, and the battle began. There was no elegance to the match, just brute force. The initial king went down under a hammering of blows. His successor lasted past the first challenger, but lost to the second. Half a dozen men claimed the title of king for one or two matches. No one lasted more than two contests.

Lieutenant Dunkin, the fourth lieutenant challenged the current king and easily took him. There was an abundance of challengers from foreward of the mast as this was an opportunity to best an officer. Lieutenant Dunkin was skilful but after besting four challengers, everyone could see that he was tiring.

Jon challenged, and was selected. Jon had barely put his foot on the hatch when Dunkin began his assault. Jon, completely in defensive mode, parried a number of thrusts as he gained the hatch. After the offensive flurry, Dunkin stepped back to get his breath. Jon launched an assault before Dunkin had time to recover. Dunkin slipped. Jon was in a position to bring down a battering blow, which he did. Dunkin anticipated it and blocked it. Jon hammered down with a second and third blow, each effectively blocked by Dunkin.

Jon raised his cutlass for the fourth blow and concurrently shifted his weight backward. Dunkin saw an opportunity and rapidly slashed toward his right. Jon saw it coming and had time to further shift backward. Dunkin's cutlass point flashed past his chest, but was closer than two inches. Jon was too far away to strike Dunkin, but he was close enough to sweep his cutlass after Dunkin's cutlass. He put as much force as he could into the sweep without knocking himself off-balance. He connected with Dunkin's cutlass and knocked it flying out of Dunkin's hand.

"Do you cede, sir?"

"I do," replied Dunkin. He recovered and left the hatch. The next man was already climbing up. It was Mullen.

Mullen had massive brute strength, which was immediately put to use. He closed with Jon and physically pushed him back. Jon was able to twist to get away and retreat to the middle of the hatch cover. Mullen turned, raised his cutlass overhead in a two-handed hold, and brought the cutlass crashing down. Jon easily understood the move and was prepared for it. If he took the strike directly, it could break his cutlass. At the very least it would drive his cutlass down and expose his head. Jon raised his cutlass on a slant with a two-handed hold and deflected the strike to his left. As the strike impacted, he stepped to his right and swept his cutlass to his right in the exposed flank of Mullen. He managed to pull his swing somewhat, but it still hit with a loud whack just below Mullen's rib cage. Mullen went down and rolled in pain to the edge of the hatch cover.

Jon lowered his cutlass and stooped over to Mullen.

"You okay mate?"

A couple of men helped Mullen to his feet and away from the hatch cover. The crowd had gone silent. Jon thought it was because he had been too hard on Mullen. When he stood and turned, he understood the reason. Lieutenant Rylett stood on the hatch.

Jon looked down, shook his head, and exhaled. Rylett smiled his little smile.

Rylett lowered his cutlass and prepared to thrust or parry, it was impossible to read him. They started to circle. Each of them thrust and parried, attempting to feel out their opponent. Rylett exploded forth. Even though he was expecting it, it was still startling. He managed to parry the assault, but only just. Rylett still managed to rake Jon's forearm. It burned like the devil. It was not an incapacitating blow, so Jon still had to continue.

The crew was so silent; it was possible to hear Rylett's breathing. Rylett had yet to work up a sweat, and his breathing was still shallow, unlike Jon's. Rylett was like a snake stalking his victim. He exploded in another strike. Jon managed to side step a killing blow, but still suffered a grazing blow along his lower left rib. If Rylett had been using a real blade, Jon would have been cut and weakening as he bled. He needed to end this before receiving any further injuries.

Rylett extended his cutlass repeatedly toward Jon's head and taunted Jon. Jon spent his time batting Rylett's cutlass away and paying insufficient attention to Rylett's moves. That was a fatal mistake as Jon next felt a hammering into his solar plexus, as Rylett's cutlass found its mark. The strike bowled Jon over and he collapsed on the hatch cover fighting for breath.

As Jon was dragged from the hatch covered by Mannion and West, there were no challengers prepared to take on Rylett. With no apparent challengers, Captain Montague ceased the drills and ordered the crew back to normal watch routine.

Luckily, Jon was not on watch, so there was time to recover. Physically, only time was needed to recover from the blows inflicted. Mentally, other types of scabs continued to form.

It would take more than time to recover from these mental wounds.

CHAPTER 10

The ship was pitching noticeably by the end of the middle watch. As the morning watch started, the crew stood by the pitching guns waiting for first light. It was a standard precaution to stand by the guns at first light to ensure any visitors received a warm greeting should they exhibit hostile intentions. It was not much fun for the gun crews this morning, however, with two and a half ton guns sliding on the deck.

As the light gradually increased, two things were absent on the horizon -- strange sails and the sun. The sky was overcast, with dark, menacing skies well to the south. Combined with the motion, any good sailor knew these indications foretold an upcoming disturbance in the weather. The guns were secured with an extra lashing.

The motion of the ship became more pronounced as the morning and the forenoon watch proceeded. A rolling motion had started as well. Given the motion and the dark skies to the south, the majority of the crew generally accepted that the weather disturbance was to the south of them. Unfortunately, based on the changing motion, it appeared the disturbance was heading north or northeast in a general direction toward them.

With the wind shifting, Captain Montague decided to move from the north side of the convoy to the south of the convoy. It would be easier to run down on the convoy from that position as the windward side of the convoy was now south. As only a tack was called for, topmen remained on deck to handle the running tackle. The ship slowly clawed its way into the new position.

Jon could see discussions between the officer of the watch and the master as to whether to strike the tops. Only the royals and top gallants could be taken down at sea. After considerable back and forth, Jon reckoned a decision had been made. He saw the officer of the watch shout something; but could not hear the words because of the wind.

"Topmen aloft. Strike down the royals and topgallants," shouted Lieutenant Dunkin, the officer of the watch.

"Aye, aye, sir," replied Jon, before hustling up the ratlines.

Striking the tops would decrease the amount of exposed surface should the wind increase further in strength. The wind strength was already occasionally gusting about thirty knots, so the task of striking the tops had changed from limited risk to dam dangerous. For extra safety, Jon personally cautioned each man to retain three points of contact and use only one hand for the assigned tasks.

The work was slow and exhausting. The noise from the wind made any communication in the tops close to impossible. The most difficult aspect of the work was the lowering of the yard and mast to the deck in the wind. The wind first pushed the yardarm outboard. Every time a rope tugged, it affected the balance of the topmen disconnecting the yardarm from the mast. Even though he was involved with lowering, Jon kept glancing around to check his men.

"Beck, grab hold," screamed Jon.

Beck grabbed the nearest line just before he lost his balance. With both feet dangling in the air, only his two-handed grip saved him from a worse fate. If he fell overboard, there would be no stopping, no going back for him. With the assistance of West, the man beside him, Beck was able to regain his footing.

There were no royals on the mizzen so the process was speedier than for the main or foremast. Finally with the topgallant yard lowered they took a short break. The hardest part was yet to commence. The fourth level mast still had to be removed. This mast was as thick as a man's thigh and heavy enough. The problem when striking it, or putting it back into position was there was nothing to suspend it in place. There were only two lines; a stay forward to the main mast, and another line aft. There were no shrouds. The process was simple. Lash on a control line, ease the tension on the support stays, undo the woolding, and let the mast slide down in a controlled movement. Remove all the woolding and lower the mast, less the supports to the deck. It sounded easy, but was scary as hell in practise especially on the pitching mast with the wind howling.

They finally got the mast lowered. The mizzen topmen descended, happy just to reach deck in one piece. They were clearly in no hurry to return to the tops.

Such was not to be however. Assistance was needed on the foremast and mainmast, so off they went. Another few scary hours were needed to finish that work.

As the evening approached, the wind continued to increase. The size of the swells rose as a direct result. On deck, extra precautions were taken. Additional ropes were placed on each gun to ensure they didn't break loose. Safety lines were rigged in the forecastle and in the waist. The topsails were furled and extra gaskets placed over them. On the courses, a second reef was taken.

The officers were debating whether to lower the topsails to the deck. If the wind increased, it would be prudent to have them down. Unfortunately, if they lowered the topsails their capability to run down on the convoy would be constrained. The challenge was that if they didn't lower the topsails now, and the wind did pick up, it might be too dangerous to lower them. If they were still up in the increased wind, the increase in pressure could rip the sails or break the mast. Although this was an officer's decision, the impact might fall totally on the topmen. Finally, the decision was made to lower the topsails. With trepidation, the topmen again ascended into the tops.

Extra gaskets were placed on the topsails before the yardarms were lowered, lest the wind pluck the sails loose during lowering. They completed work one mast at a time. It was more important to get it right without any mistakes than do it fast and have an accident.

A third reef was ordered to the courses. The mizzen lateen was furled and extra gaskets applied. It was slow, treacherous work. Jon was relieved when it was finished. While his team was aloft in weather like this he felt like a mother hen looking after her chicks when hawks were circling.

Jon had experienced a number of storms. This storm, however, was stronger than anything he had previously encountered. The winds just kept increasing and the sea was rising. When the Mermaid crested a wave, the wind shrieked and physically clutched you, ripped at your clothes, and thrust you downwind. When the ship dipped into the trough, the waves were so high that the wind was blocked at deck level.

Last light came early. There was no abatement in the storm. Jon went below and rigged his hammock for sleep. At least in the hammock, the motion of the ship was less pronounced. He was exhausted and instantly fell asleep.

Waking for the next watch, Jon could hear the wind shrieking through the standing rigging. It was an ominous sound. If anything, the storm was more powerful than before. Staggering during a roll of the ship, Jon headed toward the hatch heading up for the watch head count. A quick pat of the pocket confirmed the presence of a morsel of bread. Given the motion of the ship, it was unlikely that there would be a hot meal today or anytime soon.

Jon had donned a tarred jacket which was supposedly waterproof, but he was soon soaked, as was every other man aboard. The wind was pushing the Mermaid sideways. She was heeling at least twenty-five degrees, and making significant leeway. Her seams were working, so there was an expectation that some of the time on watch would be on the pumps.

So far, they were being sorely abused by the wind, but were riding out the storm. If it got no worse, they would be in no danger. That was Jon's assessment based on his experience. He sought out Langtry, a far more experienced sailor from his mess.

"What do you think?" shouted Jon over the wind.

"If it doesn't get any worse, we'll ride it out," replied Langtry.

Captain Montague had been able to maintain a north-westerly course. As day two of the storm progressed, the wind was shifting more to the west. It was blowing from the southwest. The captain shifted the convoy's course from the northeast to the east. He was concerned that if they continued to the northeast, then the wind would be directly to their rear and given the size of the waves, they might be 'pooped'.

Jon had only recently understood the issues with being 'pooped'. A large wave would break over the stern of the ship. Most people considered the stern of the ship the weakest point of a man-o'-war. There were transom windows for both the captain's quarters and the officer's wardroom which could be easily broken by the weight of the water smashing down. The wave could also damage the rudder or pintals, the rudder mountings. It could also smash into the men at the helm causing a momentary loss of steering control. Any of these events could jeopardize the ship.

The safest way to ride out a storm was to put the ship bow-on or heading into the wind. Turning the ship to head into the wind at this point was extremely dangerous. It was also difficult to communicate with other ships of the convoy, so turning the ship would likely result in the scattering of the convoy, which the captain wished to avoid.

As far as communicating with other ships, Jon couldn't even see any other ships when they crested a wave. He was not inclined to go aloft for a better view. In fact, the captain had removed the masthead lookouts. Even if they survived, no one on deck could hear any warnings from them in this wind. You had to shout into a man's ear just for him to hear you.

The sound and the motion were numbing. They over-powered the emotions. The motion was so bad, that many hardened sailors were puking their guts out. Luckily, since there was no food other than 'bread' there was little to keep down.

Jon stayed on deck. Below decks, water was sloshing back and forth. Everything was soaking wet. The water also had a mixture of vomit and excrement. It was too dangerous to use the jakes, so those that needed to go used a bucket. It overturned often.

The Mermaid was taking on water as her seams worked in the heavy motion. Generally, men worked the pumps for one to two hours per day. Now they worked the pumps nearly continuously. Working the pumps further drained already exhausted men. Jon took his turn like all the others. At least when you were below, the impact of the wind was reduced. It was even easier to communicate, although no one had much to say. By this point, most of the crew were wishing they had never heard of the navy.

Day three saw the wind shift further to the west. The captain altered course, if you could call it a course, back to the northeast. They followed the same dull routine for the entire day. No hot food, little sleep, wet, shivering conditions, short, nauseating dips with a sideways rolling motion, and one or two shifts working the pumps.

Jon came off the pumps at the end of the middle watch. He headed up to the upper deck to get some air after the reek of the hold. Normally, there would be light as the dawn approached, but the clouds obscured any possible sunlight. It was also raining, which was different from the previous two days. The rain was steady and hard.

He was just heading below using the forecastle hatch when he heard and felt an almighty crash. Jon wasn't sure of the location of the crash, as he had been on the stairs. Luckily, he was holding supports or he would have fallen. The sound seemed like it came from somewhere up foreward.

Jon turned and rushed back up to the deck, then up to the forecastle. He immediately looked up to see if any of the masts or rigging had been compromised. They looked alright to him. He grabbed a lifeline and pulled himself up to the bow.

A second crash occurred as the Mermaid reached the bottom of the trough and started to plough into another wave. Jon lost his footing and slammed to his knees, not that there was great footing to start. Using the lifeline to regain his feet, he resumed slow movement toward the bow. The crash had definitely come from foreward, but in the darkness it was impossible to see the cause of the crash. The bowsprit was examined. Everything seemed to be in working order on the bowsprit and the jib, which was the only sail still set. Continuing the process of eliminating potential sources, he leaned outboard to verify that the bow anchors were catted home with extra lashings. They still appeared to be secure. Since everything on board appeared secure, the source of the noise remained a mystery.

Still peering over the bow bulwark examining the anchors, Jon spotted something in the water that didn't look right. There was some object moving alongside the bow's larboard side. Several seconds, perhaps a minute elapsed before the nature of the object registered. It was a mast, or at least the jagged bottom of a mast, which had broken off some ship. Unfortunately for the Mermaid, there was still a yard attached to the mast and the rigging had snagged somehow on the bow of the Mermaid.

The sight mesmerized Jon. Every time the Mermaid lifted on a wave, the mast fell away. When the bow dropped and plunged into the next wave, the mast hit the oncoming wave first and was forced back toward the bow. Just before the Mermaid's bow hit the wave, the end of the mast hammered into the bow as it had nowhere else to go. The mast was a battering ram against the wooden 'door' of the Mermaid's larboard bow.

The question was how much battering could the bow take before it was stove-in. Once the bow was stove-in, the Mermaid would be fighting for her life.

It was unclear whether the hammering sound could be heard on the quarterdeck. Jon turned and worked his way aft to report to the officer of the watch. It took an exaggerated amount of time because of the motion.

Despite the gravity of the situation, Jan was hesitant to mount the steps from the waist to the quarterdeck. The quarterdeck was officer country, and they guarded it jealously. By stepping foot on the quarterdeck without permission, a man could be found guilty of insubordination. That was not a risk Jon was willing to take. He stood at the bottom of the steps in full view of the officer of the watch and waved his arms to gain permission to approach the quarterdeck.

After a couple of minutes of waving, the officer of the watch beckoned him to approach. Jon staggered up the steps, knuckled his forehead and reported to the officer of the watch. The captain was standing a couple of paces to windward, just to add to Jon's nervousness. There was no way Jon would speak to the captain directly without first being granted permission.

"Sir, there's a busted mast from another ship snagged on our bow. The yard is still attached, and the yard and rigging has somehow got caught on the bow. The wind and the waves are forcing the broken base of the mast against the larboard bow each time we dip into a trough. That's what's causing the crash we've been hearing up foreward. If it keeps it up, it might stove-in the larboard bow. I don't know if the caulking's been damaged yet."

Captain Montague who had somehow overheard the conversation beckoned to Mr. Mason, the bosun. "Get a party together and clear away that broken mast from the bow."

To the first lieutenant, Mr. Davis, the captain ordered, "Get the carpenter to check for damage on the larboard bow".

Mr. Mason grabbed Jon by the arm, "Get foreward. I'll send some more men up."

"We'll need rope and very sharp boarding axes," said Jon. Without any doubt, someone would have to be lowered over the bow and cut away any rigging that was catching on the Mermaid and keeping the mast alongside. Given the waves, the individual would be submerged half the time.

It took a few minutes for the bosun to roust out a working crew. They were a mixed lot. The bosun had to find strong men who weren't either exhausted or seasick.

"Who's going over?" asked Jon when the bosun appeared.

"You are," replied the bosun.

"Me?.....I'm a topman, this is a job for some landsman."

"Tough shit -- you were the one that spotted it. You were the one that identified it as a mast, and topmen look after masts. So get your ass ready," shouted Mr. Mason.

Jon looked over the bow. No one in his right mind would want to go over the side in weather like this. It was insane. There were only two options -- either to go, or not. A refusal would be disobedience of a lawful command. That was a striped back for sure, or possibly worse. A demotion from the position as senior rating for the mizzenmast would occur. It was also highly probable that every shit job they could find would be his. Someone had to go. If that snagged mast punched a hole in the bow, the odds were that everyone on this ship would be dead within an hour or two. So what choice really was there?

Shrugging his shoulders while concurrently shaking his head and muttering to himself, he leaned over the bow and examined the task at hand. Finally, after weathering another deluge of water when the bow hammered into the next wave, he straightened and turned back to the bosun.

"I'll need a regular line plus a safety line."

Mr. Mason nodded.

"You," said Jon pointing at the nearest man. "Get me a sharp boarding axe; one with a good lanyard."

Jon proceeded to undo his shirt, and remove the money-belt that he wore. He walked over to the bosun and handed him the money belt as he spoke into his ear.

"I'm giving this to you for safekeeping. I can't carry it in the water. I better not find anything missing when you return it to me, 'cause bosun or not, you'll be just as dead."

Stepping back slightly, Jon looked directly in the bosun's eyes. The bosun had a surly expression, which visibly altered as his darkened face paled.

"I'm gonna make a rope seat with a short rope. I'll secure that to one line. I want that second safety line around my chest in case the first one fails. I'll take a boarding axe with a lanyard over my right hand. I'll go out on the bowsprit and find a place to use as a fulcrum for heaving me back aboard. I'll signal to lower, so make sure there's enough slack in the lines. That should be easy. All I'll have to do is step off. To lift, I'll raise my hand above my head and rotate it in a circle. Okay?"

Mr. Mason slapped him on the back and nodded that he understood. It was easier than trying to shout.

Jon started rapidly tying the rope seat. He was committed now. There was no sense moaning about it. After the rope seat was completed, he tied on the first line. On the safety line, he made a bowline around the upper chest. Someone handed him a boarding axe.

Jon moved toward the bowsprit. Mr. Mason positioned himself to the larboard side of the bowsprit where he could see everything.

Jon slipped the lanyard of the boarding axe over the right wrist. It was now all about timing. A slow count began to assess the time between wave crests. Despite slowing edging on along the bowsprit, he couldn't find an appropriate spot for a fulcrum. Turning to look at the men holding his safety lines was a mistake. They could see what he couldn't. A larger than normal wave was cresting behind him.

The Mermaid plunged into the base of the next wave. As he couldn't see the wave, it hit him unexpectedly, propelling him off the bowsprit and into the bow. The hammering knocked the wind from him so violently he was breathless. As he sucked in air, the wave broke. The result was a mouth and lungs full of seawater. Panic overtook him and he clawed his way up the barnacled bow to the surface. The water was freezing. Sputtering and coughing, he tried to gain his orientation. The Mermaid was cresting the next wave by now so a desperate search to spot the offending rigging commenced. At least a dozen ropes appeared in his blurred vision. He paused to make sure that the ones he was cutting were not his safety lines.

Before he could fully get his bearings, the Mermaid hit the trough and slammed in to the next wave. He was only half-ready for it. He was at least holding his breath. He grabbed a rope, pulled his knife, and sawed away. By the time his head had broken the surface, the line had parted. He groped for the knife sheath and slid his knife away. A flick of his wrist and the boarding axe was in his hand. He hammered away at another rope and it parted. The next wave hit.

Wave after wave submerged him. He cut every rope he could find, but it didn't seem to make any difference. The mast was still firmly caught.

As his head came to the surface, Jon lifted his arm and circled for the deck gang to haul him in. He was hammered against the side of the bow, and scraped mercilessly as they hauled him up. The safety rope around his chest was crushing his chest and chaffing his entire upper torso. Finally, they dragged him over the bulwark and he flopped like a dead fish. Between fighting for breath and shivering, he had no strength to move.

"Make way," shouted Lieutenant Davis. The next thing that Jon knew was that the first lieutenant was leaning over him. "Report!"

Jon could hardly speak as his teeth were chattering that badly. "Sir, I cut all the lines I could reach. The sail on the yard is furled, and jammed somehow against the keel. I can't see how. It might be possible to move it further down, but if it does, it's going to run along the keel and pop up aft. It may either pop-up between the rudder and the transom or hit the rudder and knock it off the pintals. In either case we might lose the rudder."

The first lieutenant took in what Jon said. "What about cutting loose the yard from the mast?"

"From what I could see, it looked as if the yard was anchored to the mast with chains. You'd have to chop them out. I don't know if it's possible in these conditions," replied Jon.

"It has to be done," stated Lieutenant Davis. "Bosun, get another man over the side to separate the yard and mast. We have to cut away that mast."

The bosun looked at the first lieutenant, "Aye Aye sir." He knew, as did the first lieutenant that the next man had a low survival probability. He also knew they would have to keep putting men over until they managed to free the mast. The alternative was death for the entire crew.

The bosun looked around at the men mustered before him and shouted, "Any volunteers?"

They all knew the odds. One man named Henry stepped forward. They removed the safety lines from Jon and strapped them around

Henry. Henry was a landsman from the starboard watch. Although Jon knew Henry to see him, he didn't know much more about the man. The boarding axe was passed over.

"Good luck," was all Jon could mumble.

Jon was rolled into some canvas in an attempt to get some warmth back into the body. Henry disappeared over the side. Jon lost track of time, but it wasn't too long until Henry's limp body was dragged back on board. Another man volunteered. He apparently lasted longer than Henry had, but he also was a limp rag when hauled back on board.

Jon stood and staggered to the bulwark. Looking down at the mast, the marks from the previous two men were visible. The bosun called, "Any more volunteers?"

There was not one man willing after seeing what happened to the previous three men including Jon. The other two had been taken below to the surgeon already. Only Jon remained topside of the three that had gone over the side.

To underscore the seriousness of their situation, the mast crashed once more into the side of the Mermaid. Lieutenant Davis re-appeared. "What's the hold-up?"

"No volunteers," replied Mr. Mason.

Lieutenant Davis pointed at the first man on the safety line. "You're next. Rope up and get going."

"No sir, you can flog me, but that's death for sure. No sir, I'm not goin'," said the man. The others looked at Lieutenant Davis and shook their heads as well.

The Bosun started to rope up. He knew he was next, and had to show leadership or his position as bosun was finished.

Jon took a step from where he was standing along the bulwark toward Mr. Mason. He extended his arm with his palm open. Mr. Mason looked up from tying the rope around his waist. Jon shook his head and beckoned with his hand.

"You're not going over with my money-belt. I'll be having it back before you go over the side."

Jon felt a hand slap on his back. He turned to find Lieutenant Davis looking intently at him.

"Good man Smith, I'll remember this," shouted Lieutenant Davis.

Jon's jaw dropped. He sputtered, but nothing came out.

Jon turned to the bosun as the bosun slapped the boarding axe into his open hand. The bosun had a smile from ear to ear as he leaned down to tie a rope to the rope seat, which Jon was still wearing. Simultaneously, Jon's arms were raised from behind, and the second safety rope snaked down to his chest.

Jon absently tested the edge of the boarding axe. It was dull. He asked for a new boarding axe with a sharper edge -- delaying the inevitable.

Climbing over the bulwark, he waited for the waves. As the Mermaid crested the wave, he dropped and lunged through the water for the mast. He got there and established a strong grip before the Mermaid hammered into the next wave. Once the wave had retreated, Jon got in three good strokes. He hit the mast a fourth time, but the blade embedded in the wood. It took some time to get it loose. When he finally pried the blade loose, he was spun around. He hit the next wave facing forward. The yard closed in on him and he was better able to see the fitting on the yard. The yard was only a fraction of the width of the mast. They had been spending all their efforts on the mast, and probably could have already cut the yard in half. Jon put all of his efforts into the yardarm. In four waves, he managed to work his way through half of the yardarm. What little strength he had was flagging rapidly. The next wave he put all his efforts into the yardarm once again. It was not enough. He knew he had only one more wave in him.

When he surfaced after the next wave, he hammered the yardarm four times. The yardarm was weak, but had not broken. He moved back along the furled sail toward the bow. He felt a gasket and cut it. He continued and cut two additional gaskets.

Surfacing after the next wave, he knew he'd had it. He mentally cursed himself for not running when he had the chance. He muttered, "Never again, I'm running the next chance I get."

While being hauled aboard in a semi-conscious condition, the sail caught and started unfurling. It placed extra pressure on the yard. Everyone heard the snap of the yardarm over the wind, as they attempted to warm Jon's body.

The bosun looked overboard. The mast hammered into the side of the Mermaid. It was skewing sideways, whereas before it had remained largely parallel with the Mermaid. The result was that more water caught it and pulled it away broadside to the Mermaid. Concurrently, the sail unfurled. The sail tugged at that portion of the yardarm caught under the Mermaid's bow and wrenched it loose. The entire mast and yard assembly floated away from the Mermaid. In another wave it was well astern.

The crisis for the ship was over. For Jon, it was just beginning.

CHAPTER 11

Two men half dragged, half carried an inert Jon down to the sick bay. In normal conditions, this would have been a relatively simple process, but with the motion of the ship it was more challenging. Jon was rolled in canvas to provide some warmth. He was like a weight, suspended between two bookends. Each time the ship lurched, the weight -- Jon -- swung out and smashed against whatever object they were passing. If the lurch was bad enough, and one of the bookends lost his balance or had to reach out to grab something, Jon was dropped. By the time they managed to get him down to the surgeon, his battered body was well 'tenderized'.

Upon reaching the sick bay, the loblolly boys pointed them toward a hammock, where Jon was deposited and swaddled in dry blankets. How they managed to keep the blankets dry in this weather was a mystery, but of little consequence or concern now.

"Mr. Longstreet, sir, there's another one," commented one of the surgeon's mates.

"Is he in as bad shape as the other two?" asked Mr. Longstreet, the surgeon. The surgeon had just seen two similar cases of hypothermia, both of which had lasted but minutes.

"Worse. According to the men that carried him down, he was over the side twice. The two others were only in the water once," replied the surgeon's mate.

"Well, I hope that we can do better than the other two. Let's get him in here and on the table," said Mr. Longstreet. Jon was dragged in and deposited on the examining table.

"Jesus, his temperature is low. He feels like an ice block," exclaimed Mr. Longstreet. "Get some hot water from the cook."

"Captain ordered all the fires out, so no hot water, sir," replied the surgeon's mate.

"I guess we'll have to do this the hard way. Strip him and start rubbing down his arms and legs to restore as much circulation as possible," ordered the surgeon. As the surgeon's mates started work on Jon, Mr. Longstreet went in search of some medicine.

"Tilt his head back, while I pour a little of this rum into him," ordered Mr. Longstreet. He decided to explain things further to his two assistants.

"If there were hot water available, I wouldn't be giving him any rum. Hypothermia can be deadly by itself, and is often fatal when combined with exhaustion. Normally you don't give the patient alcohol because it increases the blood flow to the body's skin and extremities. You normally need to retain as much heat as possible in the body's core. Unfortunately, I don't have any other treatment that I think might work available at the present, and he needs to get some blood moving in his arms and legs. Now tip his head back so I can pour some of this rum down his throat," said Mr. Longstreet.

"Maybe I should get a mild case of hypothermia," suggested one of the surgeon's mates, smacking his lips as he watched the rum disappear down Jon's throat. The surgeon gave him a dirty look, which seemed not to faze the man in the slightest.

Jon was semi-conscious of what was happening. Mr. Longstreet seemed to have an ample supply of neat rum. So long as he felt inclined to pour it down Jon's throat, Jon felt obligated to drink it. If he were going to check out, at least he'd be feeling no pain while doing it.

Despite the alcohol and warm dry blankets, the uncontrollable vibrating continued. As the surgeon's mates continued to apply a vigorous rubdown, the body's internal functions slowed, finally resulting in Jon slipping into unconsciousness.

The loblolly boys debated whether recovery was possible once a patient lost all lucidity and drifted into an unconscious state. For the next few hours it was touch and go for sure. The efforts of the surgeon's mates slowly tapered off. They had done the best they could with what they had. They left him covered in blankets, in the hands of His Maker, while they went about their other work.

They say that just before death, you see your entire life flash before your eyes. Most people, when they hear this statement, think their life will pass by in a continuous stream from the time that they are born until the present. This is not the case. Moments in your life will appear which you have either totally forgotten or repressed. The moments will be so clear that you are again in that place and time. Somehow, your brain has stored the entire aspect of the moment, including the input that you received from all of your senses. You can smell, taste, see, feel and hear everything that happened and that you felt at that moment. The moment is fleeting however, as another image will rapidly replace it. There is no apparent sequence to these images. The images will go on until everything goes black. At that point either you come back to life or head the other way. Since no living person can describe the other path, that remains an even bigger mystery.

Because Jon was young, there weren't as many images or experiences stored away as an older person might potentially have stored. He saw his mother, as she was when he was young. His mother's features were soft, as a woman's should be in her twenties. The image skipped to his father telling him that the family was depending on him to get a good price for the produce in Rye the next day. He remembered turning his head and seeing Abercrombie strike Malcolm Cartwright in the head with a black object, then blackness.

Jon momentarily returned to semi-consciousness after twenty-four hours, still shaking from the cold. He could only slightly differentiate between the various forms of pain. He had a massive headache, probably due to the neat rum. His chest was raw from the pressure and rubbing of the safety rope. Most of his body was bruised from slamming into the bow or the mast in the water. He longed for something to ease his pain.

In a weak voice, Jon croaked, "Anyone here?"

A surgeon's mate appeared in the dim light.

"Something to ease the pain?" croaked Jon.

Apparently, small mercies do occur as the surgeon's mate provided a couple of tots of rum to ease the pain. It was also quite helpful in reducing the magnitude of his hangover. Jon again drifted off to sleep.

Sometime later, after surfacing from the depths of sleep, he could still hear the screaming of the wind. That meant the storm was still in full progress. All sense of time had been lost. Whether he had been asleep for minutes or hours was unknown, but it must have been for some time because the pressure on his bladder was fearsome. Satisfying that need was challenging because, cocooned in a series of blankets, it was nigh on impossible to even move his arms. Some light shivering was still evident but at least the uncontrollable vibrating had ceased.

"Anyone there?" croaked Jon.

"Right here mate," came a rapid response. "How are you feeling?"

Jon looked around. There was no light at all. Even the candles were out. In the darkness he had no idea who was answering him.

"Is that you Bones?" croaked Jon.

"Sure enough. You had us worried Jon. You doin' alright?" answered Bones.

"Need some water, and I gotta go," said Jon. "I'm still cold as hell."

"At least you're alive. The others never made it," said Bones.

"I'm still not sure I will," said Jon. He then realised his money belt and clothes were gone.

"Where's all my stuff?" asked Jon suddenly.

"Never you mind. We got it all secured away for you. Come on now and we'll get you up. You can do your business and I'll get you some water, some bread and some clothes," said Bones.

Bones assisted Jon in getting out of the hammock. When his feet hit the deck, they were in ankle deep water, which was sloshing around before it drained down into the hold.

"How long have I been down here?" asked a much relieved Jon a few moments later.

"It's day five of this storm, and it hasn't let up one bit," replied Bones.

"Jesus, I feel shitty. I don't think there is a square inch of my body that doesn't ache."

Bones helped with dressing, but the clothes were damp. Shivering recommenced at a stronger level than had occurred just moments before.

"I'll give you a tot, eat some bread, and get some more sleep. There ain't anyone going up in the tops until this storm is over, so you just take it easy," said Bones.

Jon drank water, rum, and munched on some bread, all the while vibrating in the hammock. Sleep was not forthcoming. He had already slept longer than he could ever remember since coming aboard. Bones saw that he wasn't asleep when he came over to check on him.

"Hey Bones, what's happening?"

"As you can hear, the storm is still goin' strong," replied Bones. The shriek of the wind could be clearly heard even this far below.

"Have many customers?"

"Enough. Most of them are busted bones. They'll heal soon enough, or we'll put them off in England."

"England......"

"Where's home, Jon?"

"About a half day's walk inland from Rye. My father rents a farm from the local squire."

"Any other family?"

"My mother, a fourteen year-old sister, Susan, and a nine year-old brother, Robbie."

"A lot of mouths to feed."

"Yeah. In a good year, the farm provides enough crops to cover the rent, food for our family, and to pay for necessities. There never seemed to be any additional money that allowed us to get ahead. In a bad year, after the rent and bills for necessities were paid, there wasn't even enough left over to feed the family until the next harvest. I started poaching to supplement the food for the family, and I wasn't the only one. Lots of folks were in the same situation."

"I can barely remember back when I was a young tyke. My father was much the same as yours I suppose. I never remember the farm rent going down," said Bones softly.

"No, it seems the local squire always needed more funds. He claimed he always needed more gamekeepers. The worse the harvest, the more he needed the game keepers. If he hadn't hired some of those gamekeepers, he wouldn't have needed such high rents and everyone would have been happier, except maybe the gamekeepers."

"Heard from your family since you were pressed?"

"Not a word. My ability to read and write is limited, and my parents can't do either. What I figure though, is that with me gone, there is one less mouth to feed. I was pressed after the harvest, so my absence shouldn't have hurt them, at least from a work point of view. I imagine that they will be missing the extra meat for the pot I was able to provide, but otherwise, I'm hoping that they will be better off."

"That's a good way of lookin' at it. No sense dwelling on the other. There's enough bitterness here, without worrying about things you can't do nothin' about anyway," said Bones.

"That's true. Just the same, I'd like to meet the bastards that did this to me in a dark alley some night. Not only did they put me through a lot, but they did the same to my family."

Bones chuckled, "That's probably been said about every press gang that ever raided a tavern."

"I'm not talkin' about the press gang. They were just doin' their job. Fact is, they probably saved my life. No, I'm talkin' about a couple of vicious bastards that worked for the local squire. I spoke to the bosun on the Winchester, my previous ship. He told me the Winchester's press gang had been approached by a man targeting me. The description of this man fit one of the squire's men I mentioned. I don't know who hit me and tried to rob me, but I saw one of those two hit the guy I was with and kill him. Believe me, if I get a chance, I'd like to pay those two back."

"You know what they say about revenge, don't you?" asked Bones. "Before you head down that path, first dig two graves..."

"Well two graves ought to do it, but I hadn't really thought it would go that far. I was thinking more along the lines of an extended cruise in His Majesty's service for them."

"What I was going to say before you cut me off, was that you dig two graves -- one for your victim and the other for yourself," said Bones. "Anyway, I can see that this conversation isn't helping, so I'll be off."

Jon wasn't put off at all by the conversation. It did cause him to review his current situation, and contrast it with what he believed might have occurred if he had not been pressed.

All things considered, Jon believed he was far better off than he could have expected. He had seen a large part of the world, although not getting off the ship in most cases. He had learned a great deal about seamanship. He had been promoted ahead of many others because of this skill. He had improved his ability to trade and was certainly richer than he had ever been. Richer in fact than his father, despite all the backbreaking labour his father had done. He was also more knowledgeable than he would have been if he had remained on the farm. He had experienced some minor supervisory roles, and had taught men. He also knew how to kill, if need be, as he had dispatched at least two men to see their Maker during the boarding of the French vessel Vigilante. He figured he had probably killed more with cannon shots, but of that he was not proud -- it was just his job. His physical condition was certainly improved. Although the food on one of His Majesty's vessels was not great, the physically demanding daily duties and steady diet had transformed his body from that of a youth to a strong, lithe adult. There was no question his self-confidence was greater. So all-in-all, Jon was grateful.

Jon also reflected on his position within the ship. On his previous ship, HMS Winchester, he had been somewhat of a pariah as he had been continuously given extra duties. He had very few friends. In fact, he was what he considered a loner. That did not bother him. He had come into this ship with a fresh start, and because of the circumstances around Beck's fall, was now in exactly the same loner position. Add to that, he was a newcomer and also a senior rating. Each of these by themselves was a small hurdle to overcome, but added together they reinforced the loner label.

The real problem had come when Beck had fallen from the mizzen during a training exercise to strike the top. Although he was not responsible for a man falling from the mizzen, there was an underlying reservation about him on the part of others because of it. He was also different from the others, as he had money, and every man on the ship knew it. At least he hoped he still had money, if the bosun could be trusted. He carried two knives for a reason. People had seen him fight. They knew he was fast. So far, he was the only man on board who had, at least one time, bested Lieutenant Rylett -- considered the ship's best fencer, in cutlass practice. As a result, no one was eager to tackle him to get at the money. Jon was also smart enough to spread a little around to protect himself. He had purchased fruits and vegetables for his mess when the opportunity presented itself.

Lieutenant Rylett posed yet another problem. He liked to stick it to Jon at every opportunity he could. During cutlass practise, this meant enduring countless painful strikes from the practice swords. Other times he was subjected to extra duties that provided no value, except perhaps teaching patience and tolerance. If Jon lost his cool in any of those situations, Rylett would use it against him. He had narrowly escaped a striped shirt on a number of occasions. All of these factors had resulted in his messmates, and all the topmen, distancing themselves from him to some extent.

The attitude that he now sensed was one of acceptance, possibly even respect, although he was not sure that he would go that far. The reservation just didn't seem to be there anymore. When supervising his team on the mizzen, he rarely shouted. Sometimes it was necessary when the officers were listening, but the men were aware of this as well. They knew the game. In most cases, if things weren't going properly, he would approach the man and quietly determine the problem. He would then show or suggest different approaches. Sometimes it didn't work, but most of the time it did. The overall result of this approach was that the mizzen team was well trained and rarely needed supervision.

Despite all of these setbacks, and what some would consider progress, Jon knew that he still didn't want to be here, or in the navy. That left one major question in his mind. What did he want?

He had made a pact with himself earlier in the voyage that whatever happened on this voyage would determine whether he stayed or ran. The fact that he had been ordered over the side of the ship meant that he was expendable, so it made his decision simple.

He would run given the right opportunity.

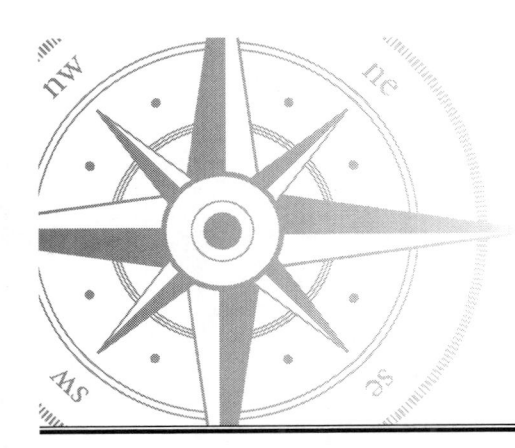

CHAPTER 12

The trials of the Mermaid continued while Jon remained confined in the sick bay.

Close to half the crew was ineffective. Most of these men were so seasick they could barely move. Others had broken bones or had been injured when they lost their footing or grip when the ship's motion violently changed.

Of those that were still effective, most were exhausted, as they spent the majority of their time working the pumps. Since the start of the storm, the pumps had never stopped. Water from rain and spray continually dripped through the joints in the deck. The seams were working hard in this sea. Either the pumps continued or the Mermaid would slowly sink.

If the men were exhausted, the officers were not much better off. The captain had rarely left the quarterdeck since the beginning of the storm. The master had been present most of the time as well. The other officers had continued their normal watches and were in better condition.

No one had consumed a decent meal since the storm had started and certainly nothing hot. All the crew had eaten in the past few days was bread. The officers hadn't fared much better, although they had jams with which to alter the bread's taste.

The wind had veered later in the day, after Jon was carried below. The convoy had been scattered, with each ship looking to ensure her respective safety rather than attempting to maintain any kind of formation. With the change in wind direction, HMS Mermaid had altered her course to keep from being stern-on to the wind.

The wind direction continued to change as the storm track shifted. This kept the officers on their toes, as they frequently needed to change course. As the storm continued, the frequency of rogue waves increased. Rogue waves were of special concern, as they increased the threat of being pooped.

Over the last two days, the wind direction had changed more rapidly. It appeared the storm was tracking to the south of the convoy, and moving at a good clip. With the wind direction changing hourly, closer attention had to be paid to the swell. Lookouts for rogue waves were posted, despite a uniform dislike of adding extra duties to a hungry, sick and battered crew.

On the fifth day of the storm, during the first watch, the wind was changing almost hourly. Two lookouts were in the forecastle, one on either side in the waist, and another two at the stern of the poop deck.

Near three bells in the first watch the aft lookout screamed, "Rogue wave."

The officer of the deck, the captain, and the master's mate all turned to see the possible threat.

"Oh my God," slipped out of Lieutenant Caharty's mouth.

The captain screamed, "Hold on."

There was no time to say anything else as a rogue wave hammered into the stern of the ship. The wave was so large, that a solid wall of water at least four feet high washed directly over the quarterdeck.

When the wave hammered the stern of the ship, the windows in both the captain's quarters and the officer's wardroom were smashed. Those officers in the wardroom were tossed around like puppets. On the quarterdeck, the two men on the wheel both lost their footing, but held onto the wheel. This kept the rudder from slewing the ship sideways into the trough. The lookouts had time to grab the bulwark and were able to maintain their position.

The officer of the watch, the captain, and the master's mate were all washed into the waist. The officers picked themselves up and rushed back to the quarterdeck. The master's mate fractured his leg both above and below the knee when he slammed into a 12-pounder.

There was general flooding on the lower gun deck, but that only meant the water was deeper than it had been previously.

Work parties were formed to repair the transom windows and assess the damage to the ship. The carpenter reported no other damage other than the loss of the transom windows. He rigged coverings over the windows to prevent any further water from entering. The loss of light was minimal because the skies were dark anyway.

Asleep in the hammock in the sick bay, Jon knew nothing about the incident until the next day when one of the surgeon's mates mentioned it.

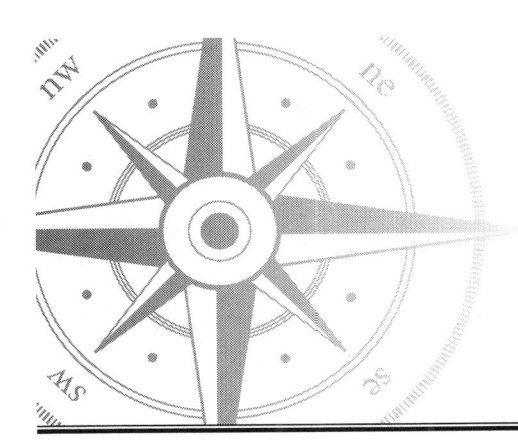

CHAPTER 13

It was the morning watch and time for the surgeon to make his rounds. Mr. Longstreet finally made his way over to Jon.

"Well Smith, how do you feel?" asked Mr. Longstreet.

"Hungry and sore," responded Jon truthfully.

"No different than most men on board," replied Mr. Longstreet. "I'm returning you to regular duties. Get your kit and get out of here."

"Aye, sir, and thank you," responded Jon. He turned to Bones, "Thanks for everything Bones." He squeezed Bone's arm as he passed him and headed for the stairs heading to the gun deck.

Water was still sloshing around on the gun deck. Men were busy attempting to mop it up, but it would take some time before they got all of it. Continuing to the upper deck, the first thing that Jon did was to scan the sea and sky like any typical sailor. He had not seen the sky in four days. The storm had dissipated, but the sea was still lively. The wind, however, had dropped considerably during the previous night.

Despite being ordered back to duty, Jon deviated. He needed to find the bosun and ascertain whether his valuables were still intact. Despite the small size of the ship, it took some time to hunt him down. Mr. Mason was busy laying into a man for some fault he had discovered. Upon realizing Jon was there, he wordlessly motioned Jon to follow him.

Somewhat apprehensively, Jon followed Mason down to his quarters. Jon had never entered any mess other than the men's, so it was a different world to him. Waiting for the bosun, he scanned the interior. Each occupant of the mess had a level of privacy that far exceeded any man forward of the mast. Personal chests were also visible. Foreward of the mast no man had a chest, as there was no place to set them. A permanent mess table was present at which sat the carpenter and others. They had mugs in hand. These were comforts not seen forward of the mast.

So busy was he looking at the interior that he failed to realize the bosun was handing him his money-belt. Snapping back to reality, he examined the contents to ensure everything was present.

"What's a matter -- don't you trust me?" said Mr. Mason.

Jon looked at him, "Would you check it if the shoe were on the other foot?"

Mr. Mason replied, "With you -- you're dam right I would."

"Well I guess you'll live another day, since everything appears to be here," said Jon as he strapped the belt on underneath his shirt. "By the way, thanks for looking after it, although I rather suspect you were hoping I wasn't going to be around to collect it."

Mr. Mason smiled, "I admit, the thought had crossed my mind. Just the same, I'm glad that you made it. I would also like to say thanks for heading back into the water a second time. I'm getting a little too old for that sort of nonsense."

"You bastard, you knew I wasn't volunteering."

Mr. Mason burst out laughing. He was struggling to get the words out, "You should have seen the look on your face when Lieutenant Davis congratulated you on your outstanding sense of duty."

Jon shook his head. His first impression when he came aboard the Mermaid was that Mr. Mason was a puffed up little rooster, but here was Mason joking man-to-man with him, even after Jon had called him a bastard. There was a human side to the man after all -- best not to push it though.

Jon continued to shake his head as he exited the bosun's mess and headed back up to the deck. The laughter from the bosun's mess chased after him.

"Sir, the surgeon has released me ready for duty," said Jon as he reported to Midshipman Farley who was his direct superior.

"Right Smith, get your people aloft. I want a full report on the condition of the ropes and rigging," ordered Mr. Farley.

Gathering the mizzen topmen, they ascended the mizzen ratlines. There was some repair work to accomplish, but in general, the Mermaid had fared well. By the end of the afternoon watch, all repairs for which the mizzen topmen were responsible, were complete. The topsails were raised, and courses were deployed, albeit with some reefs.

The captain's order to have the galley fires lit had spread around the ship. Even though the ship's motion was still lively, a hot supper would be fully appreciated after several days on ship's bread.

"I'm as hungry as a bear," said Hale.

"Me too," replied West.

"Everyone's hungry. I heard that we are getting double rations for supper. Any truth to that rumour?" asked Young.

Langtry, as senior man in the mess, replied, "We'll find out soon enough, when Mannion brings the rations."

"Now that this storm is blown out, whatcha think we are going to do?" asked Hale.

"Head north, look for what's left of the convoy. Once we find them, then we'll have to shepherd them back to England, or to France for those ships carrying the Frenchmen," said Jon.

"Anyone seen any other ships from the convoy?" asked Hale.

"Not that I heard of or saw."

"Here comes Mannion. Let's see what he's got," said West.

"Double rations, gents," said a smiling Mannion. "Pork, peas, cheese, the works -- the only thing we didn't get was the beef ration."

As Mannion dished out equal portions to each man, there was a muted eagerness to dig in to the meal. Once Mannion was satisfied that each man had equal portions, he said, "Dig in." No one had to be told a second time. The entire mess polished off their respective portions in short order without any complaints.

After the meal, Langtry said in an elevated voice, "Gents, clean up your kit as best as possible and put whatever's wet out to dry as best you can."

When the bell struck for the last dog watch, Jon stayed below. He grabbed some biscuit from the bread barge, which he shoved into his pocket before retrieving the single book he had on loan from his ditty bag. A quick search found a secluded, reasonably dry place to sit with sufficient light. The bulk of the watch was spent attempting to read. It still required slow, laborious effort on his part. Over time some improvement could be measured. From time to time, he sought assistance from someone to get help in pronouncing a word, or explaining its meaning. Since few sailors before the mast read, just finding someone to approach was a challenge. Unconsciously, he sucked on a piece of biscuit while reading. After allowing some time for saliva to soften the 'bread', the biscuit could be crushed into small enough pieces to chew and swallow. Despite the large meal, hunger was a near constant companion.

The call for the next watch triggered a quick rush back to the ditty bag. Exchanging the book for a tarred jacket, Jon dressed enroute to the upper deck for head count. Although it wasn't raining at the present, donning the tarred jack would help keep the cold wind at bay.

Standing in line for the normal head count at the start of the watch, the entire watch heard Lieutenant Rylett berate some poor bastard. As Rylett was the officer of the watch, if there were any dirty jobs to do during this watch, Jon figured he would be targeted.

The watch itself was very quiet. Each man was attempting to regain his strength after the storm. It was obviously too quiet for Lieutenant Rylett. Near the end of the watch Jon was called by the bosun.

"Smith, check the lashings on the main top to ensure they're secure," said Mr. Mason.

Jon looked the bosun. They both knew the source of the order.

"Aye, Mr. Mason."

As he started the ascent, Jon shook his head in exasperation. Everyone within hearing knew the order was a punishment, for no one on deck could even see the lashings in the fading light. Additionally, the lashings he was ordered to check were on the main, whereas Jon's responsibility was the mizzen mast.

Jon quickly climbed the mast, and verified that the lashings were fine. He remained aloft until the end of the watch, just in case Lieutenant Rylett had any further ideas on how to keep him occupied.

Jon's impression and that of many men on board, was that Lieutenant Rylett was a weasel-like bastard. He stole credit from the men in his division. He handed out punishments without any regard to the damage they caused, or to whether they were justified. If he were taken to task, he weaselled out of it by laying the blame on someone else. The worst part about it was that because he was an officer he got away with it. If he were before the mast, someone would have re-arranged his face for him by now. Jon would volunteer for that job in a heartbeat.

As the watch ended, Jon scampered down from the tops and fled below. Sleep and distance from Rylett were all that he craved.

In the morning, while the mess was together, West commented, "I see Rylett was back to his old tricks again last night. What is it with that bastard anyway?"

"Rylett just loves Jon ever since receiving that crack on the knee during cutlass practice and having that heart-to-heart chat with the previous captain," said Mannion with a grin.

"He's got it in for me, but he's not going to beat me; I'm better than him," growled Jon.

"Pride goeth before destruction, and an haughty spirit before a fall. Proverbs 16.18," said Liliput the senior rating of the foremast. Liliput couldn't read, but had somehow memorized an incredible number of passages from the bible. When he said a quote, most men in the mess paid attention.

Langtry commented, "If Rylett has enough confidence to resume his old tricks, just you wait. It won't be long before they start to impact you and me. That bastard is meaner than a snake and just as sly as a fox. He has more tricks than a sorcerer does. You can bet your last penny that he'll use some of them tricks against us before we get to England."

That comment stopped any further conversation cold, as each man took in the implications.

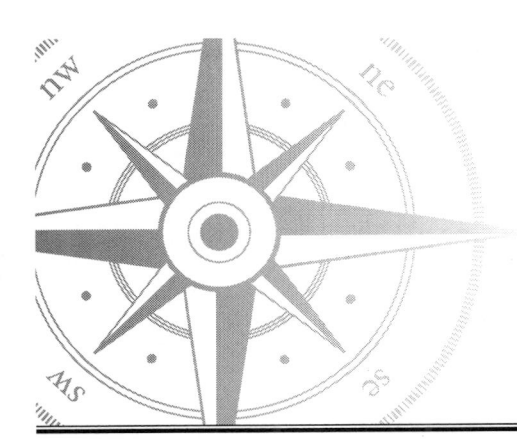

CHAPTER 14

On the morning of the eighth day after the start of the storm, Captain Montague motioned for the master to join him on the windward side of the quarterdeck. In that position they were out of hearing of the remainder of the watch.

"What say you Mr. Flynn? Given the odd nature of wind direction and the seas during the storm, which course would be the most appropriate to take to find the remaining ships of the convoy?" asked the captain.

"I would venture due north at first, captain. I imagine most merchant captains would run with the wind so we should find them all north and east of us," replied the master.

"Do you think any of them would be to the west of us?" asked Captain Montague.

"It's possible, sir. If there were any, I would imagine they would be the merchantmen bound for England, and not the ones carrying the Frenchmen. Those five ships were at the front of the convoy and should all be ahead of us," replied the master.

The captain turned and called for the first lieutenant.

Upon Lieutenant Davis's arrival, the captain issued orders. "Mr. Davis, we will proceed due north for the day. I want the topgallants and royals top put back on her and double the lookouts in the tops until we find all the ships of the convoy. They are likely to be scattered all over."

"Aye, aye, sir," replied Lieutenant Davis.

While both the first lieutenant and captain were present Mr. Flynn stated, "McFadden's seriously injured. They might have to take his leg off. For the remainder of this voyage he's out of commission."

Captain Montague asked, "So who do we replace him with?"

Lieutenant Davis replied, "Usually one of the quartermasters assumes the position. In this case, it would be either Kieffer or Williams. Who do you think is better Mr. Flynn?"

"They're both good men on the wheel -- about equal I suppose. Neither of them can read or write and I have my doubts about their capabilities in arithmetic. I don't believe they would be able to perform certain aspects of the job," replied Mr. Flynn.

"Let's get the division commanders over here. We'll see if they have any ideas," said Captain Montague.

Lieutenant Caharty, the ship's second lieutenant and larboard division commander, and Lieutenant Rylett, the ship's third lieutenant and starboard division commander, were called.

Upon their arrival Captain Montague summarized, "McFadden, the master's mate is injured and needs to be replaced. Normally one of the quartermasters would assume the position, but neither of them can read or write and their capabilities in arithmetic are unknown. Is there anyone in your divisions that can read and write, is smart enough to do arithmetic, and has sufficient knowledge to assume an acting master's mate rating? Mr. Rylett?"

Lieutenant Rylett considered for a moment, and then replied, "No one in my division, sir."

"Mr. Caharty?"

"Maybe Smith, sir," replied Lieutenant Caharty after some hesitation.

"Who's Smith?" asked Captain Montague.

Lieutenant Davis provided the information, "Able seaman Jon Smith sir. He's captain of the mizzen. He's probably the most skilled topman we have on the ship. He can read and write after a fashion, and has some capability in mathematics. He's bright. I believe he has the basis for the job. He was the man that went into the water, twice I might add, and cut away that snagged mast. He was the only one that survived. According to Mr. Longstreet, he was ordered to report back to duty yesterday morning."

Lieutenant Caharty chipped in, "He's back on duty. He was in the tops all yesterday afternoon."

Lieutenant Rylett could not contain himself. "Smith is young, and doesn't have even a fraction of the experience that either of the quartermasters have. I suggest sir, that you give the job to one of the quartermasters until we get to England, and then find a permanent replacement on shore."

"That's a reasonable proposition. What say you Mr. Flynn?" asked Captain Montague.

Mr. Flynn was well aware of Lieutenant Rylett's animosity toward Jon Smith. He wasn't sure Smith was all that much better than what Rylett was proposing.

"Before I make any decision sir, may I suggest I do a morning's test with each of them? The one that is most successful I will submit for your approval sir," said Mr. Flynn.

"That's a better solution and an immediate one. If none of them work out, we can find a replacement in England as Lieutenant Rylett has suggested," replied the captain. "See to it Mr. Flynn. I'll expect a name during the afternoon watch."

"Mr. Caharty, could you have Smith report at two bells in the forenoon watch?" asked the master.

"Certainly, Mr. Flynn. Do you need another man for the wheel as well?" responded Caharty.

"Please. We can do all three at the same time."

The little group broke up and went to complete the tasks they had been given.

At two bells in the forenoon watch Jon approached the quarterdeck. The officer of the watch was Lieutenant Rylett. Jon was wary.

"Sir, I was told to report to the quarterdeck," said Jon as he arrived on the deck and knuckled his forehead.

"Report to the master," said Lieutenant Rylett sullenly.

"Aye, sir," responded Jon, while again knuckling his forehead.

The master, Mr. Flynn was but three paces away. Jon turned, took two steps toward him and again knuckled his forehead. "Mr. Flynn sir, I was ordered to report to you."

"Do you know why you're here Smith?" responded Mr. Flynn.

"No sir."

"We need to ascertain your ability in reading, writing, arithmetic, and other such skills," said Mr. Flynn.

"I have some abilities in each, but I doubt I am anywhere near your standards, sir."

"Be that as it may, you will still go through the testing. Head into the chartroom and see Dickerson. I'll be there presently."

"Aye, sir."

Jon entered the chartroom. One of the master's mates, Chad Dickerson, and Kieffer, a quartermaster were present. Shortly after Jon entered and was told where to stand, Williams, the other quartermaster entered.

Over the next three hours, Mr. Flynn tested Jon's abilities in mathematics, reading and writing as well as Williams' and Kieffer's. After the watch ended, Jon was sure that he had not measured up to Mr. Flynn's expectations. Testing finished as the bell struck for noon leaving sufficient time for Jon to get his spirit ration and dinner.

As he sat down in his usual place at the mess table, Hale asked what was on everyone's mind. "Where were you during watch this morning?"

"Up in officer's country."

"What's that all about?" asked Young. Everyone in the mess was curious.

Jon lifted both of his arms off the table and shrugged. "I have no idea."

Little did Jon know of the surprises yet to come.

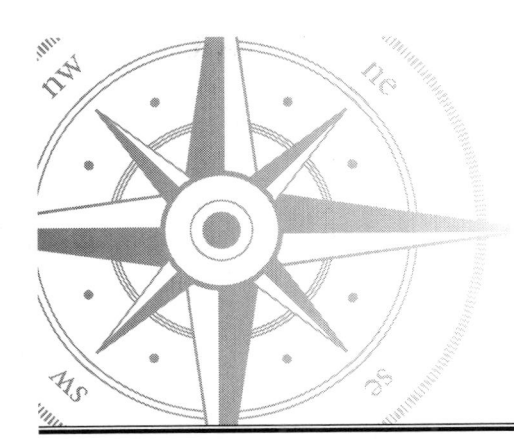

CHAPTER 15

HMS Mermaid ploughed north through still lively seas in search of the missing merchantmen. Jon spent the afternoon watch clinging to the mast top as a lookout. It was a thankless task. There was nothing to see but endless ocean in any direction.

In the first dog watch, he was sitting in the waist reading and munching on a piece of ship's bread when a messenger tapped him on the shoulder. "Smith, you're to report to your division commander."

Lieutenant Caharty was standing with Mr. Flynn to leeward of the wheel when Jon arrived and reported.

"Smith, I have what I believe is some good news for you. The captain has appointed you to be an acting master's mate until such time as the position is either made permanent, you cannot accomplish the required duties, another more qualified replacement is found, or McFadden is returned to duty," said Lieutenant Caharty. "I'll hand you over to the master who can brief you on your new duties.

Jon was shocked and at the same time immensely proud. It took a minute or so until he could find some words.

"What happened to McFadden, sir?" Jon was addressing the master, to whom he had never spoken.

"We were pooped four nights ago. The wave washed McFadden over into the waist. He landed against a 12-pounder and broke his leg above and below the knee. At present, he's in sick bay and cannot move from his hammock. They say that he might lose the leg," said Mr. Flynn.

"I'm sorry to hear that sir," said Jon. "What are my duties to be?'

"You will alternate watches with Dickerson. During the day, you will undergo training in addition to your normal watches. You are lacking even some of the basic information. I'll therefore expect you to be working every minute to get yourself up to speed. If I don't see this dedication in you, I'll send you back foreward," said the master.

The master then hit him with a second surprise.

"Smith, now that you are an acting master's mate, you need to shift aft. Get your kit and report aft to Dickerson. He will set you up in the cockpit," said Mr. Flynn. "By the way, the next time you report for duty, be in the proper dress."

"Aye, aye, sir."

Jon was of mixed opinion as he went below to shift his kit. He was first and foremost elated that he had been chosen for advancement. Even if it were only temporary, it still meant that he had an opportunity to learn. Jon admitted to himself that he was ambitious.

He did have reservations leaving his mess. He had been a member of the larboard watch's topmen mess for the past six months, only missing a period of time when he had been ashore at Louisbourg. As the senior rating of the mizzen top, however, he had not been as close to many members of the mess as he might have been if he had not been their supervisor. There had also been a reservation on the part of the members of the mess about him after Beck had fallen from the mizzen during a practice and evaluation session in English Harbour. Just the same, he knew these men, respected them and was content to work and mess with them. It was with mixed feelings, therefore, that he made his farewells. He called all his men together and gave them the news at once.

"I've been given an opportunity as an acting master's mate for the remainder of this voyage. McFadden was apparently badly injured when the ship was pooped a few nights ago. I'm to replace him. For the present time, I will be shifting aft. I want you to know that I appreciate everything that you have done for me since I came on board. Of course, I will see you each day, but I doubt that we will have much time to speak. Good luck, and who knows, I might be back," said Jon as he shook hands with each man who worked the mizzen.

In turn, each man shook his hand and expressed their good wishes to him. Others from the mess heard and wandered over to say goodbye. The only man that did not appear was Langtry. Jon spotted him a bit later and approached him.

"Langtry, thanks for the conversations we've had and the advice. I appreciated it. As you probably heard I'm shifting aft, so I will say farewell now."

Langtry was noticeably silent. He mumbled, "Goodbye," and turned back to what he had been doing. Jon was surprised when Langtry did not express his best wishes as other members of the mess had done. Jon wondered if Langtry thought he was 'stealing' the master's mate job that Langtry had perhaps coveted. Well if he did, that was his problem. Jon hadn't even known that the position was open, nor that he was being considered for it.

All in all, Jon considered the goodbyes cordial, but far from heart breaking. Since he didn't know if he would be returning to this mess at some point in the future, they were about what he expected.

After the goodbyes, Jon gathered his mug, plate and bowl from the mess bag. He ambled up forward, grabbed his ditty bag, and headed aft and down one deck to the cockpit, unsure of how his arrival in the cockpit would be accepted.

When Jon arrived in the cockpit, only Mr. Farley was present. Jon was on somewhat friendly terms with Mr. Farley, because he had assisted Jon with his reading and writing skills. It was likely that further assistance in this area would be required if any of the tests and evaluations given by Mr. Flynn were an indication.

"Mr. Farley, sir, I was told to see Dickerson in the cockpit. He was supposed to get me squared-away," said Jon humbly.

"First things first," said Mr. Farley. "Since you are joining us in the cockpit, you need to understand that everyone here is on a first name basis. My name's Kevin and yours is…?"

"Jon, sir," replied Jon respectfully.

"Jon, you're missing the point," stated Kevin Farley. "There are no sir's here. I'm Kevin; you're Jon. Dickerson is Chad, and Elkhorne is Brian, even if he doesn't like to be called by his first name. Get it?"

"Yes, sir, I mean yes, Kevin," said Jon. "It's just that it's such a change. This morning, if I had called you anything but sir, I could have ended up with a flogging."

"Yes, well…" stammered Farley.

"Where do I put my things?"

At that point, Dickerson entered and took over. "Jon, glad to have you with us, although you can appreciate that I don't like the circumstances." Jon was not sure what circumstances he meant, so he kept his mouth shut. Dickerson offered Jon his hand.

"Chad, I need to find out where I'm to stow my kit and I need to prepare the proper dress for my next watch."

"You'll take this little cubby-hole for yourself. The previous occupant isn't here to complain," said Chad.

Jon was shown to a small space that was separated from the main room by a curtain. It was a revelation to Jon. There was certainly more personal space and privacy in the cockpit than foreward.

"As for proper dress, a master's mate is required to turn out for each watch wearing a blue frock coat with white trim. You'll need a white shirt and trousers. For the present time, I think that you can get away with your slop pants. You also need to wear shoes and white stockings. As for a hat, I believe that you can forgo that for now," said Chad.

"I have shoes, but no white stockings. I have a navy jacket that will do, but I need white trim. I need to see the purser to get the white trim. Do you think he will have stockings and white shirts?" asked Jon.

"Mr. Bilbo will provide everything -- for a price," chuckled Chad. "I'll leave you to it. I'll be back before change of shift to speak to you." With that Dickerson turned and exited the cockpit.

Jon dropped his ditty bag in his cubbyhole. He pulled out his sewing kit and started to work on his jacket. He had to go and find the purser to obtain the white trim necessary to complete the frock coat. While there he also acquired those additional items he needed, thereby adding to his tab with the purser. By the time the next watch started, he would be properly attired.

As he altered his jacket and the shirts he had acquired from the purser, he sat at the common table in the cockpit. The light was better. Only Kevin Farley was present, as Brian Elkhorne was on watch.

"You sew well Jon," commented Farley.

"Not at first, I was taught by a good teacher. That seems to be the trick. With a good teacher, you can learn nearly anything," responded Jon.

"Do you mind if I explain a few things to you while you are sewing?" asked Farley.

"Go ahead."

"Well it deals with how we do things here in the cockpit. I guess you could call it the etiquette of the place," said Farley. "Let's take food for instance. We receive the same rations as the men, however, we tend to like different fare on occasion. The mess pays for any change in that fare, with each individual mess member contributing a specified amount for the extra food. Understand?"

"What you're saying is that I will be obligated to contribute funds to the mess so that extra food can be obtained. I understand, however, since we are already at sea and have no possibility of acquiring additional sources of food, am I expected to chip in money now?"

"No, not now, but when we reach England, you will," explained Farley. "That will be the first opportunity to restore the larder, so we will be expecting you to contribute your fair share."

"Fair enough," responded Jon. "Anything else?"

"Drink is different here as well," replied Farley. "You can drink anytime you want, as much as you want; but you need your own supply. You get the spirit ration, the same as the men; but you can purchase more."

"The spirit ration is enough for me," said Jon quietly.

The conversation died at that point as Farley disappeared to get some sleep. Jon kept sewing.

Finally Dickerson returned to the cockpit.

"Chad, I need to find out more information related to my duties as a master's mate. I'm not sure what I need to do."

Dickerson quickly explained. "The master's mate duties vary. When in port or harbour, you're responsible for fitting out the ship and making sure the Mermaid has all the sailing supplies she needs. It's sometimes necessary to work with the carpenter, sailmaker and bosun, as they can provide guidance on what is needed. When leaving or entering harbour, you're responsible for hoisting or dropping the anchor. Alternatively, if the ship were docked, you would moor or cast off. When sailing, you're responsible to examine the ship daily and notify the master if there are any problems with the sails, masts, ropes or pulleys. You represent the master during each watch when the master is not present and control the quartermasters or other men on the wheel."

"Now this last aspect of your duties may seem minor, but it is the most important and in reality the most challenging. You have to maintain a log, maintain the charts and know the course, present position and navigation hazards the ship may encounter. You're also supposed to train the young gentlemen in navigation," continued Dickerson.

"Wow. As captain of the mizzen, it's routine to check all the sails, ropes and pulleys for the mizzen mast. The only difference I see with that aspect of the job, is now I would be checking all masts as opposed to just the mizzen," said Jon. "As far as the rest of it goes, it's all new to me. I've never done anything like it before."

"Just look at it as a learning experience," said Dickerson. "It'll take time to learn everything, but then again, you weren't going anywhere anyway -- were you? Come on, it's time for you to take your first watch."

With that, Jon headed into a new watch, in a new position, with new responsibilities requiring him to learn new information. He was also about to develop new apprehensions.

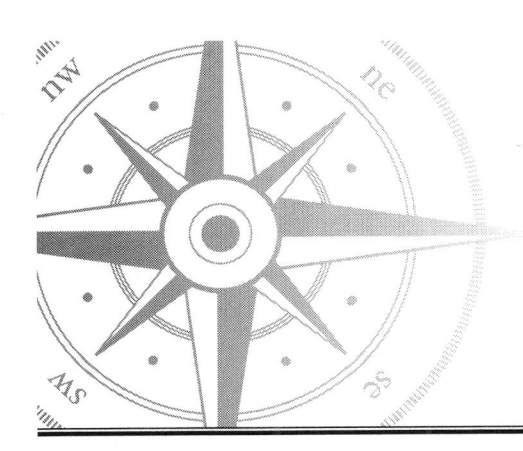

CHAPTER 16

Jon stood his first watch as acting master's mate with some trepidation. Luckily Lieutenant Dunkin, who was the officer of the watch, took pity on Jon and explained the officer of the watch's expectations of the master's mate during a watch. The information was helpful and Jon was grateful.

The Mermaid continued to head north to roundup as many ships of the convoy as possible. There was only a reduced watch overnight so everyone could get as much sleep as possible. The crew still had not fully recovered from the effects of the storm.

Starting with the bell for the morning watch, the regular routine of the ship commenced. As the forenoon watch commenced, the bulk of the crew exercised the great guns. It was the first time the guns were exercised without Jon heaving on a rope. It was a unique experience. He didn't have much time to revel in it, however, as Mr. Flynn had him undergoing training. There were times during that training when Jon wished he were back doing something simple like performing gun drill.

The first ship from the convoy was spotted just after two bells in the forenoon watch. It was over an hour later, however, before the Mermaid came up to her. She was a snow called the Lady Martha.

As the Mermaid ploughed through the waves on the windward side of the Lady Martha, Captain Montague shouted a number of questions.

Everyone on the Mermaid, and probably on the Lady Martha could hear the conversation and was listening to the responses.

"Did you encounter any problems weathering the storm?" shouted Captain Montague.

"None at all," replied the captain of the Lady Martha.

"Have you seen any other ships?" asked Captain Montague.

"Not in the past three days," replied the captain of the Lady Martha.

"Which direction were they heading when you last saw them?" asked Captain Montague.

"Due east," replied the captain of the Lady Martha

"Thank you captain. Fall in astern of us," said Captain Montague.

The Mermaid turned due east and continued the search for the other ships in the convoy.

In each successive watch as the Mermaid continued her search, Jon learned something new or improved one of his newly acquired skills. Although initially overwhelmed, he relished the new role.

While Jon was well aware of all the events going on, there was a preoccupation with learning the new duties associated with the position. In this capacity, Mr. Flynn turned out to be a blessing. As a strict disciplinarian who demanded high standards, Mr. Flynn was a great instructor who was sometimes patient, sometimes frustrated, with a student's lack of progress. Fortunately, Jon wasn't the only student; the two midshipmen were students for navigation as well. Mr. Flynn's knowledge of the sea was immense, having been at sea for about thirty years, with over ten years as a master. Even Mr. Flynn's bearing was a steadying influence. He was always clean-shaven, traditionally wore black trousers, a somewhat white shirt, and either a black or navy jacket that was always well worn. A black tricorn hat always sat atop his short, stout body to hide thinning grey hair.

When instructing, Mr. Flynn spoke quietly and reasonably slowly. It was easy to understand the words, but not always what was said. Some of the navigation terms seemed like Greek to Jon. Jon was not alone. In some cases, the navigation lessons would have to be repeated multiple times before Jon or one of the midshipmen grasped the lesson or concept.

Jon had been on friendly terms with Dickerson, prior to his being selected for the acting master's mate position. This friendship increased a little. It was challenging, however, because Dickerson and Jon were on opposite watches. When Dickerson was 'on', Jon was 'off' and vice versa. They rarely spent time together other than to hand over watches to each other. Regardless, they stayed on friendly terms. Dickerson was ten years older than Jon was, and had about fifteen years of sea time.

Jon had better rope work and sail handling skills than Dickerson, but Dickerson was far superior when it came to bookwork and the skills of navigation. Jon aimed to narrow that gap as fast as he could.

One of the biggest differences that Jon experienced was a relaxation of the rules of familiarity with all of the other ranks of the ship. Of course, there was still a strict prohibition of familiarity with the commissioned officers, but otherwise things were somewhat more relaxed. Common sense, courtesy, and timing were important. For example, if he needed some help or advice, he could approach the bosun or another mate without suffering the consequences of a breach of discipline. Cracking a joke with a member of the crew was acceptable, so long as he didn't breech naval etiquette.

The only shadow lurking on the horizon was Lieutenant Rylett. There was a sense that Rylett was just waiting for an error to occur, so Rylett could ridicule or somehow undermine Jon's position. Mistakes would undoubtedly occur. It was hoped that those mistakes would be overlooked by Rylett, or be such that recovery was possible.

Over the next two days, another nine cargo vessels, and one of the escort sloops, the Hampshire, were spotted and fell in with the Mermaid. None of these vessels was missing a mast, so it appeared that the victim had been one of the still missing vessels. Of the missing vessels, two carried French personnel from Louisbourg. The other two were cargo ships heading to England, plus the sloop escort, the Abigail. It was hoped that the remaining sloop had found these vessels and was now escorting them toward England.

As senior commander of the convoy, Captain Montague ordered the Hampshire sloop to lead the convoy. The Mermaid took up position astern and to the windward side of the convoy. Extra lookouts remained in the tops to continue the search for the missing vessels.

The Mermaid and her convoy continued eastward toward England and France without any sign of the missing five ships. Normal shipboard routines in the form of gun drill and boarding party drill continued. Jon's duties when cleared for action required him to be on the quarterdeck near the wheel. Jon, Dickerson, or Mr. Flynn would be keeping the charts and navigation log. Since he was the junior and least experienced, he expected to receive the jobs no one else wanted. This deduction was repeatedly proven correct.

Occasionally, Jon spelled the quartermaster on the wheel. It was an enjoyable experience, at least for short durations. He could feel the ship -- how she handled the waves, how she reacted when the guns fired, and how she handled stays. Each time he was on the wheel, he gained a small amount of knowledge, especially if the weather conditions were different.

Without question, the cruise eastward back to England changed him. He had seen the power of the sea and been afraid of that power. That fear had been conquered. What's more, he could conquer that fear again if need be. The change in status to acting master's mate altered the pressure on him. When responsible for the mizzen top, supervision of subordinates was required. There were no subordinates in the current position, but a greater responsibility for maintaining the course and position of the ship was present. He was learning things he never would have dreamed about a year earlier. None of this was lost on him. He wondered now if he would remain at sea. While there was no choice for the present, if he could attain the permanent position of master's mate, then he would be in a far better position than a mere sailor. He discussed these things with Dickerson on occasion.

"Chad, what are the steps I need to take to become a full-fledged master's mate?" asked Jon at the end of one watch.

"There are a number of different paths to advancement," commented Dickerson. "The first thing you need to understand is that the master's mate position is filled at the captain's discretion. What I mean by this, is that the acting, or as you call it 'permanent', position can be filled or taken away from any man as the captain deems appropriate. Obviously, the acting position is only temporary; however, the captain can remove a man from the permanent position as well and send him foreward. The only exception to this that I know is when the man has a valid master's certificate."

"You mean that you could be sent foreward?" Jon was astonished at that remark.

"Not me. I have a valid master's certificate," replied Dickerson. "You on the other hand could be sent foreward, back to your old position. You were given this position by the captain's order."

"I realize that," said Jon. "I am grateful that I have been given this opportunity. I'm just wondering where I should go next."

"Probably back to your cubbyhole to get some sleep so you are wide awake for your next watch," said Dickerson with a straight face.

"Yeah, yeah," replied Jon, not impressed at Dickerson's attempt to change the topic. "You still haven't explained to me the various paths you mentioned."

"In His Majesty's navy, there are generally two paths. The first path is to become a master. The first step toward that is to get as much experience as possible; then you write the master's exam. If you pass that exam, you have the qualification, but not the position. You have to find and attain a position on a vessel. So long as that vessel is in commission, you have a job. Once the vessel is paid-off, or for any other reason is removed from service, you lose your position and need to look for a new ship," explained Dickerson.

"If you have written your master's exam, and get your papers, then you can usually find a master's mate position on any major ship. Any qualified master's mate is more valued than a master's mate without papers, so finding a job isn't that difficult," continued Dickerson.

"There is another path which some take. As a master's mate, it is possible to write the lieutenant's exams and become a commissioned officer. In order to write the lieutenant's exams, you have to have years of experience. I forget exactly how many, but it is years," further explained Dickerson.

"I appreciate the information Chad," said Jon. "I believe that I will take your advice."

"What's that?" asked Dickerson.

"Get some sleep, so that I am wide awake on my next watch," said Jon over his back as he headed to his cubbyhole.

Dickerson just shook his head and rolled his eyes.

What Chad had said provided considerable food for thought. The last approach mentioned, becoming an officer in His Majesty's navy, didn't seem all that attractive, especially if one had to wait years before writing an exam. Perhaps being an officer in a merchantman was the path to follow.

Some of the stumbling blocks in following any path were his reading and writing abilities. They still needed to be greatly improved. Every day he exercised those skills both on duty and off duty. It was far easier to gain information and help with incomprehensible words. Anyone in the cockpit could help. As a group, they were generally very good about assisting. On the other hand, he needed to reciprocate with assistance to the others where possible. Jokes, a story, or some assistance in seamanship were payments for their assisting his reading and writing development.

Since he was taking much of the same training as the midshipmen, they often spent time together going over some of the more difficult lessons. Jon was religious about doing extra work. This enthusiasm was not shared by the others. Mr. Elkhorne, a senior midshipman whose previous attempt at his lieutenant's exam had resulted in failure, was hesitant to work. As they approached England, however, Mr. Elkhorne adjusted his attitude as he contemplated re-taking his examination for lieutenant. Mr. Farley, on the other hand was free spirited and at least two years away from taking his lieutenant's exams. He was even less inclined to undertake extra study.

With the mathematics required for navigation, Jon was working at a level far more advanced than anything previously encountered. There were significant challenges understanding all concepts or equations required for the job. The mathematics fascinated Jon, so work on the formulas continued at every appropriate opportunity. Jon knew that continuous practice was necessary to attain a skill and improve in any area. This had been proven time and again since being pressed, so perseverance was necessary.

After eight days of sailing, the lookouts reported strange sails on the horizon. The sails were to the southwest behind the convoy. Since the other escorting sloop, the Hampshire, had been stationed in front of the convoy, Mermaid signalled the convoy and escort that she was turning to investigate. Upon acknowledgement of the signal, the Mermaid went about and headed directly toward the sails on the horizon.

The drums rumbled 'Clear for Action', as the Mermaid gallantly fought her way into the wind and headed toward the sails. It was at times like this that Jon wished he were back in the tops to see what was happening. Even if stationed in the mizzen, there wouldn't be much to see. The sails on the main and fore masts would obstruct any view from the mizzen. Therefore, like every other person on the quarterdeck, he waited for information impatiently.

A major difference was that this was the first time he had been on the quarterdeck for the coming action. While ensuring the quartermaster maintained the heading that the officer of the watch had ordered, he wondered what it would be like standing near the wheel when the enemy was firing at the officers all around him, and likely at him. He had been fired at before, but no one was aiming directly at him as a specific target. A small sweat broke out on his forehead.

He could see forward over the bow. The other leading ship was still hull down below the horizon, but her sails were clear enough. English style sails. After having seen them as a lookout since leaving Louisbourg, Jon tentatively identified her as the missing escort.

"Mr. Flynn, sir, that's the Abigail, that New Hampshire sloop of ten guns. I recognize her sail configuration," stated Jon. He said it in a loud enough voice that the captain and others on the quarterdeck could hear him.

From above, the lookout called, "Deck there, the first ship is an armed sloop, English sail plan. The others look like merchantmen."

Captain Montague turned to the others, "Gentlemen, it looks like we have found our missing ships. Let's shepherd them back to the convoy. Signals, have Abigail make her number and confirm who she is. Once I'm satisfied that she is the Abigail, then we can stand-down the guns."

The Mermaid continued toward the Abigail as the signal flags were hoisted aloft. The Abigail made her reply with the correct signal flags and continued to hoist a stream of signals outlining the condition of her charges. Closer examination of two of the three merchantmen showed evident damage. Of the four ships joining the convoy, none had lost a mast. That meant that there was still one missing ship. It seemed probable the missing ship had lost the mast with which the Mermaid had run afoul.

Lieutenant Davis had the crew stand-down from quarters. Jon stayed on the quarterdeck until relieved. Before being relieved, the officer of the watch issued orders to position the Mermaid to the northern windward side of the four vessels in accordance with Captain Montague's wishes. The Mermaid came about to shepherd those vessels back into the convoy.

Signals were raised to alert the convoy and other escort that the four vessels were joining the convoy. The Abigail was ordered to position herself aft of the convoy, while the Mermaid continued to the north, the windward side of the convoy.

The convoy re-formed, everyone settled down to the familiar convoy routine.

CHAPTER 17

"Land ho, off the larboard bow!" shouted the lookout.

After being at sea for weeks and weathering a major storm, these words brought relief to more than one set of ears on the Mermaid. It had been three days since the Mermaid had met up with the Abigail. In those three days, nothing notable had happened to the crew or the Mermaid. For Jon it was a different story. He continued to learn new things, most of all navigation. He was fascinated by the ability to plot a position and determine a course based on that position. It was the first time since he had been at sea that he was aware of where they were.

Questions from the quarterdeck to the lookouts did not resolve what land they were seeing. By the charts, it appeared to be Ireland, but where in Ireland? Was the Mermaid too far north? Regardless of the position, the convoy would still have to steer a more southerly course. The signals to the convoy reflected this.

The sighting of land allowed the master to conduct yet another lesson for his students.

"Gentlemen, what you see is a land mass off to larboard. One of the navigational duties of an officer is to document land masses that they see. By document I mean, in this case, that a sketch of the land mass is made, accompanied by a written description. Your job today is to sketch that land mass and write the accompanying description. Generally, the sketch is completed on one side of the paper and the description is made on the opposite side," stated Mr. Flynn.

"You may commence your work," he said and walked away to let them get at it.

Jon was at an immediate disadvantage having never previously sketched anything. With no sketch-book and no pencil, he didn't even have an idea on how to start.

Mr. Farley helped him out in that department by directing him to the effects of a deceased midshipman who had died from yellow jack in Antigua. There was a blank sketchbook in these effects, which Jon grabbed. The previous owner certainly wouldn't complain.

Landscape sketching is an art. Jon didn't like it, and didn't find it overly useful. Unfortunately, that was beside the point. Having been ordered to complete a sketch, there was no choice but to comply with the order. Mr. Flynn had high expectations and standards.

The first attempt was a dismal failure. It looked like a raccoon had walked across the paper with dirty paws. Jon flipped the paper over and made a second attempt on the back. It was a marginal improvement.

Asking around to his fellow 'students' to gain guidance, he received little help. Five attempts later, the landscape had receded in the distance. The last version resulted in a coastline with a questionable facsimile of what it really looked like. These efforts were no better or worse than Mr. Farley's, but not nearly as good as Mr. Elkhorne's, as Elkhorne had years of practice. Also missing was any speed in the accomplishment of this task. Mr. Flynn's assessment of his work was not flattering.

The Mermaid continued southeastwardly skirting the land they could see to the east. In two days land again was observed to the north -- England.

Again Jon was tasked to sketch the coastline. This time he was more prepared.

"Well, it's somewhat better than your last attempt," said Mr. Flynn. "I doubt if it will win any artistic awards, and most masters would believe it less than the standard they would expect. You'll need to improve quite a bit, Smith."

"Aye, sir, I understand," replied Jon. "I'll do better next time."

"You'll have to," replied Mr. Flynn seriously.

The ships had been at sea for close to a month. Over a week of this had been in a storm. They were now in the English Channel, but still had some distance to go to reach France.

A request from cargo ships in the convoy to split away toward England was received before nightfall. Captain Montague considered this, and decided to turn the entire convoy northeast toward Portsmouth further up into the English Channel. There were no specific orders as to where to land the French from Louisbourg. Everyone on the quarterdeck considered Brest to be the best option.

The major problem facing them was their ability to communicate with the French. Captain Montague needed to impart to the French, without being fired upon, that this was a mission of mercy. Communicating with the enemy would be difficult by itself. To gain permission from the French to allow English vessels to enter a French port in time of war, discharge their load, and depart unimpeded would be that much more challenging.

They sailed all night up the English Channel. At first light, those merchantmen heading towards London were allowed to proceed on their own, but with a wary eye for French privateers. One escort, the sloop Abigail, was dispatched with them.

The remaining vessels of the convoy then turned south southwest and headed toward Brest.

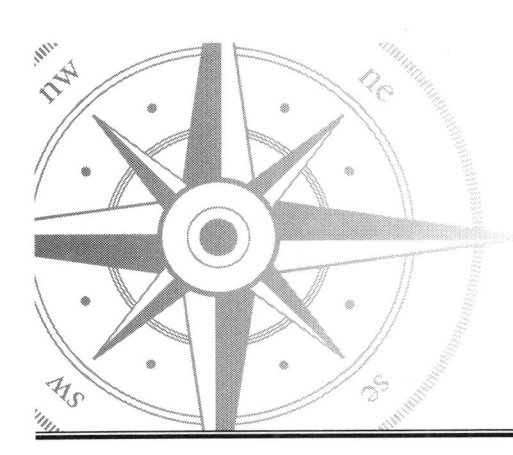

CHAPTER 18

About an hour before last light Captain Montague appeared on the quarterdeck. Immediately, the watch on duty stiffened. It was Jon's watch, so he was at his normal sailing watch position on the quarterdeck near the quartermaster on the wheel. The officer of the watch was Lieutenant Rylett. Shortly after the captain appeared, the master quietly positioned himself behind Jon on the lee side of the wheel. Captain Montague had a habit of checking the course, the logs, and standing well to the windward of the wheel. This evening he was pacing around. Something was up.

The small convoy composed of the five cargo ships carrying the Frenchmen, the colonial escort sloop Hampshire, and the Mermaid sailed at a leisurely pace toward the French coast, as there was no rush, and no deadline. It wouldn't be possible to attempt to communicate with the French before first light the next day. Sailing toward a hostile port located on a lee shore in the dark was done only with a good reason, and in the opinion of most of the crew, this convoy didn't have sufficient reason.

After several minutes of pacing, the captain turned.

"Mr. Flynn, how close can we get to the entrance to Brest without running afoul of any rocks?" asked Captain Montague.

"Rocks or obstructions are not a problem, Captain. The majority are all closer in. The primary concerns are those French batteries covering the entrance. According to reports, they have 42-pounders in those batteries," replied the master.

"Lieutenant Rylett."

"Sir."

"Mr. Rylett, we are close to the port of Brest. Our orders are simply to land the Frenchmen on French soil. I believe that we have a challenge ahead of us in that regard. The French are simply not going to allow a British vessel to sail into one of their harbours, especially an enemy warship in time of war. So, considering our orders, how would you propose accomplishing our mission?" asked Captain Montague.

"Sir, I believe that I would only send in the merchantmen, one at a time. If the first one were captured, then the remainder would be safe. We could then land the remaining Frenchmen in England as prisoners of war," replied Lieutenant Rylett.

"That sir would not accomplish our mission. As well, the owner of the ship that was taken would be after our hides, although I doubt that he would be successful," replied Captain Montague. "We need to ensure appropriate precautions are undertaken, so the French do not capture or otherwise keep the ships when those ships dock to off-load the Frenchmen. The volume of personnel, including women and children, and their possessions necessitate docking. Off-loading them at sea and rowing them to shore is simply not practical. Do you have any other ideas as to how or what precautions we can take?"

"No, sir," said an abashed Lieutenant Rylett.

"Lieutenant Davis."

"Sir."

"I propose to close with the entrance at reduced sail at first light, so the Frenchmen at those batteries can easily identify us," said Captain Montague. "We will stand off well out of range of those guns. I will send in the Hampshire to initiate communications with the French. Hoist signals so everyone in the convoy understands those intentions."

"Aye, aye, sir." The first lieutenant set about organizing the signals with Midshipman Elkhorne, who was the acting signals officer.

The captain continued his pacing. After some time, he appeared to make some form of decision. "Lieutenant Rylett, please inform all officers I will see them in my cabin forthwith." With that Captain Montague turned and departed the quarterdeck.

Jon looked at the master, who masked whatever he was thinking effectively.

All the commissioned officers, including the master carrying the charts, headed to the captain's cabin. Once assembled in the captain's cabin, Captain Montague spoke.

"Gentlemen, I have no intention of heading into Brest with the Mermaid. I don't relish the idea of having the Mermaid under French guns and not being allowed to shoot back. If I were the French, I wouldn't like any enemy ship entering any one of my ports. Given the circumstances, I believe they will restrict entrance to only the cargo ships holding the Frenchmen. So neither the Mermaid nor the Hampshire will enter the harbour."

"The entry of our ships into the enemy's harbour does provide us with a unique opportunity," continued the captain. "Think of the intelligence that we might be able to obtain. If nothing else, we could see the state of their ships, see if any new ships are under construction, determine if any ships are being readied for sea, and update our knowledge of their fixed fortifications."

"I agree sir," said Lieutenant Davis. "All we need to do is put the proper eyes on board the cargo vessels when they go into the port."

"Who in your opinion possesses the proper set of eyes?" asked the captain.

"I do sir," replied Lieutenant Davis.

Captain Montague looked at Lieutenant Davis as if he were seriously evaluating the suggestion. He stroked his lower face a couple of times.

"If you were the port admiral of Brest, or any other port for that matter, and you had to allow enemy vessels to enter your port, discharge cargo and then depart, what security precautions would you take?" asked the captain.

Lieutenant Davis pondered the question for a few moments, as did everyone else in the cabin.

"I would attempt to hide or at least camouflage anything of importance. I would know that I couldn't hide everything. I would restrict the movement of the crew of the English vessels. They would remain onboard. I would watch the officers like a hawk, possibly confine them below decks while they were docked," stated Lieutenant Davis.

"What about the remainder of the crew?" asked the captain.

"They would be needed to unload the cargo, so I suppose they would be given the freedom of the deck," replied Lieutenant Davis.

"Would they be allowed in the tops?" asked the captain.

"They would have to rig and unrig the yards for hoisting, furl the sails, things like that. I believe they would have to be given some limited freedom to be in the tops, at the very least when entering and exiting the harbour," replied Lieutenant Davis.

"What you are saying, as I understand it Lieutenant Davis, is that officers will be restricted, even to the extent that they might be confined while in port, whereas men will be allowed to freely move at least onboard, possibly even in the tops," stated the captain.

"Aye, sir, I suppose that's true," replied Lieutenant Davis.

"Now if you were a French officer boarding an English vessel that just came into port, how would you undertake to impose these restrictions?" asked the captain.

"I believe that I would assemble the crew, identify the officers and then post a guard on them," said Lieutenant Davis.

"How would you identify the officers?"

"By clothes and speech, I suppose," said Lieutenant Davis.

"Call for the master-at-arms," ordered Captain Montague.

Upon his arrival, the master-at-arms was subjected to immediate questioning.

"Mr. Pearly, in your position as master-at-arms, you have had the opportunity of securing an enemy vessel after it has been taken, the most recent being the Vigilant, I believe."

"Aye, sir."

"Mr. Pearly, if you were to line up the crew of a French vessel we just boarded and wanted to find all the officers, how would you go about it?" asked the captain.

"Sir, I would first look at the uniforms. Anyone wearing an officer's uniform, commissioned officer or standing officer, I would pull out of the line. I would go further because some of them Frenchmen are sneaky. They sometimes change uniforms. I would watch their faces and check their hands. Men from foreward of the mast all have callused, stained hands. The officers typically don't. Another trait is that foreward of the mast, men learn not to look an officer in the eye -- it might be taken for insubordination. Officers don't avoid your eyes," replied Mr. Pearly. "If necessary, I would check their speech, as officers speak differently than men, sir."

"Thank you Mr. Pearly," said the captain. Mr. Pearly knuckled his forehead and departed.

"What we need Mr. Davis, are approximately five men that know what to look for, are smart and can blend in with the merchantmen crew. We will put one of these men on each cargo ship. Hopefully with men in different ships some of them will be able to gather some intelligence that is worthwhile," said Captain Montague. "Find me those men, tonight."

"Aye, aye, sir."

"I want them on the merchantmen before first light, and I want the captains of the merchantmen told to cooperate," further instructed Captain Montague.

"Gentlemen, please assist Lieutenant Davis in getting the best men and getting them where they need to be. Dismissed."

Jon was sitting in the cockpit after handing over the watch to Dickerson. A runner appeared. "Smith, report to the quarterdeck."

Wondering what he'd done this time; Jon grabbed a coat and headed up to the quarterdeck.

Arriving on the quarterdeck, Lieutenant Davis pointed for him to remain on the lee side. Mr. Elkhorne, Langtry, another topman Jansen, from the starboard watch, and a stranger all arrived in short order.

"Follow me," ordered Lieutenant Davis. The men followed him down to the wardroom, where they circled the wardroom table.

It was the first time Jon had ever been in the officers' wardroom. He was astonished by the place. Each officer had actual cabins along each side. There was a large table near the rear transom windows, or what he suspected were the transom windows as they were boarded up since the Mermaid was pooped.

There had to be something serious happening to allow men in officers' country.

CHAPTER 19

Lieutenant Davis looked at each man and commenced his briefing by saying, "Thank you for volunteering."
Oh shite!

"As you all know we are escorting the Frenchmen taken at Louisbourg back to France. We are currently in the English Channel off the French port of Brest. The captain has decided that none of the warships will enter the port. Only the merchantmen will go in. It's been some years since a British vessel visited Brest, so the entry of the merchantmen gives us the opportunity to gain some intelligence about enemy intentions."

"Let me make this simple. Each of you is going on board a different merchantman for the purposes of gathering as much intelligence as you can while in Brest. Normally, an officer would gather this intelligence. We believe the Frenchmen will be looking for officers. That's why you are going instead of an officer. You can fit in better with the crew, and work in the tops where we think you'll be able to see more."

Jon looked around at the others. By their expressions of surprise, this was new to them as well. Since being pressed, one of the common unwritten rules that Jon had learned was 'never volunteer'. This appeared to be a dangerous mission. It was just like the officers. He was being ordered to go, yet the officers would say he volunteered if any problem arose.

Again, they considered him expendable. Jon had to swallow whatever objections he had, because Lieutenant Davis was continuing the briefing.

"Why do we need intelligence do you ask? The answer is to KNOW YOUR ENEMY. Without knowledge of your enemies' capabilities, intentions and likely actions or reactions, it is difficult to defeat them. The intelligence we need from your journey into Brest will be categorized in three areas -- capability, readiness and protection. Are you with me so far?" Everyone signalled his acknowledgement.

"Let's deal with capability first," continued Lieutenant Davis. "We need to know the numbers, and types of warships in harbour. That means from the largest man-of-war, to the smallest gunboat. We need to know the number of guns and estimated size of those guns. For example, you might see four gunboats. That's not good enough. We need more detail. What I mean by that is that of the four gunboats, one looks like it has a 6-pounder, another two have 12-pounders, and a larger gunboat has a 24-pounder with seating for forty men. Get the idea?" Everyone signalled acknowledgement.

"We also would like to have an idea of the number and size of the merchantmen in port. First off, look for flags. We need to know if the merchantmen are French, neutrals, or other countries trading with the French. All merchantmen have the potential to carry troops or military stores, and they make lovely prizes, so pay closer attention to the Frenchmen and any others that are not neutrals," continued Lieutenant Davis.

"Next look at the harbour facilities. Count the number of piers or docks and berthing spaces. We will pass the information on, so it can be compared to previous assessments. Look for their construction and repair facilities. See if you can determine what they can build or repair, and if there are any ships in those construction or repair facilities. That should cover the capability."

"For readiness, check each vessel, especially the naval vessels, to see the state of preparedness to go to sea. Are the yards up? Are there sails on the yards? Does it look like there is a full crew for the ship, and what is the size of that crew? Are any ships being provisioned? Are the hoys active? If so, to which ships and what are they carrying?"

"For the merchantmen, are they loading or unloading? What are the cargos? When do you estimate the ships will be ready to sail? Remember, it may be prize money."

"For protection, check along the entire shoreline for fortifications. If you see any, count the number of cannon ports. See if there are any troop bivouacs. Count the number of tents, troops, and cannon. See if you can assess the morale of the place, the condition of the troops guarding you, and the state of alertness. Look at the uniforms. See if you can tell the difference between army and navy uniforms. Look at cap badges. For army troops, are they infantry, artillery or something else?"

"Finally, I want all of this reported when you get back. Make sure the French don't catch you. I don't know what they would do, but I doubt that it will be very pleasant," said Lieutenant Davis. "Any questions?"

There were no questions.

"Grab your kit, and report to the bosun at the entry port. You will be shifting over to the merchantmen within the hour. Good luck," said Lieutenant Davis.

Jon turned to the man standing next to him, the stranger. "Jon Smith, quartermaster's mate," he said as he extended his hand.

"William Maynard, topman off the Hampshire," replied the man.

"You volunteered for this?"

"Captain asked me. I said yes," replied Maynard.

"More'n I got. I guess that's the difference 'tween your ship and this one."

Jon went back to the cockpit to change into his slops. He left his money belt and all valuables in his ditty bag, which the purser secured. He made a smaller bag for a change of clothes and his messing kit. He added his sketchbook and two pencils.

It was a silent boat ride over to the merchantman. Each man was thinking about the task, and the possible repercussions if caught.

CHAPTER 20

Jon climbed the wooden battens up the side of the merchantman Gloucester. He was met with hostile stares and muted silence as he stepped over the threshold. I suppose they're as happy to have me as I am to be here, he thought.

Before taking another step, Jon glanced all around him. All the sails were secure except the course on the mainmast. It would provide them steerage way, and allow them to maintain their position in the convoy. The ship had a ship-shape appearance, but there was nothing fancy or remarkable about it.

A man stepped forward silently and motioned. Jon had no idea who he was, but if he had to guess, the bosun would be his choice. Following the man, they went below into the crew's quarters.

There were intermittent lanterns along the path of their journey, as if the owners of the vessel were reluctant to spend a penny more than they absolutely needed.

The guide pointed at a bunk and said, "This is yours. You'll be on the starboard watch as a topman. You can do topman duties?"

"Probably better than you," replied Jon with a chuckle. "Could you pass on to the captain to add me to the roster about some time last fall. The name's Jon Smith. The French are bound to check it. I'll also need to see everyone, but I suppose that can wait until morning."

The guide disappeared. Jon hung his ditty bag on the end of his bunk and slid up to get some sleep.

Sometime during the night, he was woken for watch. Having never been on a merchantman before, Jon didn't know the watch keeping responsibilities. With only the main course drawing, it was immediately obvious there was little work for any topmen. With only a handful of souls present, it was prudent to find a quiet corner in which to nod off.

At first light, his guide from the previous night tossed him a holystone and motioned for him to get to work. It had been some time since Jon had holystoned a deck. He shook his head and got in line with some other men. If nothing else, the Gloucester and her captain were going to get every possible ounce of work from the extra crewman foisted upon them.

Breakfast was the first opportunity Jon had to speak to the crew. He was shunned. It appeared the Gloucester's entire crew, including officers were apprehensive about having him aboard. No one knew what the French would do if Jon was caught. In addition, although all the Frenchmen prisoners had been kept below decks while the transfer was taking place, they no doubt had eyeballed each sailor on board. It was possible; therefore, the prisoners would identify a new face and point that man out to the French authorities in Brest.

Jon's biggest concern since his arrival on board the Gloucester was his continued survival. Having fought the French, he knew not to underestimate them. They could catch him once in Brest. He could also give himself away or one of the Frenchmen 'prisoners' might identify him as a new face resulting in his capture. The way Jon saw it, his only defence was to make it appear that he was a long-term member of the Gloucester's crew. That meant he would have to learn all about the crew of the Gloucester, and them about him.

After breakfast, he went to the quarterdeck and requested permission to speak to the captain. The captain appeared after some time. He was an older man with greying hair and a completely black beard that extended to the second button on his coat. His clothes were older and dated, as if he had purchased them years ago, which by their worn appearance, might have been the case.

"I'm Captain Tilbury. What do you want, Smith?"

"Sir, I am seeking your permission to address the crew. If any of us wish to escape the attentions of the French, I believe that we need to be prepared."

"How will you do that by addressing the crew?"

"Sir, they need to see me as just another of their crewmates, not some outsider. If the French believe there is an outsider on board, it is likely we might all be punished. I have no idea what the French will do; but based on everything I've seen of them, they are not to be underestimated."

Captain Tilbury considered what Jon was saying.

"Mr. Jerkins, keep the prisoners locked below decks. Have all the men, both watches report here immediately."

"Aye, aye, sir," responded Jerkins.

As all the men came aft, Jon looked at Captain Tilbury who nodded.

"Men, my name's Jon Smith. As you are probably aware, I have been sent over to accompany this ship into Brest -- to spy on the French. You may not like it. I'm not happy about it either, but like you, I didn't have a choice. So we need to make the best of it."

"The way that I see this happening is that if we work together, we all come out of it together. I have no idea what the French will do if they catch us spying -- to me or to you. I doubt that any of us would like it. Our best defence is to prevent that from happening. We've got two problems. The first problem is with the Frenchmen on board this vessel. By now, they have probably eyeballed every member of the crew. Since I'm a new face, I might be spotted faster. We need to think of how to avoid that. The second problem is that we will all likely be questioned upon arrival in Brest. We need to know enough about each other that we won't be caught-out during questioning."

"Just what information do we need to know about each other?" asked one man.

"For your part, you need to know my name, where I'm from, and what I like. That's simple," said Jon. "I need to know the same about each of you, which given my memory won't be so simple."

At that comment, Jon got a few chuckles. It eased the tension somewhat.

"I'll start. My name's Jon Smith. I am originally from Rye, and have been a seaman for two years, topman for the last year. I'm a good seaman, like my rum, and tend to spend all my pay in each port when we have a run ashore. Everyone got that? Just to prove my point, I have no money with me, which is a condition many of us can relate to." Jon pulled out empty pockets.

At that comment, Jon got a few more chuckles and acknowledgements from the crew.

"If you get questioned about how long I've been on board, just say you don't rightly remember, maybe about a year."

Jon spent the remainder of the day getting to know each man. Luckily, there were only twenty crew members.

At first light, the Gloucester and all the other vessels of the convoy had closed in to the approaches of Brest. The smaller escort sloop, Hampshire, edged in toward land and attempted to signal the French with flags. Over the next hour, by the flag actions of the smaller sloop, it was apparent that the French were either not awake, or not interested in replying to the English signal.

Finally, after considerable effort on the part of the escort sloop, the French appeared to be replying. Jon had great eyesight. The distance to the French batteries was too great, however, to read any of the flags raised by the French.

Jon came back on duty for the afternoon watch. The ships were still standing off the coast waiting for permission to enter port. It took the entire day to relay the fact that French colonists from Louisbourg were on board the vessels. It was the first that the French were aware that Louisbourg had fallen. They were likely both sceptical of the English, and unsure what to do.

As darkness crept in, the Mermaid hoisted the signals to withdraw further offshore for the night. The Hampshire was ordered to remain close inshore. Given the proximity of English merchantmen just outside the harbour, there was no sense in risking their loss from privateers before any landing could be negotiated. By the end of the second dog watch, the convoy was loitering in a relatively safe position offshore for the night.

On board the Gloucester, Captain Tilbury was frustrated with the lack of progress. He wanted to get into Brest and get out. The longer they took doing this transfer, the more money out of his or his owner's pockets. He called for Jon.

"What's your assessment of the situation Smith?"

"Sir, I believe the French don't know what to make of us," stated Jon. "They can see the cargo vessels with escorts. That's puzzling to them. If it were to be a naval attack, there would only be men o' war, not cargo vessels. They have to assume, therefore, that the story that Frenchmen from Louisbourg are on board is true. I doubt, however, that the local battery commander has the authority to allow us into port. He would have to await instructions. I don't know if the local port admiral has that authority, or if he has to wait for instructions from Paris. I suspect the latter. I think that we will eventually be allowed in, but that it might take a few more days." Jon thought he pulled that off very well. He had heard Lieutenant Davis say the same thing to Lieutenant Caharty prior to departure from the Mermaid.

All the next day, the ships stood off the entrance to Brest as the escort sloop Hampshire communicated back and forth with the closest fort. At the end of the day, the Hampshire finally received permission to allow the merchantmen only, to proceed into Brest. They were to discharge their passengers and cargo as soon as possible, and leave.

After first light on the third day off Brest, the merchantmen began to enter the harbour. The Gloucester was the third of the five vessels to navigate into Brest.

The level of danger was about to go way up.

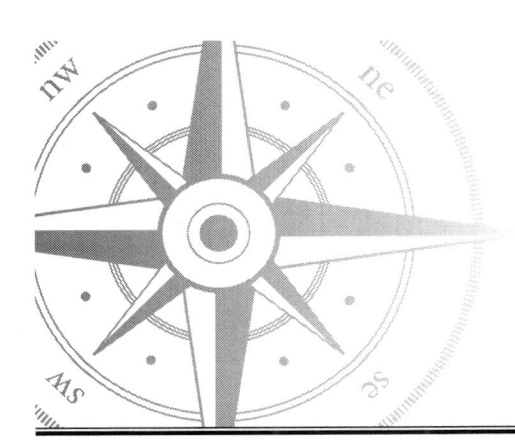

CHAPTER 21

Sailing into Brest was like placing your head in the lion's mouth. Every man on board felt it.

Jon shrugged it off. He had work to do. Jon headed to the tops, as the Gloucester started inshore towards the entrance channel, prepared to stay there for the duration of the trip into Brest or for the daylight hours, whichever took longer. There was a rationale for this approach. The best lines of vision were to be achieved from the tops. Since the mission was to gain as much intelligence about Brest and its approaches as possible, it was only logical that the tops be used to achieve that goal. An alternate purpose, but more valid from a survival perspective, was to remain out of sight of the Frenchmen on board.

The French prisoners were allowed the freedom of the deck each day for a limited time and under close supervision. A new face was less likely to be noticed in the tops, or at least a clear identity would be more challenging, lest a Frenchman report crew changes once they entered Brest. When descending from the tops, it was necessary to head straight below to keep out of view.

During the trip into Brest, the search for fortifications was continuous. On the north shore, there was an outer fort. An outer fort called Fort de Bertheaume had been mentioned during the briefing. Without access to a chart, it was not possible to confirm the exact location of the fort at that time. Given the distance, it was impossible to count the number of gun emplacements.

While in the tops, Jon carried neither glass nor paper. There was a possibility that the reflection of a glass would be spotted and reported. A topman never carried paper. Both would be indicators as to the true nature of activity being conducted. The result would be capture by the French and whatever that might entail.

As the Gloucester approached the narrows, everyone could see another fort on the north shore. This fort was later identified as Fort du Petit Minou. On the south shore, it appeared that there were approximately ten emplacements at îlot des Capucins, but no fort. Each emplacement appeared to be wicker baskets filled with soil in front of each gun. No gun muzzles were spotted. It was an assumption, therefore, that guns were actually present. There were twenty medium sized tents on the island. Each tent was big enough to accommodate six to eight men. It looked like a dreadful place to be stationed, in Jon's opinion. The position was exposed on three sides. On the fourth side -- the side facing the mainland, there was a steep drop to the water. Although it appeared from most angles to be part of the mainland, îlot des Capucins was, in fact, an island.

As they passed along the narrows, most men remarked on another fort spotted on the north shore. That was Fort du Dellec. It was an old position that the English knew about, so there had been a warning to keep an eye out for it. There appeared to be at least twenty 42-pounders at that fort. With their field of fire, those cannons could cover the entire width of the passage.

Finally, the port of Brest came into view. It was on the north shore of a large body of water. Jon had knowledge of a number of ports such as Portsmouth, Rye, English Harbour, and Louisbourg, to make a comparison. The inland area at Brest was far larger than any of these ports. From the lack of ships anchored anywhere in this vast area, Jon surmised that the depth of the water was too deep for anchoring.

The actual piers at Brest were up a river. Both sides of the river mouth had fortifications covering the entrance. Although only a portion of it was visible as they were coming in, it looked as if the entire city were surrounded by massive walls which were angled something like the fortress of Louisbourg.

Jon finally grasped the magnitude of the task assigned. Just the number of fortifications and detail that were currently visible was too much information for any normal person to remember. The task seemed unrealistic when added to all the requested detail related to shipping. The only possible way to capture all the information was to document it segment by segment. Unfortunately, as soon as paper was produced, especially by a man foreward of the mast, the French would suspect and react. It was a daunting task.

A longboat approached the Gloucester filled with hostile looking French troops and navy personnel. These transferred to the Gloucester prior to the ship entering the river. One of the transferred men was the pilot. Jon remained in the tops.

Once on board, the French military mustered everyone on deck, except the men in the tops because they were needed to handle the sails. They sorted out the Frenchmen coming from Louisbourg to determine a leader. The captain spoke on behalf of the Gloucester's crew.

There was a lot of commotion on the deck. Jon tried not to concern himself with it. He was concentrating on counting the ships and berthing spaces as the Gloucester worked her way upstream to where she was going to dock. He counted twelve piers with a berthing position on each side of the pier. A cargo ship occupied each berthing space. Naval vessels, with the exception of oar-powered gunboats, were conspicuously absent.

The Gloucester finally docked. Jon remained occupied furling sails and ensuring everything was ship-shape up top. He was finally beckoned to come down to the deck. That's when the fun started.

Bayonet wielding French troops shoved Jon, as well as the other topmen, into line. The Frenchmen were continuously shouting something at all the Englishmen on board, but no one had any idea what they were saying. When no one complied with the Frenchman's orders because they didn't understand, the French troops just screamed louder, as if by sheer volume they could achieve compliance with their wishes.

Finally a Frenchman - possibly an officer came over.

"Form a line," said the English-speaking French officer in an authoritative voice.

The Gloucester's crew slowly shuffled into line at a relaxed pace. A bayonet nudge to a couple of the Gloucester's seamen ensured a bit more speed in their actions. Once in line, a rapid survey of the entire deck confirmed the absence of the captain and the mate of the Gloucester. They were already confined below decks.

"Put your hands out in front of you," said the French officer.

Another Frenchman walked down the line and examined every man's hands. He was looking for calluses and tar stains to ensure the man was a crewman, not an officer in disguise.

The French officer next walked down the line and randomly pointed to a man. That man was roughly jerked out of the line and propelled across the deck.

The French officer walked over to the man and started to interrogate him.

"What is your name?" asked the French officer.

"Mercer, James Mercer," replied the man. Mercer was obviously frightened. In fact he was shaking like a leaf.

"What is your position on this vessel?"

"Topman on the foremast, sir," replied Mercer.

"Who is that man?" asked the French officer. He was pointing at Jon.

"Him -- that's Jon Smith, sir?" replied Mercer.

"What is his position on this vessel?"

"Smith is a topman on the mainmast," replied Mercer. If possible, Mercer appeared even more scared than he had before.

"What do you know about Smith?" asked the French officer.

"He's a good seaman. He's originally from Rye. When he has a run ashore he tends to like his rum and always comes back broke," replied Mercer. A flicker of a smile came to the Frenchman's face.

"How long has he been on this ship?"

"Don't rightly remember, sir. Maybe a year," replied Mercer.

"Get back in line," ordered the officer.

"You there, come here," ordered the officer. He was pointing to Jon.

Jon stepped forward. One of the French troops pushed him with a musket butt to speed him up.

"Name?" asked the French officer.

"Jon Smith, sir," said Jon. He made sure he didn't look at the French officer directly.

"Where are you from?" asked the officer.

"Why the Gloucester, where else," replied a confused Jon. He was acting the part of a simple sailor.

"Originally?"

"I was born near Rye, in England," said Jon.

"What's a rhumb line?"

"Don't have any idea. I suppose it's a line of rum bottles," said Jon. This French officer was smart thought Jon. He well knew that a rhumb line would be a term very familiar to officers, as it was a standard question used during navigational training.

"What was the name of that man I was just questioning?" asked the officer.

"Who, Mercer?" responded Jon.

"Tell me about him," ordered the officer.

"Let's see -- Mercer is a topman on the foremast. He's on the starboard watch. I'm on the larboard, so we don't get to talk much. He was onboard when I got here. He has a family, wife and two kids in Plymouth, I think. Most of his pay goes back to them, so he's not much fun on a run ashore," said Jon.

"How long have you been aboard?" asked the officer.

"Don't rightly remember, maybe a year," replied Jon.

"Get back in line," ordered the officer.

A couple more men were pulled from line and similarly questioned. The French officer appeared to be satisfied that all the officers had been accounted for, and that no 'hidden' officers were present to spy on them. Finally, he ordered the crew to off-load the Frenchmen they had carried from Louisbourg.

"Rig the yardarms for cargo hoisting," cried the bosun. The crew sprang to work. They much preferred to have something to do than stand in front of bayonets.

As the Frenchmen and cargo were unloaded, Jon had the occasional opportunity to view his surroundings. He tried not to be too curious, as the French troops guarding them were edgy.

At dark work ceased. All the crew were herded below and hatches shut. No one was allowed topside. The men ate and went to sleep. At least everyone would have a good night's sleep. Jon started to write down everything he could remember. He sketched the port and harbour as best as he could remember it. When that was completed, he took all of the documents and carefully hid them. He ensured that none of the crew observed him when he secreted the documents away, lest they be able to betray him.

In the morning after breakfast, the crew re-commenced unloading. It took all day. During the day the level of French alertness seemed to slide. Maybe it was the monotony. Jon was able to observe his surroundings with more intensity and thoroughness. He noted additional detail he had not noticed the previous day.

They were ready to sail on the evening tide. It was none too soon for all members of the Gloucester's crew. The French authorities, however, denied the Gloucester permission to leave until the next morning. The stated reason was that the tide was after dark.

Any ship needed a flooding high tide to exit the river. To back the ship out from her berth into the channel, the tide needed to flood upstream to neutralize the normal river current. Without that neutralization, the ship would be pushed stern first down the river, with little control.

Most of the crew thought the real reason was that the French didn't want any enemy vessels wandering around in the dark near one of their largest naval ports.

Although the crew were again locked below decks, none of them seemed to mind -- it was another full night's sleep. The anxiety that everyone had felt the first day slowly dissipated. If the French were going to do anything, everyone believed it would have happened by now.

Jon spent part of the evening updating his documents. He was still surprised that he hadn't seen any large warships.

The next morning, in preparation to sail, Jon went to the peak of the mainmast. He was supposed to be readying the royals; but in reality he was observing areas that he hadn't had the opportunity to see since arriving.

From this height, it was possible to see over buildings. The top masts of several large ships could be seen further up the river. He counted the masts and divided by three -- seven large ships. By the height of the masts, these ships were likely two-deckers or possibly three-deckers. There was no way to tell. There were a number of smaller masts. Jon estimated another ten smaller ships. There were no sails on most of the yards, so most of these ships were not ready for sea.

The Gloucester finally was allowed to cast off from the dock. It was tricky manoeuvring the ship. The courses and topgallants were dropped, to back the ship out into the river. Once they were sufficiently out in the river, the jib and spritsail had to be immediately raised and catch wind to swing the bow around to point downstream. This was difficult as the stern of the ship was already in the current and being pushed downstream. Luckily, the river current was extremely weak as the tide was running inward. Jon could not imagine being able to get the bow around fast enough if the tide were not running, or even worse, if the tide were against them.

Slowly the bow started to come around. As the bow shifted to larboard, the backward motion eased as the wind pushing the courses and topgallants had less surface area for the wind to catch. The captain shouted for the yards to be swung to a larboard tack. This would increase the area for the wind to catch and keep the backward momentum.

Jon could see the captain's concern. His bowsprit had not yet cleared the neighbouring ship. The Gloucester's bowsprit could collide with the ship in the adjoining berth without more backward motion.

It seemed that everyone was holding his breath. The bowsprit just skimmed the neighbouring ship. Once it was clear of that ship, orders rapped out to haul the yards over to an extreme starboard tack.

The French troops still on board were nervous, but ignorant of the closeness of the manoeuvre. The French officer was very aware of it. Once the Gloucester was safe out in the river channel, he berated the captain. Jon could hear it all the way in the tops.

Jon had to chuckle. It wasn't the captain's fault in truth. The pilot was responsible for manoeuvring the ship in these close quarters of the port. That was why he was there, and why it was mandatory to use a pilot in this port. The French officer could not take out his outrage on the pilot as the pilot probably outranked him, so he let Captain Tilbury have it. Even more humorous, was that Captain Tilbury's orders to swing the yards to a larboard tack while backing, had saved the pilot, and the ship from damage. Captain Tilbury was berated for doing the right thing.

The Gloucester slowly made her way down the river and into the open water off the mouth of the river. A guard boat met them, where all the French troops, the French officer and pilot transferred over. Prior to leaving the captain was summoned by the French officer.

"Captain, under the conditions of this mission of mercy we have not kept your ship or harmed your crew. You are to head directly to sea. If there is any deviation in your course, you will be fired upon. Is that clear?" said the French officer.

"Yes it is," replied Captain Tilbury.

"This is a nice ship. It would be a very nice prize. Until that time captain, I bid you farewell," said the French officer as he turned and climbed down to the waiting gunboat.

The captain lost no time in complying with the wishes of the Frenchman. He hoisted all sail and headed directly for the narrows.

As they exited Brest, Jon came down from the tops. He went below, grabbed pencil, paper and a glass. Returning to the tops, he put these tools to work. He sketched the coastline and the fortifications as best as possible in the time available. He used the glass infrequently and with caution to gather better details, in case the French spotted a reflection and opened fire on them.

There was one significant advantage provided as they exited Brest. The wind was directly against them slowing their passage. They had to tack back and forth to make any type of progress. The captain was very nervous about the orders he had received from the French officer not to deviate from his course. He kept his tacks of short duration and limited divergence from his true course. It was a tedious transit of a long duration back out to meet the Mermaid and other waiting ships. It provided considerable extra time for Jon to sketch and document the forts they were passing.

Despite leaving in the morning, it was mid-afternoon by the time the Gloucester joined up with the convoy. She was only the second cargo ship of the five to come out of Brest. The Mermaid signalled the Gloucester to heave to while they dropped a boat in the water to recover Jon.

As the Mermaid's gig hooked on alongside, the entire crew of the Gloucester seemed to exhale a sigh of relief. Jon said thanks to all the crew and especially Mercer for covering for him on the first morning in Brest.

With as much relief as the Gloucester crew, Jon tossed his ditty bag down to the gig and scrambled down the battens after it.

It was time to report on his mission.

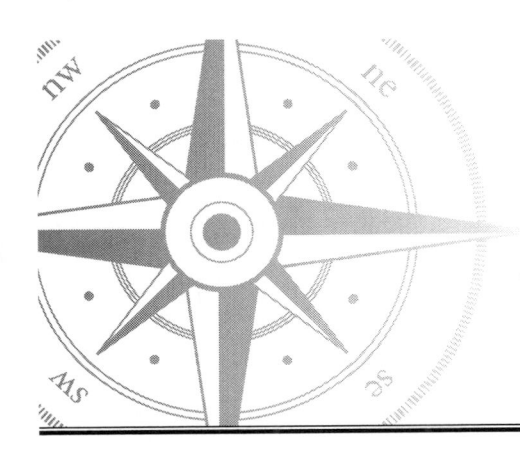

CHAPTER 22

As the gig nudged alongside the Mermaid, Jon had a single regret. He would have preferred to be forgotten on the Gloucester. It would have solved his dilemma about running.

Lieutenant Davis was waiting for him as he climbed the quarterdeck.

"Sir, I'm back aboard. I tried to make some sketches while returning. They need some more work. Would it be possible to delay my report until I finish redoing the sketches?"

"You think the report would be improved by better sketches?" asked Davis.

"I do sir."

"Report to me when ready. We still have some more time until the last three ships arrive."

Jon knuckled his forehead, preparing to disappear to the cockpit. He hadn't taken two steps when Mr. Flynn said from the door of the chartroom, "Smith, I would like to see your sketches of the coastline inside Brest harbour, and match them to the charts that we have."

"Aye, sir, I'll be finished with the copies for Lieutenant Davis in a couple of hours or so," said Jon. "After those are finished, then I'll prepare a copy for you, sir."

"Before you get too carried away, let's take a look at what you have," said Mr. Flynn.

Jon laid the rough sketches out on the chartroom table. Underneath the sketches, Mr. Flynn had been studying an older chart of Brest. Jon was able to match the locations on the charts where each sketched fortification was positioned.

"There are three forts on the north shore that are fixed and cover the majority of the entrance. These inner two forts house what look like 42-pounders and therefore have the range to completely cover the narrows. The outer fort can only cover about half of the wider first portion of the entrance. On the south shore, there are no fixed forts, although there is a temporary location just at the entrance to the narrows. The cannon located at that temporary position are smaller, as they had to be dragged up to the top of that small cliff. I can't be sure if they were 18-pounders or 12-pounders, as I didn't see them. With the fixed fort on the north side, and this temporary battery, the narrows entrance is well covered. The other fort further in towards the narrows can take care of anything that gets past this first outer ring of forts. Then there are the fortifications at the mouth of the river. All-in-all, there is no way we can force our way into that place," said Jon.

Mr. Flynn examined Jon's sketches with a critical eye.

"Your sketches need some improvement. They are barely workable, and lack any flair," said Mr. Flynn.

Jon shrugged his shoulders, but in a way that Mr. Flynn didn't notice. Two weeks ago, he didn't even know how to sketch. Mr Flynn had taught him. To hear that his sketches were workable was an improvement in his mind.

It had been Jon's intention to prepare two copies of the sketches -- one for Lieutenant Davis's report and the other for his own logbook. Mr. Flynn asked for a copy, which was the same as an order.

Over the next three hours, Jon prepared the required copies of each sketch. The best one was selected for submission to Lieutenant Davis. The second best, he kept for himself. The worst copy he put aside for Mr. Flynn.

Clutching all the papers, he headed first to the quarterdeck, then to the wardroom to report to Mr. Davis.

"Excuse me sir, I'm looking for Lieutenant Davis," said Jon to Lieutenant Caharty in the wardroom.

"Wait here, I'll see if he's available," said Lieutenant Caharty. Caharty went and knocked at a small cabin in the back. Some whispered discussions occurred. Both Lieutenant Davis and Lieutenant Caharty returned.

"What have you got for me, Smith?" asked Lieutenant Davis. Lieutenant Caharty was an onlooker.

Jon pointed to the wardroom table as he stepped forward, "If I may, sir?"

Lieutenant Davis nodded his permission. Using the wardroom table, Jon rolled out a chart of Brest harbour. Lieutenant Caharty, Mr. Flynn and Lieutenant Dunkin observed.

"As we sailed in, there was a fort located here," said Jon, speaking rapidly. He used his finger to point the route the Gloucester took into the harbour and location of the fort. "You can see it yourself with a good glass. It's called Fort de Bertheaume. We weren't close enough for me to count the number of emplacements, as I didn't have a glass. Also, I didn't sketch it on the way in, as I didn't want to get caught with a sketch by the French."

"As we continued in, there is another fort on the north shore at the start of the narrows -- Fort du Petit Minou. Both on the approach and exit, I was too far away to count the number of emplacements. I have tried to sketch it as best as possible for the quick look I had through a borrowed glass. This is the sketch, such as it is," said Jon. He showed everyone the sketch. He handed a spare sketch to Mr. Flynn.

"We were closer to the south shore. Here at this point called the îlot des Capucins, there is a temporary battery set up. There are what looks like ten emplacements made of wicker baskets filled with dirt, but no permanent fort. There were twenty medium sized tents on the island. Each tent was big enough to accommodate six to eight men. This is my quick sketch of the point," said Jon. He showed everyone the sketch. Again Mr. Flynn received a copy.

"We entered the narrows and about two-thirds of the way down, at this point, there is another permanent fort of stone on the north shore called Fort du Dellec. There looked to be at least twenty 42-pounders at that fort. This is the sketch, such as it is."

"The narrows open up to a huge area. Brest is on the north shore. The entire area is immense compared to Portsmouth, and much larger than the bay at Louisbourg just to give you some perspective of its size," said Jon. "The actual port of Brest is up the river with the city on both sides. There are strong outer walls, which appear to be all around the city. Since I was unable to leave the ship, I could not confirm this or verify the state of these walls. On both sides of the mouth of the river are strong fortifications." Jon again provided a sketch of the mouth of the river.

"I counted twelve piers with a berthing location on each side of the pier. A cargo ship occupied each docking space. There were no naval vessels present, however, the last morning as we were departing, I was able to get up to the royals. I took a good look around and spotted the top masts of several large ships further up the river. I counted twenty-one masts, so dividing by three I assumed there were seven large ships. By the height of the masts, these ships are likely two-deckers or possibly three-deckers. There was no way to tell. There were a number of smaller masts, which I estimated belonged to another ten smaller ships. There were no sails on most of the yards, so most of these ships were not ready for sea."

"As far as smaller vessels, I only spotted ten gunboats, but there might have been more. Five of these had what looked like an 18-pounder in the bow. The other five had 12-pounders for sure, because I was able to see them at close range."

"As for the troop morale, all we saw were those troops sent to guard us on the ship. The men were nervous, but had reasonable training, were alert and disciplined. The officer who did the questioning on board our ship was smart and dangerous. He locked up the captain and mate immediately. He then checked every man on board -- his appearance, his hands, his bearing -- and then cross checked each man's story with other crew members. From what I saw, he didn't seem to trust the Frenchmen from Louisbourg any more than he trusted us."

"I don't know if I can provide anything more, sirs," remarked Jon as he nervously finished his short presentation.

"What you are saying Smith, is that any attempt to attack Brest by ship is likely doomed," said Lieutenant Caharty.

"All it takes is any one of these forts to spot you and fire; then every one of the forts will be ready. If you start by taking out the first fort, by the time you reduce it by bombardment; you are going to take a number of hits. Those big cannons can out range anything we have. Once past that fort, you'll have to do it all over again twice more just to get to the city. Getting up to the port in that river would be like running a gauntlet, with the same result."

"I knew their defences were strong, but not that strong," muttered Lieutenant Davis. "Any other questions for Smith?"

No one had any additional questions.

"Very well Smith. You've done well," stated Lieutenant Davis. "Once the other men report, I'll see if the captain wishes to speak to you directly. Until then you are dismissed."

"Aye, sir," said Jon and fled from the wardroom back to the safety of the cockpit on the deck below.

Jon collapsed at the cockpit table. He was hungry, worn-out and drained from preparing the sketches. As his hand dropped into his lap, he also realized that something important was missing -- his money belt. Despite his fatigue, he made a beeline to the purser's storage room to retrieve that critical item. After pounding on the door, a purser's mate finally coughed up his ditty bag. Jon carefully verified the contents of the money belt. Satisfied that everything was present, he trudged back to the cockpit.

Another surprise awaited him. Jon had missed his watches while absent on the Gloucester, so both Mr. Flynn and Dickerson were eager for him to resume his duties. He was, therefore, placed immediately back in the watch rotation without any regard to sleep.

There's no justice, he thought. I've worked as hard as, or probably harder than either of them while I was gone and certainly took more risk. You'd think they'd give me at least one watch to rest.

Late the next day, the other three cargo vessels appeared exiting from Brest. Langtry and Mr. Elkhorne were both recovered from the cargo vessels and reported to Lieutenant Davis. Jon wasn't privy to what they passed on.

While they were giving their reports, the Mermaid and her little convoy headed north to England. In the morning, all the cargo ships headed for London to obtain loads for North America, with the Hampshire sloop to escort them.

HMS Mermaid headed to Portsmouth to re-provision prior to heading back to Antigua. The men were eager for a run ashore.

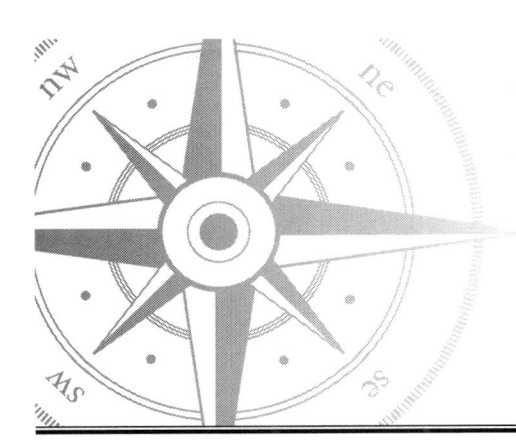

CHAPTER 23

An orphaned ship arrived in Portsmouth harbour late on a Thursday afternoon.

HMS Mermaid was officially a member of the Leeward Island squadron on detached service to the North American station. She was on detached duty from that station to escort a convoy back to England via France. In simpler terms, HMS Mermaid was like an orphan begging for any support from the Port Admiral.

It had been years since the Mermaid had seen an English port. It was months since she had last been near a naval yard. Her bottom was foul and she needed stores. She was like an impoverished second cousin that lands on your doorstep.

In some ways, Jon considered his position on the Mermaid somewhat the same as the ship itself. He also felt something like an orphan. He was a pressed man elevated to a senior topman position and then given an acting master's mate position. He had no true friends, and numerous others questioning his right or suitability to hold his current position. He could speak to the other master's mate Chad Dickerson, but he could not confide in him. Everyone else around him was either a superior or a subordinate. He dare not say what he was thinking to anyone.

Jon put all this to the back of his mind as they sailed in on shortened sail. Standing by the anchor, in the duty position for anchoring, he nervously waited with the men assigned to the anchoring detail. The nervousness was justified. It was the first time completing this function. The correct commands were not known. No one had ever provided instruction in these duties, and he had never even been present at the anchor during anchoring. The only hope was that the men assigned to the position knew what they were doing.

"Take the lashings off the anchor, and prepare it for letting go."

The men were already working on it, without having to be told. There were a couple of rolled eyeballs, but no one said a word in response.

"You think we'll get any shore leave," whispered a member of the anchor detail to his mate.

"Silence on the deck." More rolled eyeballs.

"Let go the anchor," came the shout from the quarterdeck when the ship reached the place the guard boat identified for the Mermaid to occupy.

"Let go," said Jon. It was a redundant order as the men were already acting on the orders from the quarterdeck. They could hear those orders as well as Jon.

Once the anchor dropped and grabbed, Jon's work was complete. He heard the orders from the quarterdeck, "Lower the captain's gig. Gig crew to assemble aft."

Jon looked at the four hands working the anchor detail. There was a subdued hostility in their eyes. Jon considered that he had earned that. He hadn't handled the anchoring all that well. In fact, if it wasn't for the knowledge of these hands, they might not have been ready to anchor. What should he do about it? He instinctively knew that he couldn't show any weakness, but he also knew that he had been throwing his weight around -- at least from their perspective. He hated when a midshipman or bosun's mate had thrown his weight around, so he understood how these men felt.

"Men, you all appear to have experience working the anchoring detail. What are the procedures if we had to anchor at a designated buoy or marker?"

The question caught the men off-guard. The men knew the answers, but were uncertain as to the purpose of the question.

Jon smiled. He had been in these men's shoes before. They didn't know if they were being asked to see if they knew their duties, or if Jon was just looking for a reason to berate them. The possibility that Jon didn't know the answer was not a consideration.

Jon pointed at one man, "Explain the steps."

The man hesitantly explained the steps they would take. Jon soaked up the knowledge.

"Alright, now explain the process for raising the anchor," said Jon as he pointed to a different man.

The man explained the steps as Jon again took mental notes. By this time the four men were puzzled, as indicated by their facial expressions.

"How long have each of you been working the anchor detail?"

"Four years, sir," "Two years, sir," "Two years, sir," "Two years and a bit, sir."

"Given your experience, can you see any way to improve any of these steps to make it easier, faster or safer?"

There was some looking at each other, and then a chorus of, "No, sir."

"Good enough, dismissed."

The men shuffled off while Jon headed back to the quarterdeck. He was feeling pleased with how he handled that situation. Instead of four pissed-off men that would have resisted working with him the next time, the men went away curious. To add the butter on the bread, he now knew the steps for dropping and raising the anchor.

His pleasant feeling was short-lived, however, because the second he set foot on the quarterdeck, Mr. Flynn was shouting at him.

"Smith, I want all the requirements for stores ready for delivery to the naval yards at first light tomorrow," said Mr. Flynn.

Chad had already warned him that Mr. Flynn would be requesting these requirements, so both he and Chad had been working diligently on compiling the list and appropriate requisitions since Jon had returned from Brest.

It still meant a long night with little sleep.

CHAPTER 24

Although old and outdated in size, the Mermaid was still a line-of-battle ship of the Royal Navy. Upon arrival at Portsmouth, Captain Montague was obliged to make his manners with the port admiral. This was especially important if he wished any provisions, as the port admiral could provide or deny.

These weren't the only concerns that Captain Montague had about his ship. After the problem with yellow jack the previous year, the Mermaid was still short of crew. She was also an old ship that had been employed in the West Indies for some time without a refit. Her bottom was in poor condition. You could see the weed trailing. She needed to be careened and cleaned. The crew also needed a reprieve. They hadn't been placed 'out of discipline' in months and deserved a break.

Captain Montague was no fool. The efficiency of a ship was a fragile thing. Both the ship and the crew needed to be cared for. The navy said it was his duty to care for the ship first. Captain Montague knew that in reality the crew needed looking after first. If the crew were looked after, they would look after the ship.

As he entered the port admiral's office, Captain Montague halted in the position of attention in front of the admiral's desk.

"Captain Montague of His Majesty's ship Mermaid, sir," said Captain Montague as he introduced himself. "Mermaid was tasked to escort the surrendered French personnel from Louisbourg back to France. We have successfully completed that task. In addition, while the French were off-loaded in Brest, I had men positioned on each of the cargo ships to gather intelligence about Brest and the French naval capacity and readiness."

"Yes, yes, reports have been received about Louisbourg," replied the port admiral. "As far as the intelligence about Brest, pass it over to my flag lieutenant. He will add it to the other intelligence we have collected."

"HMS Mermaid you said. Wasn't the Mermaid involved in that action when the Vigilant was taken?" asked the admiral.

"Yes sir. The Mermaid conducted the boarding action. She was supported by the Superb, Launceston, Eltham, Shirley, and some smaller colonial ships," replied Captain Montague.

"Good, good, you can tell me all about it over supper this evening," said the port admiral.

"That's very kind of you, sir," said Captain Montague. "However, I don't want to sail under false flags so to speak. I wasn't the captain of the Mermaid during that action. I was the captain of the Shirley. I participated in the action, but saw things from a different perspective."

"No matter, you were still there and saw the whole action. It will be an interesting tale over dinner. We dine at seven. You can ask the flag lieutenant for directions when you pass him the intelligence," said the port admiral.

"Until seven then, sir," said Captain Montague and withdrew from the port admiral's office.

Captain Montague next saw the port admiral at his residence at seven. After a before-dinner drink of sherry, Captain Montague, the port admiral, the flag lieutenant and a couple of other officers were seated to a lovely meal.

"Tell me about the Vigilant action, captain," said the port admiral.

"Well sir, I can only relate certain aspects of it, as I was not present for all of the action," stated Captain Montague. "According to Captain Douglas, who was in command of the Mermaid during the action, and has since been given command of the Vigilant, the Mermaid was on the Louisbourg outer patrol. At about two bells in the afternoon watch, strange sails were sighted by the lookouts. The Mermaid charged out to investigate and identified the ship as a French man o' war of sixty-four guns. Since Mermaid is only forty guns, Captain Douglas decided to get some more help to take the Frenchman."

"The Mermaid withdrew, but kept the Frenchman close, offering herself as a target so the Frenchman wouldn't lose her. The Frenchman was firing high the whole time, but did no major damage. There was a fair bit of fog. As they closed on Louisbourg, the fog hid the anchored fleet and other escorts from the Frenchman. When he popped out of the fog, the Frenchman took one look and turned tail. The Mermaid had popped out of the same fog bank a few minutes earlier and hoisted 'Enemy in Sight'. Every escort in the area responded. I was one of them in the Shirley," explained Captain Montague.

"We were all charging toward the Frenchman, but only the Mermaid was close enough to get in a shot. After coming out of the fog bank, the Mermaid reversed course after she had given the fleet warning. When the Frenchman appeared out of the fog bank, the Mermaid got in a full broadside; then she chased the Frenchman back into the fog bank. By this time it was in the dog watches," continued Captain Montague.

"As the Frenchman ran, the Mermaid engaged with her chase guns. She was the only vessel within gun range of the Frenchman. As Captain Douglas tells it, about two bells into the first watch he offered an extra spirit ration to the chase gun crews if they could knock down the mizzen on the Frenchman. The very next shot; they missed the mizzen, but hit the wheel. The Frenchman was knocked off course to the larboard. She went into stays. That left her entire stern exposed. Mermaid crossed her stern and poured a full broadside into her from the larboard battery. That broadside blew the stern out of the Frenchman. Captain Douglas reversed course and put another double-shot broadside into her from the starboard battery. The Frenchman had managed to come around somewhat so the second broadside wasn't able to rake her stern, but it did considerable damage."

"The Superb came up and was able to get in a broadside. By then the Mermaid was closing for boarding. The Mermaid came up to the Frenchman's starboard aft and grappled. They boarded and after a short fight the Frenchman gave up. I can understand it from the Frenchman's perspective. They were carrying an additional five hundred troops to Louisbourg. The Mermaid's two broadsides caused considerable carnage, especially on the lower gun deck. There were another three line-of-battle ships present, and two smaller sloops. There was no way they were going to win," explained Captain Montague.

"I take it the Vigilant was taken back to port and repaired?" asked the port admiral.

"She was taken back to Gabarus Bay, which is where the expedition fleet was anchored. Carpenters and men from a number of ships were employed to repair her. By the time they were finished, she was ready to join the line. I believe she is being taken back to Antigua. I'm not sure about crew however. We were all stretched mighty thin in that department," explained Captain Montague.

"What is the condition of the Mermaid at the present?" inquired the port admiral.

"We're short crew and she desperately needs to be careened and have her bottom cleaned. Once re-provisioned, she will be ready to head back to Antigua," said Captain Montague.

"Not until November," said the port admiral.

"Excuse me, I don't understand, sir," said Captain Montage. To say he was surprised would have been an understatement.

"I have no ships to spare for convoy duty to the Indies. You will have to provide escort for the next convoy. As you know, sailing to the West Indies between August and October is problematic as it is hurricane season. The earliest a convoy to the West Indies will be formed is late October, when it is reckoned safe from any hurricane," said the port admiral between bites.

"What are we to do between now and then, besides careening and cleaning the ship's bottom?" asked Captain Montague.

"You will be stationed here, under my command," said the port admiral. "You will assist in patrolling the channel. There are still a number of French privateers, operating from St. Malo, that are an irritant. The Admiralty is under increasing pressure from the big combines and houses in London to put a stop to them. We need to increase the number of patrols and increase the safety of the sea-lanes around England, and specifically in the channel. Your ship will aid in that effort. That is far more important than cleaning your bottom and it must take priority."

Captain Montague was not happy, but he could do little about it. The Mermaid was ideal for a convoy escort, being big enough to thwart French raiders, but not as valuable as the newer larger warships. Additionally, the port admiral of Portsmouth was not one to waste an opportunity when it presented itself in the form of an extra ship for patrol.

"How long do we have before sailing on patrol?" asked Captain Montague.

"You should be able to store tomorrow and sail the next day. I need you out on patrol," said the admiral.

"Sir my ship hasn't seen England in years. It's been six months and one major action since we have seen a naval yard. My officers and men haven't stepped ashore in over a year. The ship hasn't even been anywhere where it could be placed 'out of discipline' in months. Can't you give us at least a couple of days, sir?"

"You will get your sailing orders tomorrow, captain," said the admiral.

HMS Mermaid was about to become the exact opposite of a happy ship.

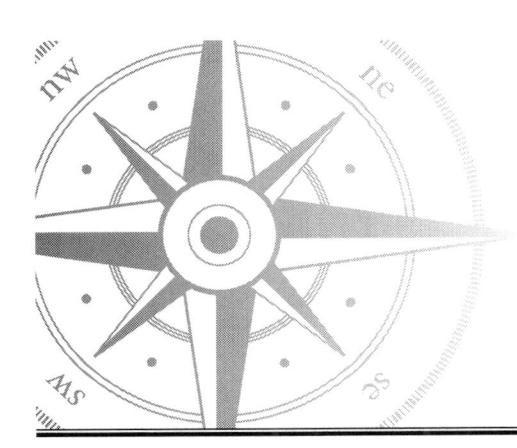

CHAPTER 25

Normal harbour watch routine was instituted moments after the anchor hit bottom.

Since commissioned officers did not perform harbour watch duties, all these duties fell on the non-commissioned ranks. Much to his chagrin, Jon learned he would stand harbour watch in addition to his normal duties. The master's mate's normal duties involved checking all sailing stores and ensuring the correct requisitions were prepared for needed items. These sailing stores included rope, sails, and a host of other items necessary for the operation of the ship. Given that HMS Mermaid had not been in a harbour with a naval establishment in months, it made these regular duties even more pressing. Considerable time had been devoted to the identification, listing of requirements and preparation of requisitions.

Virtually every function required was either new, or his experience was limited to the time since becoming an acting master's mate. There was an apprehensive approach to each of these assigned tasks, but concurrently there was also some anticipation or eagerness. This eagerness was due to a hunger to learn new things. There was also value in doing a good job, especially if one wished to continue in an acting position.

Until he had become an acting master's mate, Jon had no idea that there were such onerous requirements for paper. Lists and ledgers seemed to be required for everything. The amount of each type of rope, sails, and stores of various types made these lists a necessity for there was no possible way to remember all the detail. Everything under the eye of the sailmaker, carpenter and bosun had to be checked and accounts tallied. After checking these items, requisitions for new items from the naval yard had to be prepared. It seemed never-ending.

"Jesus, Chad, doesn't the paper ever stop?"

"Just be thankful that we don't have another change of command. When Montague came on board, we had to complete the inventory of every single item before he would sign for it. I spent hours counting every nail and spool of thread on board. I'd not wish that on anyone -- except maybe you," chuckled Chad.

"Thanks a lot."

"If you're looking for sympathy, you've come to the wrong place. If you don't want to do this, you can always request that you go back foreward," said Chad, who was pulling Jon's chain. Jon was so determined to keep the acting position, it was pathetic. It was amusing at times just to jerk him around.

"I'll suffer through it alright."

"If you think this is fun, just wait until you have the watch tonight. It shouldn't be too bad, but you have to keep a sharp eye out for runners. Just thank your lucky stars that we aren't 'out of discipline'. That's generally a pain," said Chad.

Jon was not looking forward to standing a harbour watch. Previously, he had stood harbour watch, but only as a lookout. Standing a harbour watch as a master's mate had a negative aspect, primarily because it created a dilemma. As the senior man on the watch, he was responsible for everything that happened during the duration of the watch. An important responsibility was to keep the men from running. That was a difficult proposition to swallow. Having been pressed, Jon could relate to a man's motivation for running. Many times, he had considered it, and even vowed to run. How then could he enforce actions that would keep a man from running?

The crew of the Mermaid was kept busy until the end of the dog watches. They were then stood down until the start of the morning watch. Jon was assigned the first watch, and Chad the middle watch.

Jon paced the quarterdeck continuously during the first watch while wrestling with the dilemma. Thankfully, there was still daylight, so the probability of someone running was limited. The port admiral also had a standing guard boat patrol as an incentive for the men to stay put. It had the added benefit that the ship didn't have to man a guard boat, which was one less worry.

The ship was not as yet placed 'out of discipline', so the biggest challenge during the first watch was to ward off the few bumboats still heading out to the Mermaid. The captain had not yet granted permission for them to approach the ship.

When the captain returned after his supper with the port admiral, he broke the news to the officers that Mermaid would be based out of Portsmouth for the next couple of months. To temper the immediate enthusiasm, this news was quickly followed with orders they would engage in patrol duties off the south coast for the bulk of that time.

It didn't take long until the rumour spread that the ship would not be placed 'out of discipline'. The men's attitude turned foul in an instant. A majority of the crew were happy to remain in English waters. They would rather be here than in the West Indies. Here they were in a more familiar environment, closer to home and there was no threat of yellow jack. If a man were to run, this was a better place to do it.

Despite this natural affinity for home waters, these men were itching to spend some time ashore. Many of the men had not seen England in years. A large portion of the crew had not placed a foot on solid land in over a year. Certainly, no one had stepped ashore since Jon had joined the ship the previous December with the exception of the watering party that had landed at Louisbourg.

Unfortunately, as far as Jon could see, very few men would go ashore. It was more a matter of trust than anything else. Very few men could be trusted not to run. Senior positions would likely all return. Even though many of the men had prize money and a year's pay coming to them, they would gladly forgo that for freedom from the Royal Navy. More than half of the men foreward of the mast on this ship had been pressed. Even many of the so-called volunteers would run if given the opportunity.

Would he run? He was now in a different position than the remainder of the men. Since being pressed, numerous opportunities had been presented that otherwise might never have happened. Those opportunities had been used to learn new skills and increase the level of knowledge in many areas. Mr. Flynn and the captain had put their trust in him. As a master's mate, a different side of the navy had opened up that so far was intriguing. Despite these conflicting feelings, Jon knew that he was less inclined to run. Another factor for consideration was the potential loss of a year's pay and prize money. The navy had robbed him of his freedom. He'd be dammed if he was to be robbed of what they owed him as well.

A sailor's expectation when anchoring in port is that things will be more relaxed and there will be an opportunity for some downtime. That notion sank faster than a cannonball sinks once the Mermaid's hook hit bottom. It was partly due to the incredible amount of work that needed to be completed. What was more exasperating was watching the commissioned officers, with the exception of Lieutenant Davis, just idling away while Jon was working his ass off.

Hoys, loaded with stores, approached at the beginning of the forenoon watch. The hoys were a direct result of his efforts, and those of the purser. The crew looked on the hoys with disdain. The previous day when it appeared the ship would be placed 'out of discipline', the crew would have enthusiastically emptied the hoys and stowed the provisions. Now that they were not to receive any liberty, they took their time.

Any idea that he might have a bit of relaxation during the day was quashed when Mr. Flynn advised him that he had only out-dated charts of the English coast. This would have to be rectified by Jon that morning. After a quick bite to eat, Jon reported to Mr. Flynn.

"Speak to the first lieutenant and get us a boat to take us to the port administration offices," said Mr. Flynn. "While you're gone, Dickerson will stand your watches."

That was the first indication Jon had that he would be going ashore. Here was temptation placed in front of his eyes.

Disembarking at the docks, Mr. Flynn ordered the boat back to the ship. Jon and Mr. Flynn were left standing there. It would be easy to run from Mr. Flynn. They were still within the naval yard, so Jon bided his time.

"Mr. Flynn, sir. May I ask what we are doing?" They headed toward the large administration building, which housed the port offices.

"You're probably not aware of the restrictions on charts in His Majesty's navy. Every master is responsible to acquire, update, and maintain his own charts. My job is to find the appropriate charts. Your job will be to update them," said Mr. Flynn. The simplicity of Mr. Flynn's response posed some questions. In the short time he had known Mr. Flynn, Jon had become very wary of his short simple answers. They had invariably led to something more serious than anticipated.

"Just how am I supposed to update them, sir?"

"Once I acquire the required charts, I will determine their age. We will visit other ship masters and see what information they have on their charts that are not on the ones we just acquired. If there are differences, you will be responsible to copy those differences onto our newly acquired charts," explained Mr. Flynn.

"Alright, sir." Jon was baffled and didn't see the point.

Jon received an eye-opener as he accompanied Mr. Flynn. First, they went into the port administration offices. They were bounced from one unhelpful clerk to other equally unknowledgeable clerks. They finally left the port administration offices in disgust and continued out of the naval yards into Portsmouth. Temptation reared her ugly head. If there ever was an opportunity to run, this was it. It was doubtful if Mr. Flynn could run ten yards, so escaping from him would be child's play.

Curiosity got the better of Jon as he was interested in where Mr. Flynn was headed.

Following the directions from a passer-by on the street, they arrived at a chandler's shop. Mr. Flynn perused a number of charts and decided on several of them. Jon scooped them up, along with oilskins to cover them.

Reversing course, they next headed back to the dock steps where several ships' boats were waiting. Jon listened as closely as possible while Mr. Flynn engaged in conversations related to charts with a number of midshipmen or coxswains on the various boats. Mr. Flynn appeared to be determining which masters had the best charts of the English southern coast. Finally, he made a decision.

"Coxswain, would it be possible to get a lift out to your ship to see your master," asked Mr. Flynn.

"Aye, sir, step aboard," responded an older coxswain. The jolly boat was rowed out to their vessel -- a small sloop.

After getting permission to board, they were led to the rear entry and introduced to the master and commander. Since the sloop was employed in coastal patrols and revenue duties, the charts they had were far superior to the ones just acquired by Mr. Flynn at the chandlers.

Jon was busy on the sloop for the next few hours updating chart after chart with information gleaned from the sloop's charts. It was surprising the amount of information that the sloop's charts had compared to the newly acquired ones. Given some of the navigation hazards identified, the value of checking another master's chart became very apparent to Jon. Despite the tedious work, it was a lesson he would not forget.

Late in the last dog watch, Jon managed to get a lift back over to the Mermaid from the sloop's crew. By that time he was famished, as he had only nibbled over the course of the day on some bread he had placed in his pocket. He was also too exhausted to think about running.

As his feet touched the Mermaid's deck, Dickerson smiled at him and relieved him of the charts.

"Good to see you back, Jon," said a smiling Dickerson. "You have the first watch."

"You must be joking," said an incensed Jon. "I've been working all day without a break, without food or drink. Now, once I'm back, I'm expected to immediately stand another watch. Where's the justice in that?"

"You expect justice? Me' thinks you are in the wrong place," said a chuckling Dickerson. "Besides, where do you think I've been while you were away? Sleeping?"

"All I'm saying, is there is no justice on this ship. I can understand why a man would run," said Jon in a muted tone. "Hold on for a couple of minutes while I go below and grab my jacket."

With that comment, he disappeared below. In the cockpit, he found that his rations, including his spirit ration had been set aside. It was cold, but he wolfed it down regardless before returning to the deck.

"Chad, thanks for setting aside my rations."

"Least I could do," replied Dickerson as he touched Jon's shoulder and turned to go below.

Jon checked each member of the watch, and retreated to the chart area to ensure the new charts were properly stored and protected against the elements.

Jon walked around the deck a couple of times during the watch just to ensure all members of the watch were awake and alert. It was a quiet watch. When Dickerson relieved him at midnight, it didn't take much time for Jon to get below and fall asleep.

He was barely awake next morning when the commotion started. By the sounds of it, whatever occurred wasn't good. A quick trip to the deck to see what was happening confirmed that assessment. Two men had failed to report for duties on the morning harbour watch. A fast check below failed to locate the missing men. A detailed search of the vessel was ordered, again without any sign of them. It appeared that they had deserted sometime during the night. Jon knew that he and Dickerson would be 'on the mat' over this loss.

Lieutenant Davis called Dickerson and Jon forward. "Well, what do you have to say for yourselves?"

Dickerson replied, "There was no indication that they deserted on my shift, sir."

Jon said, "I assumed the first watch and handed back over to Dickerson at midnight. During my watch, I went around the deck on three separate occasions checking every member of the watch. I always found them awake and alert. There was no indication of any noise, no splashing, or nothing out of the ordinary reported at any time. I have no idea at what time these men deserted. I would also point out that no member of my watch reported seeing the guard boat during the entire watch."

"Well they just didn't vanish into thin air, did they?" said a visibly upset Lieutenant Davis. "The captain is not going to be happy when I inform him two men deserted last night. I wouldn't want to be in your shoes."

Jon apprehensively went to work, expecting a call into the captain's cabin at any minute. He had been called there before and it had not been a pleasant experience.

CHAPTER 26

Jon apprehensively waited throughout the day for the axe to fall.

That was not to say that Jon sat around waiting and fretting about things. On the contrary, it was necessary to update ledgers continuously because throughout the day a procession of different hoys brought stores out to the Mermaid. Bumboats appeared, as the captain had finally given permission to allow them to approach, although the ship was still under discipline. With so much going on with the loading from the hoys and bumboat traffic, it appeared that Lieutenant Davis was going to have an apoplexy. Davis and the other officers were avoided as much as possible. Just listening to the officers grumbling about not being allowed ashore was aggravating. Why they were grumbling so much, he had no idea. He had been ashore, and a fat lot of good it had done him.

The re-provisioning, resulting from the arrival of the hoys, was a strong indication that the Mermaid was getting ready for sea. It appeared that no one else was going ashore, which appeared to upset the officers even more. When the officers are upset, their bitterness and resentment tends to flow down to the men. The Mermaid sunk from a disgruntled ship to lower depths.

During the first dog watch, Jon disappeared below. Out of sight, out of mind was the appropriate approach. Although curious about the abnormal movement on the deck and boats in the water which he heard, any impulse to investigate was curbed. Instead he used the time more appropriately attempting to read, until it was time to report on deck to assume the watch.

"Jon, you probably heard some noise earlier. Lieutenant Rylett took a press gang out. Keep your eyes open for them. I doubt that they would be back during this next watch, but you never know," said Dickerson.

"Thanks for the heads up Chad," said Jon as he assumed the watch. The press gang made sense. They had been short-handed for months. The desertion the previous evening only aggravated the situation.

The desertions the previous evening and the fact that the press gang was out tonight, only highlighted the predicament in which Jon found himself. Regardless of what he felt about the press, if he let any men escape tonight; his ass would be on the line. Jon decided to hell with any debate with respect to the right and wrong of pressing men. Tonight shear self-preservation was his concern.

As he made his rounds on deck, Jon spoke to each man, "Last night two men deserted. If any desert tonight, we are all going to have to pay the piper, so keep a sharp lookout, and listen for any abnormal noises. Keep your eyes open for boats returning to the ship. The press is out. I doubt if they will return in the dog watch, but be vigilant just the same."

After being relieved by Dickerson for the first watch, he quickly occupied his hammock. Nothing disturbed him until he was shaken awake for the middle watch. Jon got up, and headed bleary-eyed back on deck to assume his watch duties.

"Jon, the press gang is not back yet. Keep your eyes open. You know how Rylett can be," said Dickerson.

The mention of Rylett was sufficient incentive to arouse Jon. He went round the ship checking each man and reinforcing his earlier caution. About one hour into the watch, a cry from foreward alerted Jon and the rest of the watch that boats were approaching. The press gang returned empty-handed. This was not surprising in Portsmouth, as the inhabitants were well aware when a press gang was about and took appropriate precautions. It was never the less disappointing for the Mermaid. They would remain under strength.

In his typical fashion Lieutenant Rylett came aboard, ordered, "Secure the boats astern," turned and disappeared below. Rylett would say he needed to report the results of the press to the captain. In truth, there was little concern for the men. They were abandoned and left to secure the equipment. If anything was improperly secured or missing, they would feel Rylett's tongue at the very least.

"Give the press gang a hand," ordered Jon to the closest men. "You men forward in the bow, keep a weather eye on the bow just in case others are interested in swimming."

The bosun appeared on the quarterdeck, as did the master-at-arms. Jon joined them. They were discussing the lack of results in Portsmouth. The bosun turned to Jon and said, "Thanks for the help."

He had no sooner said that when a cry came from foreward, "Men in the water."

The master-at-arms immediately grabbed a few men on deck and propelled them toward the entry port. Jon shouted, "Pull the boats from aft up to the entry port."

It took about four minutes to bring a boat alongside and the impromptu crew to cast off. By this time, Jon had received a report from foreward. At least two men were in the water. Jon passed this information on to the master-at-arms in the jolly boat. Off they went in pursuit of the men in the water.

About fifteen minutes later the jolly boat reappeared. Two bundles were in the bottom of the boat.

"Rig a sling from the main course yardarm," ordered Jon. To a man standing beside him Jon said, "My respects to Lieutenant Davis. Tell him we have two unconscious deserters. Ask him if we send them to the surgeon or straight to confinement?"

Once rigged, the two bodies were hoisted up from the jolly boat and dropped on deck. By the time Lieutenant Davis appeared on deck, the jolly boat had again been streamed aft, and the impromptu crew had dispersed. The master-at-arms maintained guard of the two men. As they were unconscious, it was unlikely they would escape.

Lieutenant Davis inquired, "Who is it?"

Mr. Pearly, the master-at-arms lifted the head of one man, "Perkins, landsman, starboard watch, sir". He then moved to the next one, "Rory Kelly, ordinary seaman, starboard watch. These two are messmates, sir."

Jon knew the two to see them, but had never dealt with them.

"Take them below, and put them in irons. I'll have them up before the captain tomorrow. Now if there's nothing else, I'm going back to sleep. We'll be sailing tomorrow," ordered Lieutenant Davis.

"Aye, sir," said Jon. "You two men, assist the master-at-arms in moving these bodies below."

As Jon made his rounds, he mused that he was glad he was not in the deserters' shoes. Each time he stopped to check a man on his watch, he said, "We'll be sailing in the morning. Between now and the end of the watch, be extra cautious. There's but a few hours for any would-be deserter to escape. I expect any additional attempts will be made in the next two or three hours."

The extra precautions and noise were enough to alert any would-be deserters that now was not the time. As a result the watch ended without the loss of any additional men.

The morning watch had the men mustered as if they were at sea. Regular sea-going routine was initiated. Just before the start of the forenoon watch, the guard boat appeared carrying the port admiral's flag lieutenant. He passed on written orders to the captain and departed.

The captain held a summary trial in his cabin at four bells in the forenoon watch. Kelly and Perkins were brought before him. Jon was standing by in case he was called as a witness. His presence was not necesaary. Kelly and Perkins were marched out of the captain's cabin by the master-at-arms. Mr. Pearly whispered as he passed Jon, "Twenty-four lashes."

Jon reflected, it could have been a lot worse, but twenty-four lashes were still significant. He didn't feel any remorse for the men. He was thankful that they had been caught, or it might have been him in the captain's cabin instead, and he might have been wearing the twenty-four lashes.

Jon turned and went back on deck seeking Mr. Flynn. Finding no tasks assigned to him. Jon grabbed a navigation book and commenced studying it in the chart area.

Out of sight, out of mind.

CHAPTER 27

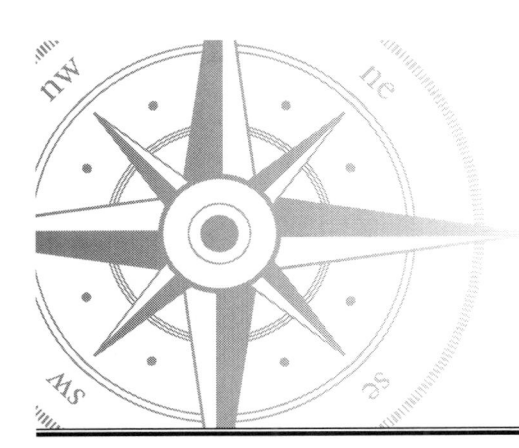

A dispirited crew looked forlornly at a receding Portsmouth as the Mermaid sailed on the afternoon tide.

Once out to sea, the Mermaid turned west toward Plymouth. When the ship was out of sight of land and any prying eyes, the grates were rigged while the crew was piped to witness punishment. Kelly was led up in irons to the grate. The master-at-arms removed his irons and tied him to the grates. The drum roll began and the cat o' nine tails tickled Kelly's back. Kelly was a bull of a man, but even he rapidly succumbed to the lash.

It was not the first time that Jon had ever viewed punishment by the lash, but it was the first time that he had viewed it from the quarterdeck. His location didn't change his opinion at all. It was still a barbaric form of punishment.

When the twenty-four lashes had been applied to Kelly, he was cut down and dragged away to the surgeon. Perkins was led forth to receive his due. The drums rolled again and the lash whipped down. Where Kelly had been stoic, Perkins screamed as the lash cut his flesh. The screams didn't last long as Perkins passed out after the sixth stroke. Conscious or not, all twenty-four lashes were applied before Perkins was cut down and sent below to the surgeon.

Jon contemplated the effect of the lash on the two men. Each would be even more resentful of the navy and authority. It was highly likely that each would be much more cautious of attempting to run again. Would they run? Most likely, but they would be wary. Was the lash necessary? It depended upon how you looked at it. Without it, it was likely there would be no navy. The question still in Jon's mind was whether it was fair to press a man and then punish him when he attempted to leave? Legally it was allowed, but morally the answer was no.

Jon couldn't see any solution to this dichotomy. Surely a volunteer navy would be better, but how many would actually volunteer? Not enough to man all the ships needed to protect the sea lanes and British commerce around the world. There had to be a better way. He just couldn't see himself ordering the flogging of a man just because that man ran or attempted to run after he had been pressed. That just confirmed in his mind that the option to write the Lieutenant's examination was not for him.

The Mermaid sailed on, unmindful of the trials or tribulations of the crew confined within her wooden walls. For her there was only the incessant wear, the pounding on her skin caused by the sea, the constant rubbing on her rigging and sails by the wind. There was always the working of her joints by continuous motion.

It had been some time since Jon had last sailed in the English Channel. That had been well over a year ago on HMS Winchester. What a difference a year had made. Virtually every day, since being pressed, he had learned something new or improved an existing skill. Musing about this while standing watch, he idly wondered what it would be like once all the necessary skills were attained. Learning interested him; what would take its place once he reached the appropriate level? Such musings were interrupted when the mainmast lookout shouted down.

"Deck there, sail on the larboard quarter. Looks like a brig, possibly French."

The officer of the deck was Lieutenant Dunkin, the fourth lieutenant. He turned to the midshipman of the watch. "Up you go Mr. Farley. Take a glass and tell me what you see."

"Smith, my respects to the captain. Tell him that we have a possible French privateer on the larboard quarter," said Lieutenant Dunkin.

"Aye, aye, sir," said Jon as he rushed towards the captain's cabin to pass on the information.

The marine saw Jon coming and knocked on the captain's cabin door.

"Master's Mate Smith to see you sir," announced the marine sentry.

"Enter," said Captain Montague.

Jon entered the cabin and knuckled his forehead. "Sir, Mr. Dunkin's compliments. We have spotted a vessel off the larboard quarter. Sails appear to be a French brig, possibly a privateer. He has sent Mr. Farley up to the tops with a glass for a better look, sir."

"Very well, Smith. Tell Mr. Dunkin to investigate and keep me informed," replied the captain.

"Aye, aye, sir" replied Jon. He knuckled his forehead and departed.

Upon his return to the deck, Jon reported to Mr. Dunkin. "Sir, the captain wishes you to investigate and keep him informed."

"Thank you, Smith," replied Lieutenant Dunkin. "New course southwest. I'll try and position us between him and the French coast."

"Aye, sir, course southwest," replied Jon. The quartermaster on the wheel, Williams, repeated the order.

The Mermaid had been tacking north and south on a mean west course all afternoon. The tack to the south was nothing extraordinary, and the brig did not take any avoiding action. The Frenchman probably thought the Mermaid was an East Indiaman when no apparent reaction on their part was observed.

"Deck there, she's definitely a brig with French sail plan. No flags visible," shouted Mr. Farley from the main top.

"Deck there, she's turning," shouted the lookout. From the deck it was possible to see her topsails, but the actual vessel was still hull down and could not be seen over the horizon. The turn meant the brig was approaching the Mermaid.

"New course -- head directly toward her," said Lieutenant Dunkin.

Williams repeated the order directly, "Head directly toward her, aye, sir."

"Smith, my compliments to the captain. The brig is closing with us. I would like permission to clear for action," said Lieutenant Dunkin.

"You have my permission," said the captain, who had quietly climbed the stairs as Lieutenant Dunkin was turned speaking to Jon.

"Clear for action," shouted Lieutenant Dunkin. The timbre of his voice betrayed his enthusiasm.

The marine drummer appeared and the drum roll announcing 'Clear for Action' commenced.

It took approximately eight minutes to clear for action. During that interval, the two ships closed until they were hull up to each other.

"Load the bow-chasers. Maximum elevation, aim for her mizzen mast" shouted the captain. "She'll turn tail in a minute when we're recognized."

Now everyone on the quarterdeck and on the gun crew knew that chain or bar shot would be more effective against the brig's rigging, but at this range, that type of shot would not reach the brig. Only round shot could cover that distance. There was no need to specify that ball should be loaded.

Sure enough, very shortly after the captain had made his prediction, the brig turned and headed due south. The Mermaid altered her course to follow.

A shout came from up foreward. "The bow-chasers think they can reach her, sir," said Lieutenant Davis.

"Open fire," said Captain Montague.

"Bow-chasers only, on the uproll, FIRE," shouted Lieutenant Davis.

Both bow-chasers waited for the uproll and when the Mermaid reached the top of the wave, they both fired. Everyone heard the crack of the guns. It added to the excitement.

"Deck there, both balls hit the courses," shouted Mr. Farley who was observing from the tops with a glass.

"Continue firing, but lower your point of aim," ordered Captain Montague.

All the officers on the quarterdeck were observing through their respective glasses.

"Sir, look at the number of men on the deck," shouted Lieutenant Davis from up foreward.

"Yes, it appears they have at least a double crew for prizes and to overwhelm any victim," said Captain Montague. "It would be nice to take that vessel and rid the seas of that menace."

"Aye, sir, that it would," replied Mr. Flynn, who was standing between the wheel and the captain.

The crack of the bow-chasers caused all deck officers to lift their glasses again to see the effects. Where the first ball went, Jon had no idea, but a ball hit the stern bulwark. Even with the naked eye it was possible to discern that hit.

"That must cause them some concern," chuckled Captain Montague.

The bow-chasers continued to fire, but it was apparent that the distance between the ships was increasing over time.

After two hours of chase, everyone knew it was inevitable that the brig would be able to get away, unless something vital were struck. The captain, however, was not quite yet prepared to give up.

"Mr. Davis, the brig will be shortly out of range. I'm going to try a broadside on the chance that we might hit something important on her. I am going to come to starboard to the west. That will put us in stays and should provide a stable gun platform for at least one broadside from larboard. I want all gunners to aim for the mainmast with maximum elevation. We'll fire on the uproll. The 24-pounders should reach. I hope the 12-pounders will too. Tell every gun captain that this is the last chance they are likely to have for prize money on this ship, so make their shot count," explained the captain.

"Aye, sir," replied Lieutenant Davis as he rushed off to pass on the orders.

When Lieutenant Davis signalled ready from the waist, Captain Montague shouted, "Stand by. Put your helm over to starboard."

Williams replied "Turn her to starboard, aye, sir." The ship heeled as she turned to starboard.

"Fire on the uproll," shouted Lieutenant Davis.

There was a pause as the Mermaid hit stays and forward momentum dropped off. No guns fired. Seconds passed and still there was no firing. The Mermaid finally stopped her forward motion. She was perpendicular to the oncoming swells. Finally, the larboard side started to rise as the starboard side canted downward. It wasn't a huge difference -- somewhere between five and ten degrees. As the gun platform reached the top, cannon after cannon discharged. It was a ragged broadside, but it indicated that each gunner was aiming as carefully as possible.

Only those with glasses could see if the balls struck home, and even then, not that well. One thing was certain. It appeared that not one ball had fallen short as there were no visible splashes this side of the brig.

The brig continued to sail away. The amount of damage done by the broadside, if any, would never be known. Certainly nothing of importance was damaged, as the brig's sailing qualities did not seem to have been impaired.

"Secure the guns," ordered the captain. "Bring us back on course for Plymouth."

The captain quietly headed back to his cabin as Lieutenant Dunkin returned to the quarterdeck and brought the ship around to a west northwest course in accordance with the captain's instructions.

There was a noticeable disappointment in all ranks as the brig continued to sail out of sight in the direction of St. Malo. The reason was obvious -- no prize money.

CHAPTER 28

The morning watch was subdued.

Perhaps everyone was still disappointed at missing the French brig the previous day. Jon was not on watch, so he had remained in the cockpit for the first half of the watch. During the second half of the watch, first light occurred.

Standard ship's procedure at first light was for the crew to stand by the guns. A silence permeated the stand-to. Only the ship's rigging could be heard. Even the occasional whisper was missing. When the order to secure the guns was heard, there was little increase in noise. Only the shuffling of feet could be heard as men headed below. It happened like that sometimes. The excitement of the chase got to them; then men's hopes were dashed. If they had been successful the previous day, there would be dozens of conversations about what a man would do with his prize money. Since they weren't successful, there was nothing to talk about.

After a quick breakfast, Jon again reported to the quarterdeck for the forenoon watch.

"Clear for action," ordered the captain at two bells in the forenoon watch. "We will exercise the great guns."

Jon took station near the wheel. The Mermaid was cleared for action. The sea was quirky. The gaps between swells were much narrower than normal. The wind was steady, blowing at strength from the west. The tops of the swells showed no white, but the motion was far different than Jon had ever felt. The deck was still steady enough for gun drill, so it proceeded.

"The motion is very odd, isn't it, Mr. Flynn," commented Jon to Mr. Flynn when he came over to check the compass and the glass.

"Aye, that it is," replied Mr. Flynn. Just by his repeated looks at the glass and proximity to the wheel, Jon sensed that Mr. Flynn was uneasy.

Jon kept his mouth shut. As the drill progressed, the captain approached Mr. Flynn. They had a discussion, which Jon could not overhear. It was apparent that the captain was uneasy as well.

"Secure from gun drill," said Captain Montague to the first lieutenant. He in turn passed it on to the crew. You could hear the sighs of relief from the crew when the gun drill ceased.

"Place double lashings on those guns," ordered the first lieutenant. "Make sure they're well secured."

This was an indication of heavy weather coming.

Time went on. The sea changed only slightly. The swells got higher, but the wind didn't pick up or shift in direction. There was still a degree of apprehension on the part of the master and commissioned officers. Jon was more interested than worried. He wondered how the weather would change, and what effects it would have on the Mermaid. The routine of the ship didn't alter however.

By dawn the next morning, the swell had risen approximately five feet more. As the morning watch continued, the wind shifted, coming more from the south. By the time the pipe for 'Up Spirits' sounded, the wind had shifted to almost due south, which was not normal. The swells now had some white on the tops. Luckily dinner was cooked. The fires were ordered extinguished. The entire crew gobbled up their dinner. There was an expectation that it might be some time before they had another hot meal.

The captain ordered a course change to the south, directly into the wind. This meant tacking back and forth. It was infinitely better than running before the wind into a lee shore. There was a question however, in some minds as to whether it might be better to put into a port and anchor, rather than riding out the storm at sea. Any speculation was futile, since the captain had decided to remain at sea.

The storm hit with some force. Compared to the storm they had endured in the North Atlantic, this one was puny. There was wind, rain, and a strong running sea. There was no lightening, no apparent rogue waves, and based on their course, no lee shore to worry about.

Jon was standing the first watch beside Williams, the quartermaster on the wheel. It was raining steadily. Darkness was early as the storm clouds obscured the setting sun. Jon was soaked and miserable. As the watch continued, the rain drizzled down unrelentingly. Even with a towel wrapped around his neck, cold rainwater was dripping down his back and chest.

"Light in the distance off the starboard bow," shouted the bow lookout at about four bells in the watch.

"Mr. Farley, my respects to the captain. Tell him there is a possible vessel in distress to our southwest. I request permission to investigate," said Lieutenant Caharty. Mr. Farley disappeared below.

In a few moments Farley reappeared.

"Lieutenant Caharty, sir. The captain wishes you to investigate. He'll be up presently," said Farley.

"Bring her around, course west southwest," ordered Lieutenant Caharty.

"Aye, sir," replied Jon.

"Course west southwest, aye, sir," replied Williams.

"Bosun's mate, call the watch, we need to trim the sails," ordered Lieutenant Caharty.

The watch materialized from their sheltered positions in the waist. The sails were trimmed, and the Mermaid lumbered toward the last known position of the light.

It was a tricky course, as they would have to take the swells broad on the larboard bow to reach the last reported position of the light. If the swell pushed the bow around too much, the Mermaid could find herself broadside to the next swell. That was risky, if not outright dangerous. Jon therefore stood by to add extra strength on the wheel if it were necessary.

"Williams, just shout if you need extra strength," said Jon to the quartermaster on the wheel. There was a second man on the wheel to William's right, but Williams was senior and more experienced. If they needed help, it would need to be provided instantly to prevent the bow being pushed back.

Williams expertly turned the bow inward before reaching each swell. The course was a bit corkscrewed in nature but it was heading in the right direction and safer than tempting the more direct course. Lieutenant Caharty had the watch, although Captain Montague and Mr. Flynn the master both appeared on deck. No one faulted Williams' actions.

Twice, as they proceeded to the last reported position of the light, Jon was called to add additional brute strength on the wheel.

The Mermaid had been on what was hopefully a converging course toward the light for over an hour. No further sight of the light had occurred, even though additional men had been posted as lookouts. Everyone believed the light was from a ship in distress, but there was no sign of that ship.

The Mermaid continued forward. After another quarter hour a shout from foreward was heard, "Wreckage in the water, starboard quarter -- off the bow."

The Mermaid was in the trough between two waves. The wreckage was visible climbing the swell to the starboard. All eyes on the quarterdeck focused on the wreckage, attempting to decipher what it was and it's source. Jon and the men on the wheel were not interested in the wreckage. They were concentrating on ensuring the Mermaid turned inwards before the next swell.

Jon was not sure whether he or Williams saw it first. They both levered the wheel with everything they had to turn it as far larboard as possible. For towering on the top of the swell above them was the bow of a ship.

"Ship to larboard," screamed Jon.

Time seemed to stop. The Mermaid's bow was coming around to larboard, but slowly, ever so slowly. The bow of the oncoming ship seemed to hang on the top of the swell. The bowsprit of the oncoming ship came crashing down like a falling javelin as the oncoming ship started to slide down the swell toward the Mermaid. It hit the bowsprit of the Mermaid with a great crack. The Mermaid's bowsprit shattered in hundreds of splinters and disappeared. Unbelievably, the bowsprit on the oncoming ship remained intact. It was the only thing that saved the Mermaid.

The oncoming ship's bowsprit plunged further and went below the starboard bulwark of the Mermaid in an instant. The result was that the oncoming ship first smashed into what remained of the Mermaid's bowsprit and figurehead. These too were shattered like a hammer hitting a walnut on a flat surface. Both ships reeled to their respective larboard sides and the bows collided on the respective starboard side of the keel. Planks were immediately staved-in and water surged through the holes.

The Mermaid kept coming around, scraping down the starboard side of the oncoming ship. The Mermaid's rigging out board on the starboard side snagged and was tugged apart on the broken bulwark and other damaged portions of the unknown ship.

Jon was able to see the other ship clearly, the images burned into his mind forever. The other ship had been a two-mast vessel -- a brig. The foremast was completely gone. Only a small portion of the mainmast was still standing. The remainder of the mainmast had snapped off just below the first top. He saw no one present on the deck.

Mermaid was caught in stays. The parted lines on her starboard side caused the sails to fly loose. There was no jib sail or any other sail at the bow to bring her around. That in itself was highly dangerous in these conditions. What was worse was that her starboard bow was staved-in. The Mermaid was afloat, but in a desperate state.

"Permission to go forward and check the damage, sir," requested Jon to Lieutenant Caharty.

"Go."

Jon reached the damaged bow and grabbed a severed line to secure himself while he peered over the bow at the damage. There was a large hole in the bow and the sea was literally pouring into the ship through the hole. He pulled himself back. The bosun grabbed his arm.

"How bad?"

"Worst I've ever seen. There's at least a five-foot hole in the bow and the water is just pouring in. If we don't reduce the amount of water pouring in within the next few minutes, we'll lose the ship. Take a look," replied Jon.

Mr. Mason took the line Jon was holding and looked over the bow. He shook his head. Jon pulled him back.

"We gotta plug that hole. And you know as well as I do that we don't have anything for a hole that size," shouted Mr. Mason.

Jon shrugged.

"The only thing I can think of is to use a sail," said Mason.

"How? Those jagged edges will cut through any sail in minutes,"

"We'll have to lower someone over the side and chop away the sharp edges as best we can. We'll put something over the sharp edges and lower a sail over that. We'll have to secure the sail top and bottom so it doesn't work as much. We'll have to use the heaviest canvas -- winters sails. What do you think?" shouted Mason.

"Might work. I can't think of anything better at this point," shouted Jon.

"Cut out this bow section of the bulwark. Drag a sail up here. Double it over. We probably need a course because of the size. Nail the loose end of the course to the deck. Run a rope through the other end, and sew it in just in case the sail separates. Anchor that folded end of the course with weight so it sinks past the hole -- use the wood from the bulwark. Throw it over the side and use the anchoring rope to walk it down each side as it sinks. That should cover the hole. It won't stop all the water, but it might reduce it enough to allow the pumps to keep up," ordered Mason.

The captain grabbed the bosun's arms. "Can we save her?"

"We're sure as hell gonna try sir. I can't swim. If we can fother her, it should reduce the inflow enough so the pumps can keep up," replied Mr. Mason.

"Do it," shouted the captain.

Jon looked around at the bow and started to figure out how to rig the ship for both fothering and an improvised bowsprit. Men appeared beside him.

"Get boarding axes," shouted Jon.

The bosun pushed every man he could grab to the bow. As they arrived, Jon pointed out the area to clear. The sailmaker appeared. "We need the heaviest course you can get me in the next five minutes. After you get the sail, I'll also need the three longest spare yardarms you can find."

The bosun reappeared with additional crew. By this time, Mr. Sinclair, the bosun's mate, was directing the clearing of the bow. The removal of the bow bulwark commenced. Jagged edges of the figurehead and bowsprit were chopped away as fast as possible.

The sail appeared, and was nailed with wood to the forecastle deck. Portions of the bulwark were rolled into the far end of the sail with a rope and rapidly sewn in by a dozen sailors. Additional safety ropes were attached to each end of the sail so it could be dragged under the ship.

Ten minutes passed. The bow was noticeably lower and in danger of losing any freeboard momentarily. They threw the sail overboard as they crested a wave. The weight of the wood from the bulwark dragged the entire sail over the side. The crew worked feverishly to pull the sail under the ship by walking the lines down each side.

Ten minutes later, they were still afloat. A bucket brigade had been established below and was keeping pace with the reduced inflow of water. They needed to lower it, so they could get to the pumps, which were submerged further below.

In the meantime, Jon lashed two spare yardarms together on one end to make a 'V'. He lashed the third yardarm to the other yardarms he had just prepared to form a 'Y'. He then lashed one end of the bottom of a jib sail to the very bottom of the 'Y'. The other end of the bottom of the jib sail was secured at the junction of the three pieces. He had the foremast topmen rig two separate lines from the foremast top above the foremast topsail. The first of these he secured to the junction of the yardarms. The second one was tied to the top of the jib sail.

He put eight men on either of the two yardarms and had them move to each side and push the yardarms out over the bow. In this way, the base of the 'Y' was extended foreward of the bow much like a bowsprit. This was his attempt to replace the bowsprit. A further crew heaved on the rigged line to take the weight as the yardarms slowly moved out over the water in front of the bow. Once they were in place, he had each team lash the ends of the yardarms to the remaining bulwarks which had not been chopped away. It was ugly looking, but functional. Until they could fix the bowsprit, it would have to do.

It was not possible to fix the bowsprit until the flooding was under control. In order to fix the bowsprit, they would have to cut holes in the fothering. That would likely result in the failure of the fothering, which they could not afford. As it was, the fothering was not as good as it might possibly have been. If there had been more time, wool and oakum used for caulking might have been sewn into the sail to improve the seal. There just wasn't the time.

Once the jury-rigged jib sail was ready, Jon went aft to report to the officer of the watch.

"Sir, we have a jury-rigged jib sail that should allow us to come about," reported Jon. It was not clear whether he should be reporting to the captain or to Lieutenant Caharty, so he spoke loud enough so both could hear him.

"Thank you, Smith. Resume your duties," said Lieutenant Caharty.

Jon stepped over beside the wheel. Dickerson was there. He whispered, "You're off watch at the present. Grab a bit of shuteye in the chart room, you look like you could use it. I brought your ditty bag up there -- the cockpit is partially flooded."

Jon nodded and disappeared into the chartroom and collapsed in the corner. He was still in his wet clothes, but didn't care. He craved sleep. Despite his awkward position, he felt nothing until shaken awake.

Once he had regained his senses, he realized the deck was tilted. Obviously, they hadn't got rid of enough water yet. He was hungry, exhausted, wet and still shivering when he went on deck. The first thing he noticed was that they were running with the wind, back toward England. They were moving at about six knots by his reckoning. It was raining, but it was not a hard or heavy rain. It was more annoying.

He approached Dickerson by the wheel and completed the normal watch hand-over.

"Chad, thanks for letting me sleep. I needed it," whispered Jon.

"Mr. Flynn thought it advisable," said Dickerson.

"How's the jury-rigged jib sail holding up?" asked Jon.

"Fine so far," replied Dickerson as he took his leave and went back to the cockpit.

Jon stepped back inside the chart room to check the charts. Lieutenant Rylett the current officer of the watch was there, sheltering from the rain.

"What are you doing in here? Get back to your position," snarled Rylett.

Rather than arguing that he had more right to be in there than Rylett, Jon just turned and walked back out. He glanced at Williams, who was back on the wheel. Williams just rolled his eyes and turned his attention back to the front.

Jon sensed rather than heard a tread behind him. He glanced rearward. Captain Montague stepped up beside him.

"That was fine work you did this morning, Smith. Every man on the Mermaid owes you a debt of gratitude."

The captain stepped away over to the windward side of the quarterdeck.

Williams whispered out of the side of his mouth, "Well, that's somethin' you don't hear every day."

Jon turned to look at Williams and just nodded. He stepped forward, and swiped away the water on the compass so Williams could better see it. He spelled Williams shortly thereafter to allow him to stretch. It was hard work in this weather to hold the wheel.

Lieutenant Rylett finally came out of the chart area. Jon was sure that Captain Montague had noted Rylett's absence. It fact, there was very little that escaped the captain when he was on deck.

Just before the watch ended, the wind shifted from the south to west southwest. Rather than trimming the sails, the captain ordered a change of course so that the Mermaid was still running with the wind. Given her damaged bow, it was probably the best point of sailing to reduce the amount of water still pouring in. Jon went back into the chart area to annotate the chart and log. He was still marking the chart when the master appeared.

"If it keeps this up, we'll be back in Portsmouth tomorrow for supper," stated Jon.

"Maybe," replied Mr. Flynn cautiously.

"What happens then, sir?" asked Jon.

"The dockyard authorities will survey the ship. They will assess the damage; determine what it will take to repair her, and when she can be repaired. It could take weeks," responded Mr. Flynn.

"What happens to us in the meantime, sir?" asked Jon.

"Well that depends. First, we'll have to empty the ship of water, and then remove damaged stores including all the powder. We may have to off-load the guns. After that, it all depends on the port admiral," responded Mr. Flynn grimly.

"How so?"

"If the survey indicates that it will take a month or two to do the repairs, then some of the crew may be shifted to other vessels. You're likely to lose your acting position and revert to being a topman," stated Mr. Flynn.

"Oh," mused Jon. "What about you, sir?'

"I'll likely be on the beach, until the Mermaid is repaired or I can find another ship," said Mr. Flynn. Jon could now understand why he was so grim.

"Wouldn't they just keep you on until the ship is ready again for service, sir?" asked Jon.

"Maybe. It all depends on what the survey finds. Until we can get the water out of her, we haven't any idea about what they will find," stated Mr. Flynn.

Jon crossed his fingers, first to make Portsmouth, and then to allow the Mermaid rapid repairs.

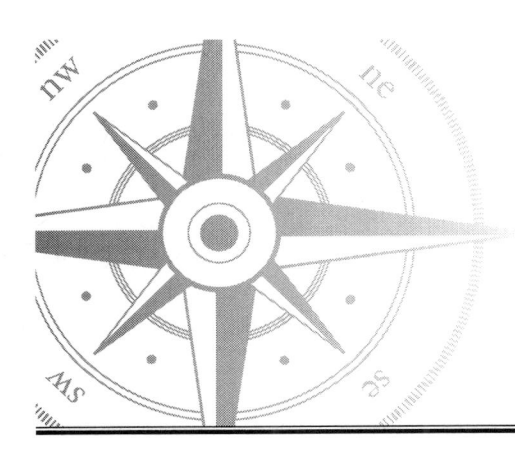

CHAPTER 29

HMS Mermaid limped in to Portsmouth harbour late in the afternoon. The closer she got to Portsmouth the more the wind had diminished and the slower her subsequent progress.

"Head her up the harbour toward the dry docks," ordered Captain Montague as the Mermaid wallowed through the outer harbour.

"Steer toward the dry docks, aye, sir," replied Williams, the quartermaster on the wheel. Jon, who was standing beside Williams and privy to all the conversations, declined to say anything.

"Shorten sail. Courses only once we come into the inner harbour," ordered the captain.

"Topmen aloft. Furl all sails but the courses," ordered Lieutenant Caharty, the officer of the watch.

"Keep the bucket brigade going until we are anchored or docked," said the captain. "If we stop too soon, she might not make it."

"Aye, aye, sir," replied Lieutenant Caharty.

"Sir, where should I steer her if the dry-dock is not available?" asked Lieutenant Caharty.

"We need to find the shallowest water possible to anchor if the dry-dock can't take us. How well do you know the harbour?" asked Captain Montague.

"Not very well, sir," replied Lieutenant Caharty.

"Mr. Flynn, can your charts provide any guidance as to where good shallow anchorage can be found in this harbour?" asked the captain.

"According to the charts, the water on the west side of the harbour appears to be shallower than the east where the navy yards are located. That is about the best I can offer, sir," replied Mr. Flynn.

"Guard boat off the starboard quarter seems to want us to anchor out here," said Lieutenant Caharty.

"I have no intention of anchoring out here. Explain the situation to them, although for the life of me I can't understand why they can't see our damage and necessity for shallow water," said the captain to Lieutenant Caharty.

"Bosun, call over to the guard boat and explain our need for the dry dock or at least shallow water. Ask them to go get some instructions for us," ordered Lieutenant Caharty.

"Aye, aye, sir," replied the bosun. He rushed off to the bow to comply with his instructions. Snippets of the conversation could be heard, as well as the bosun's exasperation as whoever was in charge of the guard boat insisted they anchor in the outer harbour. After several attempts, the bosun gave up.

"Sir, those idiots in the guard boat have orders that any incoming ships are to anchor in the outer harbour -- no exceptions. I can't seem to get it through their thick skulls that we need to get to the dry dock," said the bosun. His voice was rasping after shouting back and forth with the guard boat. Jon had a slight smile, although he made sure that no one noticed it. He would have never thought the bosun would ever get a hoarse voice over a little shouting, seeing how much shouting he normally did during a day.

"You did your best bosun. We'll just ignore them," said Lieutenant Caharty.

"Maintain your course into the inner harbour, Smith," said Lieutenant Caharty.

"Aye, sir," replied Jon.

Midshipman Elkhorne who was looking after the signal flags, shouted, "Flags being raised at the port admiral's building, sir."

Various glasses were raised to see the signal flags.

"Appears to be -- 'retire', sir. I think they are attempting to order us back to the outer harbour," said Elkhorne.

Jon glanced over at the captain. It looked as if the captain was swearing under his breath.

"Mr. Elkhorne, signal in clear language the word SINKING. Spell it out to them. Hoist it and leave it hoisted," said an exasperated captain.

"Aye, SINKING, sir," replied Mr. Elkhorne.

"Appears to be another boat heading our direction from the port admiral's building, sir," said Lieutenant Caharty.

"I wonder if this one has any more sense than the guard boat," said the captain to no one in particular. No one dared to venture a reply or comment.

"Looks like they're carrying the flag lieutenant, sir," said Lieutenant Caharty.

The boat rowed alongside and the flag lieutenant scrambled aboard as the Mermaid was still under way.

"Captain, sir. May I understand your signals and intentions?" asked the flag lieutenant politely after saluting.

"Lieutenant Davis, take the flag lieutenant foreward and let him see for himself the extent of our damage," ordered Captain Montague.

Lieutenant Davis and the flag lieutenant moved foreward. They entered the forecastle hatch and were immediately splashed as water was transferred up from below. The foreward part of the lower gun deck was under a foot or more of water. The orlop and the hold were completely immersed. If the Mermaid sank any lower, water would be flowing in through the gun ports on the gun deck. The fires in the galley were out and had been since the collision. The men were thirsty, hungry, cold, wet and exhausted. It took but a minute or so for the flag lieutenant to discern this.

"The men haven't had more than a couple hours of sleep in the past three days. They've had no food for three days as the bulk of the stores are under water. Our biggest problem is fresh water. All we have been drinking since the collision is rainwater. The bucket brigade that you see is the only thing that is keeping us afloat, otherwise we would be in Davey Jones' locker somewhere in the English Channel," stated a weary Lieutenant Davis.

The flag lieutenant and Lieutenant Davis walked back to the quarterdeck.

"Sir, the dry dock is full at the moment. The closest I can get you is the dock near the mast pond. I believe that is too deep for you, as it has been dredged to take sixty-fours with a full load. The only other place I can think of is to take her around Burrow Island. It's shallow there and you could ground her until we get a survey team over to check her," stated the flag lieutenant.

"So be it. I will accept those as directions from the port admiral and so enter it in the log," stated Captain Montague.

Directions from the flag lieutenant were given and the ship slowly manoeuvred inshore of Burrow Island. Out of the shipping lanes, she gently nudged ashore. Jon, as his duties required, stood by the anchor.

"Let go," shouted Lieutenant Davis.

The anchor was released. The courses were taken in, and yards crossed. A second bow anchor was lowered. A boat was lowered into the water and carried the second anchor closer inshore. This ensured the Mermaid would not come adrift in any wind.

Once the Mermaid was anchored, the order was given to cease the bucket brigade. Water kept seeping into the ship and the Mermaid slowly settled on the bottom. The result was that the water rose about an additional foot on the gun deck. Water was now able to flow into the Mermaid from the first few gun ports.

They had made it. The Mermaid could no longer sink, but neither could she go anywhere. Where did that leave them?

More importantly, where did it leave an acting master's mate?

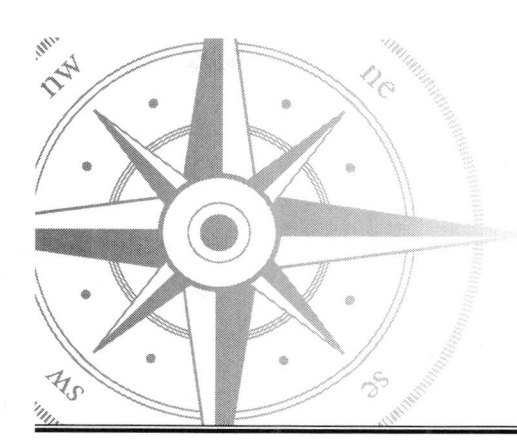

CHAPTER 30

A forlorn HMS Mermaid sat grounded to the west of Burrow Island.

A weary Captain Montague turned to the flag lieutenant, stranded on the Mermaid as his boat had long since departed company.

"You can accompany me to the admiral's office as I make my report."

"Aye, aye, sir," replied the flag lieutenant.

"Lower my gig and have it stand by," ordered Captain Montague to Lieutenant Davis. "When I get to the dock yards, I'll see about getting a portable pump and some hoys. We'll need to lighten her so we can get that hole above the water line. Open up the hatches. We'll hoist the guns out of the gun deck and land them. If we can get a portable pump in action, we'll empty out the orlop and hold."

"Lieutenant Caharty. You'll accompany me. I'd like you to go with the flag lieutenant and see about water, meals and quarters for the crew," continued Captain Montague.

"I'll meet you in the gig gentlemen," said Captain Montague before turning and heading to his quarters to fetch the written report for the admiral. Jon had returned to the quarterdeck after anchoring. He had been standing near the wheel and overheard the tail end of the conversation.

As the captain's gig pulled toward the port admiral's office across the harbour, work began on lightening the ship. The hatches were opened and yardarms rigged for hoisting. The men on the wheel were dismissed. Not having any specific task, Jon went into the chartroom and secured all of the charts. He checked and filled in the logs, ensuring they were properly completed.

Just before the last dog watch two hoys came alongside. The first had a large portable pump and some barrels of fresh water. These were hoisted on board, and the water was distributed. All the 24-pounder cannons from the lower gun deck were placed on the two hoys and they departed separately. By this time it was dark. The men were in a foul mood. They were hungry and completely exhausted. They were wet, and had no dry clothes or bedding. Their normal berthing area was still a foot under water.

The ship's longboat, which had departed sometime in the late afternoon, appeared. There were no available quarters for the men at the present. The boat did return with fresh bread, cheese and some freshly cooked beef, which the crew eagerly hoisted aboard. Each man received a thick slice of bread, a wedge of cheese and a slice of the beef. The men wolfed down the meal. Some adventurous souls recovered the spirit barrel, so the pipe "Up Spirits" was made and the men queued up for their grog. Once all the rations were issued, the crew was stood-down. Men flopped on the main deck wherever they could find a space. Within minutes, only a scaled-down harbour watch was left awake.

Standing the first watch, Jon's main occupation was trying to keep those men on duty awake. There were limited concerns about men escaping -- they were all too exhausted. In order to stay awake, Jon made continuous rounds with frequent stops to speak to each man. Jon went so far as to pair off the men on watch, so they could keep each other awake. It was a struggle never the less.

A barrel of ship's biscuit had been brought on board with the rations the previous evening. This 'bread' was distributed for breakfast in the morning before work commenced. Having just completed three days of back-breaking work without rations, and looking at another back-breaking day with less than one day's meals, the Mermaid's crew were fed up. The grumbling could be heard everywhere, even at the senior ranks. Jon wondered what it would bring once dark occurred.

The first hoys arrived at the start of the forenoon watch. The 12-pounders were hoisted over to them, as a second crew rigged the portable pump and commenced pumping.

Slowly throughout the day, as the portable pumps worked, the water level dropped. When it was chest high in the orlop, men went in to manoeuvre materiel to the hatches for hoisting out. Both Jon and Dickerson were employed in logging and accounting for, the equipment transferred to the hoys. Each kept a separate inventory tally. As a hoy was filled, cross checking was completed to ensure that both tallies matched, before releasing the hoy back to the dockyard.

With the decreasing weight of the absent guns, stores and seawater, the Mermaid lifted off the mud on which she was resting. The majority of the hole in the bow was above the water line, but not all. The hold was still flooded, and water continued to seep in. The portable pump was slowly gaining on the water. Lieutenant Davis ordered the pump's operation all night, so the hold could be emptied the next day.

With the water level much lower, it was possible to light the galley fires. Wood had to be acquired, however, because all the wood on the Mermaid was soaked. A further problem was the lack of fresh water or suitable rations on the Mermaid. These had to be brought across in a hoy and hoisted on board.

The Mermaid was a shambles. Rigging not used for hoisting was being used to dry out sails, sailors' clothes, hammocks and other ship equipment. Lieutenant Davis who prided himself on running a taut ship for the captain, was a frustrated man. The crew did everything he asked of them, but the deck was complete chaos, and would be until they were finished repairs. Davis appeared resigned to this fact.

Jon again had the first harbour watch and for a change was happy to do it. The alternative was to spend two 2-hour shifts on the portable pump. Things were starting to change slowly for the better. Everyone had a normal hot meal. With the hot food, the grumbling decreased marginally. The crew was able to rig hammocks below for the first time in five days. Although still somewhat damp, with all the gun ports opened to allow the gun deck to dry out, it was preferable to the open deck above.

All the crew had worked hard during the day. Most hadn't fully recovered from their efforts over the past few days. Virtually every man would have a shift at the pumps overnight. Still, given the proximity to land and lack of a guard boat, the possibility of runners on his watch had Jon concerned. The open gun ports meant slipping into the water was even easier.

Luckily, there were no desertions on any watch overnight.

The next morning they began to empty the hold. This actually went faster than anticipated. All the water butts were started. The water was added to what was already in the hold, so it made little difference. By midday, sufficient water had been emptied and stores removed that access to the Mermaid's pump was possible. A second crew began pumping and the level of water in the hold dropped rapidly. The hole in the bow rose far enough that it was now above the water line. Continued pumping until dark emptied the bilges. By that time all the stores had been removed from the hold. The hoys had departed earlier, so some of the pipes and casks from the hold were left on the deck overnight.

The slackening pace as the day went on meant men began to get rested and restive. That didn't bode well for the night watches. The watch was increased in size as a preventive measure in case anyone wished to go swimming. Jon paid special attention and roamed around the ship continuously. If a man deserted on his watch, he was likely to lose his master's mate position. That was something Jon wished to avoid at this point.

The following morning all remaining stores were transferred to the hoys. The survey crew from the dock yard appeared and commenced the survey. The fothering was removed from the bow and a close examination of the damage was completed. The majority of the crew did their own inspection after the survey party had completed their work.

Since the dry dock was currently occupied, the captain began to speculate whether the repairs could be completed if the Mermaid were careened. He discussed this with the carpenter. The ship had already been lightened considerably. They could still take the sails, tops and yards off her to lighten the ship further. After that she could be careened. That would expose the damaged area. A plan was proposed and a written outline prepared for submission to the port admiral.

After the survey crew left, the crew was in limbo. There was limited work to be completed. They still had wet powder on board that had to be removed carefully. That task was scheduled for the next day. The topmen would likely strike the tops after the powder was removed. Other than these major tasks, there was limited work to do, and virtually no stores with which to work.

Now all the Mermaid crew could do was wait until a decision was made on how to complete the needed repairs.

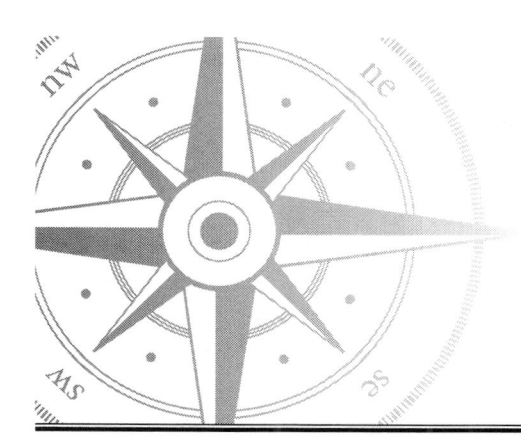

CHAPTER 31

A tired, idle, dejected crew left on board a ship vacant of stores creates a situation with which many officers have little experience. In a typical situation, a good officer would organize work, even make-work projects, to keep the men busy. Busy men have less time to reflect on their lot in life. With virtually no stores and all repairs suspended, the officers were unsure what to do with the men. It was a recipe for trouble.

Add to this recipe a ship close to shore crewed by a majority of pressed men disgruntled with the service. An officer might wonder how many of his men might take the opportunity to leave. Such was the situation of HMS Mermaid.

As a senior officer of the harbour watch, Jon was acutely aware of the situation. He was more nervous than the other officers were. If men ran on his watch, his position would be in jeopardy.

He had only held this position for a matter of weeks. In those weeks, he had been elevated in numerous ways. The commissioned officers, with the possible exception of Lieutenant Rylett, held him in higher esteem than during any other period since joining the Mermaid. The midshipmen and petty officers such as the bosun considered him an equal. His maritime knowledge had risen dramatically. He had been introduced to new areas such as navigation, charts, logs, and acquisition of supplies.

Anything that put this new position in jeopardy was an enemy. The desire to maintain this position was clearly absolute, which in turn influenced his attitude toward runners. Anyone who ran on his watch was his enemy.

With no forthcoming decision on repairs for the Mermaid, few stores on board and limited or no work for the men, the captain decided to place the ship 'out of discipline'. This was well received by the crew. They had felt that they were abused not having an appropriate 'out of discipline' period the last time they were in Portsmouth. They also had worked excessively for the previous week since the collision, and felt they were due a break.

No sooner had the 'out of discipline' flag been hoisted, than the bumboats were heading for the Mermaid. How they could even see the flag over at the port was beyond Jon. It was as if they had a sixth sense that told them when to venture forth -- and venture they did.

The commissioned officers absented themselves from the ship. The exception to this was Lieutenant Rylett, whom the captain had ordered to remain on board. A sulking Lieutenant Rylett retreated into the officer's wardroom, not to be seen again.

Jon retired into his still damp cubby. He was tired, and did not wish to spend any money at the present. He hoped there would be no disturbances -- either now or when he was on watch. To be safe, he ensured all of his valuables were on his person and that both knives were very handy. As an extra precaution, he placed a belaying pin within arm's reach in the cubby.

In his dreams, he sat at a feast with a mug of rum in one hand and shapely lass in the other. These dreams were rudely disrupted by some noise outside the cubby. Shaking his head to clear the sleep, he decided an investigation of the noise was warranted. Treading silently in bare feet from the cubby, he came upon an unknown man rifling through Dickerson's sea chest.

Rather than warn the man and potentially provoke a fight, Jon silently reached behind him to grasp the belaying pin. Padding toward the bent over man, Jon needed little stealth. The man was too intent on rifling the contents of the chest to notice anything. A quick flick of the belaying pin behind the man's ear rendered the intruder senseless. A swift kick delivered to the kidneys ensured the man wasn't faking it. Jon rolled him over with his foot. The man wasn't a member of the Mermaid's crew.

Jon considered his next move. The man could be secured by tying his hands. It would then be necessary to go on deck and fetch the watch. Since the man wasn't a member of the Mermaid's crew, he would have to be passed over to the civilian authorities. That would require time and paperwork. Both would further interrupt his sleep.

At some time in the future, Jon would have to testify at the man's trial. This trial would be held somewhere in the port. If the ship were at sea, he wouldn't be able to testify and the man would go free. That wasn't right either.

Additionally, if Jon left the cockpit to get assistance, in the time it took to return, the man would likely be gone with whatever he could carry. Others might be involved. They usually were.

Jon searched the man. He found some coins, a knife and some carvings in the man's pockets. These he emptied on the deck. He stepped over the man, hoisted him over his shoulder and carried him up the stairs to the nearest available gun port on the gun deck. There was no one present. He headed to the larboard side, which was windward at the moment. The bumboats always queued up on the leeward side of the ship. Cracking open the gun port, Jon quickly surveyed the area and determined no boats were present. Ducking back in-board, he dragged the unconscious thief over to the gun port and tossed him out. Problem resolved, Jon wiped his hands and secured the gun port.

Jon was turning to head back below when Lieutenant Rylett appeared with some doxie in hand. "Smith what are you doing here?" asked a somewhat intoxicated Rylett.

Figuring that Rylett would have no idea who was on duty, Jon replied, "Making the rounds sir." He was about to add a snide remark about how

Rylett was checking out the visitors, but figured it was more prudent to keep his mouth shut.

"Well carry on," muttered Rylett as he disappeared with the doxie into the wardroom. Jon just muttered.

Back in the cockpit, Jon pocketed the coins, and knife. The carvings were set on the mess table, as they were probably stolen from someone on board. The last step was to close and stow Dickerson's chest, prior to heading back to the cubby to get some more sleep. Despite the noise, Jon slept soundly, without any qualms about the manner in which he had handled the thief.

Mr. Farley was in the cockpit when Jon emerged from his cubby in time for his watch. Farley was examining with interest the carvings left on the cockpit table.

"You might want to watch your valuables, Kevin. Those carvings you're looking at belong to someone foreward of the mast. One of our visitors tried to abscond with them." With that comment, Jon exited for the deck to complete his handover with Dickerson.

"Chad, you need to check your sea chest. I caught a guy rifling through it," whispered Jon.

"And?" asked Dickerson.

"I took care of it," said Jon. At this Dickerson raised his eyebrow and looked at an unresponsive Jon.

"Thank you," replied Dickerson. Although curious, Dickerson refrained from asking any additional questions. If Jon had captured the man and formally charged him, Dickerson would have known about it, being the officer of the watch. Since there was no prisoner, Jon must have taken alternative actions. It was sometimes better not to know what those alternative measures were.

During the watch, Jon made several rounds throughout the ship with the master-at-arms. The primary concern was to ensure that no theft of ship's stores or crew kit occurred. With virtually no ship's stores on board, there was little concern in that area. On one occasion there was a requirement to arbitrate a dispute between a member of Mermaid's crew and a civilian of questionable character. Once a more reasonable price was arranged, the dispute fizzled.

No one could say the watch was quiet. There was dancing and music on deck, a raunchy coupling of willing participants on the lower gun deck and some shady affairs on the orlop. With the lack of ship's stores on board, Jon tended to ignore the happenings on the orlop.

To ensure no crewman had tagged along on a departing bumboat, each bumboat had to be checked before leaving. Luckily, it appeared the men were busy elsewhere and not inclined to run.

The ship stayed 'out of discipline' for two days. By the end of the second day, things had quieted down considerably, as no one had any money left, or anything to trade.

The captain and the officers came back aboard. Lieutenant Rylett appeared for the first time. The flag for 'out of discipline' was lowered before last light.

The arrival of the commissioned officers indicated imminent news regarding repairs. How long those repairs would take and who would do the work were the subject of considerable bookmaking.

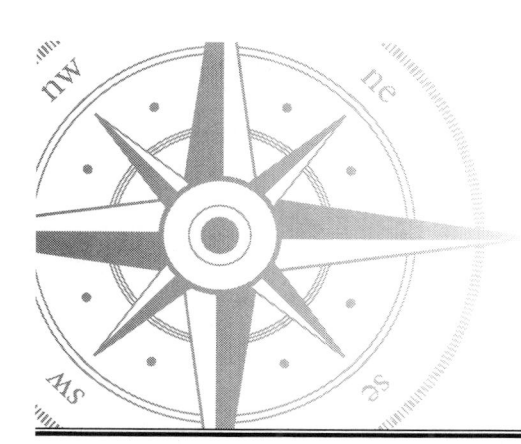

CHAPTER 32

The guard boat appeared with a message for the captain at the start of the forenoon watch the next morning. It was a summons for the captain to report to the port admiral at ten o'clock that morning.

Speculation was rampant and the bookmakers were capitalizing on it. This summons had been anticipated. Everyone expected details would be forthcoming as to when the Mermaid would enter the dry dock and the anticipated duration of the repairs. Dressed in his best uniform, Captain Montague departed in the gig well in advance of the ten o'clock appointment.

Dinner was occurring when the captain returned. Rather than disturb the ship's routine, the captain allowed dinner to proceed. The pipe 'All hands' effectively terminated any thought of an extended dinner.

As the crew mustered to hear the captain, speculation on whether the Mermaid would be going to the dry dock or would be careened dried up. The ship's bookmakers closed their books.

"Men, I have some good news and some bad news," said the captain. "First, the good news -- you will be getting paid tomorrow. For the bad news, as you know, a survey crew from the dockyard went over the Mermaid thoroughly after we got her pumped out. In addition to the damage on the starboard bow, they found damage on the larboard bow where we were hit by that mast in the North Atlantic. The entire bow would have to be replaced. Unfortunately, it doesn't stop there. The Mermaid has been stationed in the West Indies for a number of years. Much of her bottom has been eaten. There is rot in parts of her keel and in some of the knees. Given a full load and a reasonably heavy blow, the entire bottom might fall out of her. In short men, the Mermaid has been condemned."

There was silence initially as the shock of this announcement sank in. That silence quickly turned to murmuring.

"Silence on the deck," shouted Mr. Pearly, the master-at-arms.

"The Mermaid is to be paid off. England is still at war, however, and we still have need of your services. Once you are paid off from the Mermaid, you are going to be allowed to volunteer for another ship. Tomorrow morning the paymaster's party will arrive here. Each man will receive a voucher for his service pay, less the amount he owes the purser. A second voucher will be issued for prize monies due from the capture and sale of the Vigilant," continued the captain.

"After you are paid, you have two options. First, deputations from other vessels will come aboard. You may speak with these deputations and volunteer for any of these ships. You will receive a signing bonus. If you do not choose one of these ships, you will be escorted to the holding ship for reassignment as service needs dictate. That is all. Mr. Davis, dismiss the men," said the captain. He turned and retreated into his cabin.

Once the captain left, the vocal discontent from the crew was immediate and loud. The more experienced and skilled members of the crew were not happy, but the change did not affect them too greatly. In most cases, the only difference would be getting to know a new ship and their new crewmates. They would still go to sea in their present ratings. The discontent was serious among the landsmen and ordinary seamen. In most cases these men had been pressed, had seen little or no advancement, and had virtually nothing to show for their time on board the Mermaid. Now, instead of freedom, they would be transferred to other ships and end up starting again in potentially worse conditions than at present.

Jon didn't know where he stood. He would have liked to get more training so he could apply for his master's mate papers. In any move to another ship, he would lose his acting rating and revert to an able seaman. He wondered if there was any way he could take an examination or whatever testing was necessary to get the master's mate papers. He decided to ask Mr. Flynn.

Jon headed to the chart room where he found Mr. Flynn as expected. Both Mr. Flynn and Dickerson were discussing the situation. Jon held back, not wishing to intrude on a private discussion.

Dickerson turned, nodded to Jon, and brushed past him. Mr. Flynn looked at Jon and said, "What's on your mind Smith?"

"Sir, I'm looking for advice. I realize my acting rating is finished once the ship is paid off tomorrow. I have liked working for you sir, and I value your opinion and counsel. What I would like to know, is how would I go about securing a master's mate position? I know I'm a good topman. I believe I can be just as good a master's mate. I don't know how much more knowledge is required. I do know that I'm short experience. So I guess what I'm asking sir, is how can I convince whoever I need to convince in my next ship that I am deserving of a chance to obtain that needed experience?"

Mr. Flynn looked hard at Jon. His eyes were searching Jon's face, but for what Jon didn't know. Jon had been subjected to a search this intense before in the Winchester by the bosun and the sailmaker. Mr. Mason and Lieutenant Davis had also subjected him to similar looks the day he boarded the Mermaid. In each case, they had been assessing Jon to determine if he was honest and truthful.

"Let me think about it," said Mr. Flynn quietly. "I'll speak to you tomorrow morning."

"Thank you sir." He turned and headed for his cubby. He wasn't sure what he should be doing. In this case, he figured the old line 'out of sight, out of mind' would be appropriate guidance.

When he arrived back in the cockpit, he saw that every member of the cockpit was there. There was little talk. Each was assessing the captain's announcement and its impact on them.

After some time, Jon approached Dickerson. "Chad, can I disturb you?"

"Sure."

"What I'm wondering, is how would I go about getting my master's mate papers. I mean, you got your papers, so you know more about the process than I do. Can you tell me how it works?" inquired Jon.

"Well, from what I know there are different ways of achieving the rank. As you know, only the Navy Board can issue a warrant for a master. There are no clear cut rules for a master's mate. The captain can rate you, which is the most common way. You can write the Trinity House master's examination. If you pass, you have the master's qualification. Only the Navy Board can assign you to a master's position. Any captain would bring you on as a master's mate with a master's qualification. That's how I got my position on the Mermaid. A number of men opt for the commissioned officer path," explained Dickerson.

"You mentioned that to me before. Could you explain that to me again?" asked Jon.

"A master's mate can apply to take the examination for a Lieutenant. He has the same knowledge, and in many cases more experience and seamanship skills than a midshipman. If he passes the examination then he awaits the next open position and is promoted lieutenant. If he fails, he is no worse off than he is at the present. There are two catches, however. Before you can write the exam for master, and thereby be assured of a master's mate position, you are supposed to have a minimum of three years service. And to write the exam for lieutenant, you are supposed to have six years experience," explained Dickerson.

"So what you're politely trying to say, is that despite knowledge and skill, without experience, I am not likely to progress to the same position I'm currently at in the Mermaid?" stated Jon. He smiled as he said it. He did not begrudge Dickerson. Dickerson didn't make the rules.

"Jon, let's be honest. I like you. In fact, I think of you as a good friend. When I heard that you were coming aft as an acting master's mate I was shocked. I knew you were a good topman. I honestly had no idea of your skill until the collision. I knew you had guts. You proved that during the boarding of the Vigilant and again during the storm in the North Atlantic. Being so young, I knew you didn't have the level of experience that some of the others had. For example, Williams as a quartermaster, has more time behind a wheel than you have in the navy. What I figured appropriate for you was to put you in the quartermaster position and move Williams to the acting master's mate position," said Dickerson.

Jon said nothing.

Dickerson continued, "Look, part of the master's mate duties is to assist the master in teaching the midshipmen in navigation. That's part of your job. When you were brought aft, you didn't know anything about navigation, so how could you complete that portion of the job? Heck, you still are only getting by in reading and writing. You see what I'm getting at? You have to see it from a new captain's perspective."

Jon continued to look at Dickerson without really seeing him. He was trying to see what Dickerson was explaining.

Dickerson, not getting a response from Jon was worried that he had gone too far. He would hate losing Jon as a friend, especially after all they had done for each other.

Finally, Jon shifted his gaze to Dickerson's eyes. "Chad, I appreciate your perspective. I don't know why I was selected for master's mate. Other men on this ship have more time in, and have considerably more experience than me -- but none of that matters. What's past is past. The fact is I am now at a different position in life than I was a couple of months ago. I've seen a different world; a far better world than the one from which I came. You're saying I'm going to be sent back to that other world; that I have no hope of getting out of that world for at least two more years. You've seen me at work. I can do this job. Maybe I'm not as good as you are at the present, but given time, I could match you. What I'm looking for is some way of keeping what I have. If I have to shift foreword, then I need some way of ensuring I can shift aft again in a shorter time than two years. Possibly I need another option on how to get the extra skills and knowledge I would need to pass the master's examination after three years of service."

"Jon, no offence, but I think you're dreamin'," said Dickerson.

"If you want to call it that, then yes, I am dreaming," replied Jon. "Chad, I want something better for myself, same as you did. The only real difference between you and me is age. You want the same things as I do. Because of your age, no one will even question you. But when people see me, the first thing they see is some 'wet behind the ears' lad who couldn't possibly have the knowledge, nor have the required skills at that age. Why do they assume this? It's because they base it upon what they were like at that age."

"I know that I can hold my own in any seamanship skill with any man on this ship including the petty officers. What's more, most of the men know it. The next logical step for me is the same path that you chose. On this ship, I have been given that opportunity. For that, I'm grateful. Like I said, it's opened the doors to a different world for me. I'm ready for that world. My problem is that I will have to convince others that I am ready, and I don't know how to do that," continued Jon.

Dickerson could see that Jon was determined. He still thought Jon was 'whistling in the wind'. Rather than discourage him, Dickerson decided to say, "Good Luck" and left it at that.

Mr. Farley had been listening to the exchange. After Jon moved off to allow Dickerson to pack his chest, Mr. Farley approached Jon.

"Jon, there are still a number of books here on seamanship and navigation from the previous occupants, so to speak," said Mr. Farley. Jon smiled at the polite way Mr. Farley spoke of the midshipmen that had died of yellow jack the previous fall. Jon looked at Mr. Farley. He would miss him.

"And?"

"Well I've got my own. There's no sense leaving them on the ship for the dockyard workers to take. Why don't you take them? You can use them. It will help you improve your reading and increase the knowledge you'll need to pass the exams for master," suggested Mr. Farley.

"They would, but if I'm sent forward, I can't carry them," replied Jon.

"Yes, you're right. I hadn't thought of that," said Mr. Farley. "What if you put them in a chest in the orlop and could take one book at a time and put it in your ditty bag. I'm sure that some arrangement could probably be made?"

"It's something to consider. Although I have no chest, and am not likely to make one by tomorrow morning," said a smiling Jon. "Just the same, let's take a look at what books are still lying around."

Mr. Farley knew just where to look. There were seven additional books to the two Jon already had that he thought would be beneficial. Jon was unsure about four others.

"Well if you don't want them, just leave them here. The dockyard workers are sure to find them. They'll use them for ass wipe if nothing else," joked Mr. Farley.

It was sombre that evening in the cockpit. There was no drink, little food other than some biscuit, and little inclination to engage in conversation. They all knew they would depart in the morning to go their separate ways. Jon and Dickerson still had to stand harbour watch.

Jon was unsure if men would try to run before morning. This was a lousy place from which to escape. There were too many patrols in the Portsmouth area. There was also the strong possibility extra patrols would operate until after the Mermaid was paid off and the crew transferred.

The men were to be paid in the morning and it was unlikely that a man would wish to forgo a year's pay to run at this point. Finally, once the ship was paid off, each man was technically discharged from the navy. He had to be placed on strength on another ship before he was legally subject to the Articles of War. A man could legally run at any point between discharge and being placed on strength on a new ship. If caught that man could not be accused of desertion.

Jon had the middle watch. The men assigned to the watch were silent and morose. If others attempted to run, it was doubtful that these men would announce it. As a result, Jon was continuously walking around the ship spending more time on the forecastle than on the quarterdeck.

His relief at the start of the morning watch could not come fast enough.

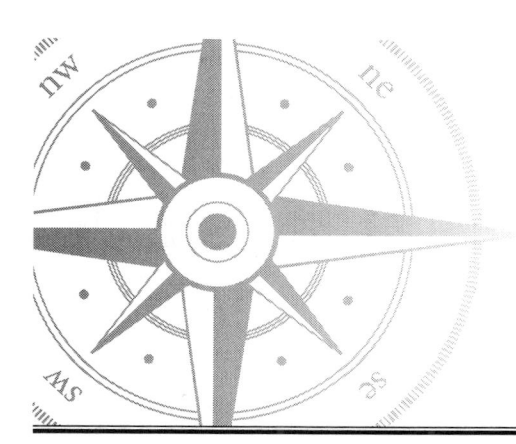

CHAPTER 33

The final morning on the Mermaid was overcast. The weather fitted the mood on the ship.

At ten in the morning, a paymaster team set up shop in the waist. They had been on board for some time going through the ship's accounting and the purser's books. The port admiral had sent a considerable number of guards to ensure no man wandered too far.

Mr. Pearly, the master-at-arms called men one at a time. The called man went to the first table and reported. His identity was confirmed. He was advised of the amount earned since the last pay, and the amount that he owed the purser. A voucher for the difference was prepared and handed to him. A notation was made on the purser's account. The man went to a second desk where he was advised of the prize money he was to receive. A second voucher was issued to the man. The man then went to a third table. Lieutenant Davis made an annotation in the ship's book that the man had been paid off and discharged.

At this point, the man was escorted to the forecastle where representatives from eight ships currently in the harbour were present. The man was allowed to ask questions about the respective ship and select which one he wished to serve on. If he were not inclined to sign on to one of these ships, he would be sent back to the waist where extra guards were positioned. He picked up his ditty bag, and went over the side into a waiting guard boat.

The first man through the process was the first man to complain, albeit after he had been marked discharged by Lieutenant Davis. He was a married man. His complaint was that the voucher was useless unless it could be converted into cash. It had just been explained to him that to get full value for the voucher, it would have to be presented to the Admiralty in London. Since he was going to be sent to another ship, he couldn't go to London. There were no money exchangers present, nor was there any means of passing this money or voucher to his wife for their kids. It was a valid complaint. Every man on board believed it a valid complaint whether he was from the Mermaid or not.

Captain Montague sensed it before the rest. If he didn't resolve this issue immediately, he would have a riot on his hands. If men who had been discharged were involved, there would be no recourse, as they were effectively discharged.

"Men, can I have a show of hands of how many wish to transfer funds to their next of kin?" asked Captain Montague from the quarterdeck where he stood watching over the entire operation. About twenty-five men raised their hands.

Captain Montague turned to Lieutenant Caharty. "Take my gig. Go see the flag lieutenant. Tell him the paymaster has not provided any way to exchange the vouchers for cash. Figure out how these men can convert the vouchers. Get back here as fast as possible before things get out of hand."

"Men, I am sending Lieutenant Caharty to see the admiral. He will be back as soon as possible bringing with him information on how you will be able to convert your vouchers into cash. I will see if we can figure out some way to forward monies to your next of kin for those who indicated that need. In the meantime we will proceed. I promise you no member of the Mermaid crew will leave here before Lieutenant Caharty returns," said the captain.

While all of this was going on, Jon had gone up to the forecastle. He started chatting with men from the various ships. He asked around each ship to determine if they needed a master's mate. There was no requirement for a master's mate from any of the ships represented.

He worked his way back to the quarterdeck to seek out Mr. Flynn. He did not find him.

Lieutenant Caharty reappeared shortly before dinner. He had men with him. They were money exchangers who were all too willing to assist in the transfer of vouchers into cash.

By the number of men, Jon had assumed there were a number of money exchangers. In reality, there was only one. The remainder of the men were guards. The moneychanger apparently had previous experience with dissatisfied customers.

The money exchanger had a commanding position as far as exchange was concerned. He was the only possible source of exchange these men were ever likely to get. He set the exchange at fifteen shillings to the pound, a twenty-five percent exchange rate. The men were outraged, especially the pressed men.

A pressed landsman who had spent a year on board the ship was entitled to only fifteen shillings a month less what they owed the purser. The average man was, therefore, receiving a voucher of approximately five or six pounds depending upon how often he had availed himself of tobacco or other items from the purser. Now that amount was to be reduced by twenty-five percent. This was a fraction of what a general labourer or farm hand was paid. To add insult to the payment, any general labourer did not have to put up with twelve-hour days, seven days a week and navy discipline.

Jon heard the discontent. He had nearly fifty pounds in cash from various trades over the past year. The trader in him immediately saw opportunity. He went to see his old mess mates. He spoke to them and managed to exchange sixty-five pounds of vouchers for almost all of his cash. Now, all he needed was to get to London to exchange them, or get to shore and find someone to exchange them at a better rate than he paid. The trade was good for him as well. The vouchers were easier to carry, and had little value to most sailors. The possibility of being robbed was therefore significantly reduced. He folded the vouchers, placed them in oilskins and secured them in his money belt.

Jon said goodbye to many mess mates and men he knew, as they left for other ships.

Jon spotted Mr. Flynn on the quarterdeck. He made his way aft and approached him.

"Excuse me, Mr. Flynn, you asked me to see you this morning, and I haven't seen you until now. Did you still wish to see me, sir?" inquired Jon.

"Ah, Smith," said Mr. Flynn absently. "Have you been paid off yet?"

"No sir, my name hasn't been called yet," replied Jon. He looked around. The ship looked deserted compared to a few hours ago. The forecastle was empty. The crew was gone, including most of the petty officers. A few men were lowering the captain's effects over the side into waiting boats. The standing officers and commissioned officers appeared to be the only remaining personnel on board. The paymaster appeared to be finishing up with the officers and midshipmen.

"Smith, Jon," called out the master-at-arms, standing in the waist.

"Excuse me sir, I am being hailed by the paymaster. With your permission sir?" asked Jon politely.

"Certainly."

Jon rapidly went down to the paymaster and reported. He received his voucher for pay and the second for prize money. He was surprised at the amount of prize money. He had been paid at a master's mate rate as opposed to the able seaman he was at the time. It was rare that the navy made that type of mistake, and Jon was not about to bring it to their attention.

He stepped over to Lieutenant Davis's table. He knuckled his forehead and reported.

Lieutenant Davis leaned back in his chair. He was tired, and it showed on his face. He examined Jon carefully. A slow smile appeared on his face.

"Well Smith, here we are again, you standing in front of my desk, and me trying to figure out what to do with you. The last time you surprised me by displaying speed and skills I would have never thought possible from one so young. The tables are turned today. It is me who is going to surprise you."

"It is custom to leave a small caretaking staff aboard any decommissioned vessel until its final demise. Normally, the caretaker party is composed of the carpenter, gunner and bosun. As there is no need for a gunner here, he has been assigned other duties. A third person in the form of Jon Smith was suggested, so Smith, you will stay on board for the next three months or so. You will work with the bosun and carpenter to strip the ship as ordered. You will assist the dockyard authorities as required."

"Just to ensure you are fully occupied, the master has recommended you also study for your master's examination in December at the Navy Board. Now there is a touchy situation here with respect to rank, so I have placed the bosun in charge, as you are only acting rank. Is that clear?" asked Lieutenant Davis.

"Aye sir, very clear," replied Jon. He was clearly taken aback, stunned even, by what had been proposed.

"If what I think is going to occur, happens, in a few more years I will see you wearing this uniform. I wish you well," stated Lieutenant Davis. Like the gentleman he was, he stood and offered his hand to Jon.

Jon shook Lieutenant Davis's hand and retreated to the bulwark in stunned silence.

A completely new opportunity had just been presented to him.

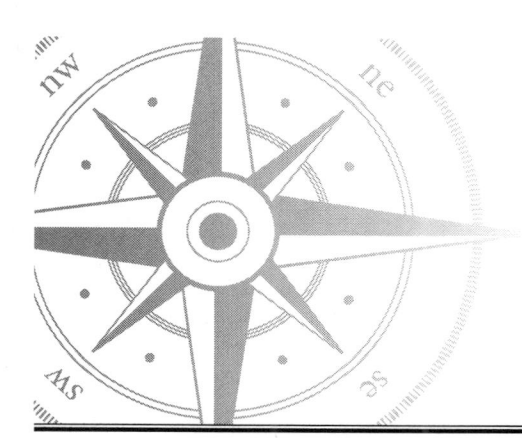

CHAPTER 34

By the last dog watch, HMS Mermaid was a deserted ship, except for the three souls who comprised her caretaker crew.

First and foremost on Jon's mind was food. He had consumed a biscuit for breakfast and nothing since. Because the ship was being paid off, the cooks had not prepared any dinner. Everyone had expected to be gone. Jon started to scrounge around the cook's area and the purser's stores to find anything edible. He found some forgotten cheese and ship's bread. There was enough for a couple of meals, so he collected it all and carried it back to his cubby.

As the last light of day slowly receded, Jon sat on the quarterdeck reading and attempting to digest the ship's bread. The bread was as hard as a cannonball and about as tasty. Slowly reading through a navigation book, his mind wandered. It was the first time since being on one of His Majesty's ships that Jon had experienced this level of privacy. It was totally foreign and didn't sit well. As the light faded to the extent that reading was impossible, he retreated to the cockpit.

Accustomed to sleeping only for a watch at a time, he woke several times through the night. Lack of noise from the watch affected his ability to return to sleep. Finally, in the morning watch he rose to see what the day would bring.

There was no movement on the ship whatsoever. First light was still an hour or so away, so the time was frittered away by munching on the remaining rations. At first light, the work day commenced. In this case, it was sitting on the quarterdeck bulwark and reading. After about an hour, Mr. Freemount poked his nose out of the hatch and looked around.

"Morning, Mr. Freemount."

Freemount swivelled his head around to see who was speaking. He spotted Jon, nodded, and continued scanning for a few seconds before disappearing back down below. It was somewhat like a turtle retreating back into his shell. Jon didn't know what to make of it.

Jon reflected that yet again things had changed for him. Since being pressed, he had been under rigid navy discipline. After being elevated to the acting master's mate position, this discipline had relaxed slightly, to the point where conversations could be instigated with the standing officers without fear of punishment. Despite the easing of restrictions, the rigid structure remained in place.

Now, as one of the three members of the Mermaid's decommissioning crew, that structure wasn't clear. Frank Mason, the bosun, was in charge. Lieutenant Davis had made that clear, even though yesterday, as a master's mate, Jon had outranked the bosun. As far as Ernie Freemount, the carpenter was concerned, Jon outranked him. He was unsure how to deal with these men, so he would have to 'play it by ear'. It was apparent he would have to swallow some pride and adapt to the different circumstances, he was after all still under naval discipline.

Even the routine was unlike anything previously encountered on one of His Majesty's ships. He had no inkling what duties would be assigned, or what time would be allowed to study for the master's examination.

Around the start of the forenoon watch, both Mason and Freemount appeared on deck. The exact time was unknown, because without the watch ringing the bell, no one could accurately say. Even though Jon had a timepiece, he did not use it. It was whatever time Mason said it was. Welcome to his new reality.

On seeing the two of them in the waist, Jon rose and sauntered over to the foreward edge of the quarterdeck.

"Morning."

Both the men acknowledged Jon's presence, but said nothing. Jon descended to the waist.

"Frank, never having been in a situation like this, how are we going to play it? For example are we going to attempt to stand any type of watch?"

"No watches. We operate by daylight. The nights are ours. If either of you want to head into town, let me know," replied Frank. "First things first. We need to get ourselves squared away. Quarters first. Jon, I want you to shift into our mess," stated Frank.

The first hurdle was over. We're going to call each other by our first names.

"No problem, but can I make a suggestion?" asked Jon.

"Go ahead," said Frank.

"I've seen your mess. The cockpit is not all that much better. The officers' wardroom is much larger, has better lighting from the transom windows, and has cabins. If we move in there, we can also get to the deck just as fast in case of any problems," said Jon.

"Good idea," said Frank. "We'll all shift our kit to the officers' wardroom."

The second hurdle was over. Frank is willing to take suggestions.

"Next point -- we need to eat. There are no rations on board. Jon, you and I will head over to the navy yards and see what we can requisition." Jon just nodded. "Once we manage to get those rations, we need a cook. Since both Ernie and I are senior, Jon you're elected," said Frank.

Whoa.

"I've never cooked," said Jon apprehensively. "Aren't you two taking a big risk?"

"I discussed this with Ernie. Neither of us can cook either. Since coming aboard, you have mastered everything that has been thrown at you. We both think that you can handle this as well. So as far as we are concerned, you're it," said Frank.

Ernie nodded his concurrence and said, "Just to ensure you understand, I will castrate you with a dull knife if you poison us."

"That's assuming you're still alive," shot back Jon.

The three of them chuckled at that, which took some of the sting from the words and assignment.

They split up, and went back to their respective areas and grabbed their kit. Jon picked a small cabin in the wardroom and started setting up his kit. Frank called out as they were working.

"We have a bit of a problem. All the boats are gone. We will have to scrounge a ride from someone over to the navy yard. Before getting our provisions, we'll have to recover the gig. It's the smallest boat," said Frank. "Jon, see if you can attract any boats in the water over here."

Jon trudged up to the quarterdeck. He didn't like the way things were heading. It appeared that he was going to get every bum job while the others sat around. The worse part about it was that he would likely have to swallow it, whether he liked it or not. There was no one to whom he could complain. Both Mr. Flynn and Captain Montague had done him a huge favour, but they were long gone.

Jon saw a boat in the distance. Grabbing a flag from the flag locker and waving it vigorously, he captured the attention of the boat. Hollering down the hatch, Jon summoned Frank, who had appeared on deck by the time the guard boat arrived. It was simple to scrounge a ride across the harbour to the navy yards.

It took considerable searching, but they finally found the Mermaid's gig. There was no one around the shoreline where the boat had been beached, so they just took it. If anyone had a problem with that, Jon figured it was Frank's problem. He was the man placed in charge.

Frank headed off to find the commissary, tasking Jon to move the gig around to the main steps -- just one more shit job. Frank did seem to be adept at getting things done. He managed to scrounge a week's worth of rations for the three of them from the commissary. Since they were in harbour, with a little persuasion, the commissary had provided fresh victuals.

Jon was thinking things were starting to get on track when Frank disappeared again. As there was no one else to transport the victuals from the commissary to the gig, it was obvious who had to do it.

By the time Jon rowed them back to the Mermaid, it was approaching dinner. All three of them were hungry. After hoisting the food aboard and securing it in another empty cabin in the officer's wardroom, Jon realised it was up to him to make dinner.

The first challenge was fire. There was little firewood left on board. Although Ernie's endeavours while they visited the dockyards were unknown, it sure didn't appear that he had done anything to improve their overall comfort. For sure Ernie hadn't collected firewood. The first priority was to scrounge for driftwood and any other wood for making a fire. Once sufficient wood had been gathered and carted back to the ship, a second problem arose. The only cooking utensil on board the Mermaid was the big copper cauldron used for the entire crew's meal, which was inappropriate for their needs.

It was now well into the afternoon watch, and his two companions were fuming at the delay.

"I'm sorry, but there will be no hot dinner," said Jon. "There is nothing onboard I can use to cook any of the rations. We have fresh bread and cheese. I'll issue portions of those, and try to get something hot for supper."

"Ernie, we need something we can use to boil water. Seen anything onboard that might work?"

"We'll take a look around after dinner," said Ernie. The tone of his voice indicated he was clearly unimpressed with everything that Jon had done.

After munching on the bread and cheese, Jon and Ernie started checking the orlop and hold for anything. Using the carpenter's tools, they disassembled the large copper cauldron. Taking one section of it, they hammered out a bowl-like appliance. It fit over the existing galley fire hearth. Jon could start a fire in the galley hearth and either boil water or grill meat using the appliance.

Part of the provisions they had drawn from the commissary was an entire shank of lamb for the week for the three of them. Jon had the option to either boil it or grill it. Unfortunately, both types of cooking could not be completed at the same time. When it came to preparing a meal, he had to grill the meat first and then boil water for peas afterwards or vice versa.

It was improvised cooking, but the meals were tastier, mainly because of the fresh rations. In Jon's opinion, it was better than anything they had consumed in the past few months. The only comment he got from Frank or Ernie was a grunt.

By the end of the first full day, Jon was fuming. Shafted with every dirty job so far, there was no end in sight. It was difficult to identify anything the other two had accomplished. If the first day provided any indication of what was coming, the prognosis was not good. If something wasn't done about it, it would only get worse. Hard work wasn't a problem, but doing all the work while the other two sat around was a different story. Swallowing one's pride was one thing, but this was totally different.

The dog watches saw him back on the quarterdeck; book in hand, studying for his master's certificate. It was the primary reason for assignment to the caretaker party. That was what he needed to focus on.

The decommissioning crew had specific duties, which was the reason they were being paid to remain on the Mermaid. Each day, there was a limited routine to be accomplished. Small cleaning tasks were undertaken. Certain areas in the ship were prepared for work, and standing rigging was stripped down. Since he was the only man with topman experience, Jon was tasked with all of the work on the standing rigging. He continued to work twice as hard as the other two men combined.

It began to dawn on Jon that he was playing into Frank and Ernie's plans. If the gunner had been left on board, there would have been an equal share of work. The actual completed work would be far less than what Jon was accomplishing, simply because the gunner wouldn't have the necessary skills. As he realized this Jon became angry with himself, almost as much as he was frustrated with Frank and Ernie. He needed to find a resolution to this predicament.

Frank and Ernie were obviously smarter than Jon had thought. That they had considerable experience was beyond doubt. How that knowledge or experience could be harnessed was the challenge. How could things be changed from the way they were -- Jon doing almost all of the work -- to having them help him accomplish what he needed to accomplish?

'Change the questions we ask ourselves, and we change the way we look at things, and therefore change the results we get,' was something that Jon had learned before. He needed to put it into action.

How could Ernie be inspired to help instead of dumping all the shit jobs on him? What did a carpenter know about the duties of a ship's master? At first glance, not much, however, one of the responsibilities of a ship's master was to ensure the loading of a ship. To do that properly a man needed to consider several things including the construction of the vessel, and the impact weight had on the vessel's performance. A good carpenter knows something about design, so why not find out how knowledgeable a carpenter Ernie was.

At breakfast the next morning, Jon asked, "Ernie, as a master, it's my responsibility to properly load a ship. What can you tell me about ships and this ship in particular, that would assist me in stowing things in the correct location?"

Ernie's response was like a plug coming out of bilge pump hose. A torrent of words started, as Ernie warmed to the discussion. Frank looked at Jon with a surprised expression on his face. Neither of them had heard this much talk come from Ernie in the few days they had been together, perhaps much longer on the part of Frank.

Ernie said, "Come with me, and I'll show you." Jon followed Ernie for the entire morning while Ernie gave a detailed explanation of the ship layout, issues for stowing such as weight and availability of critical supplies and equipment, and issues for sail handling such as design considerations for leeway, thrust and counter thrust, and a variety of other details. He was still in full flood when Jon had to interrupt him to prepare dinner.

Two things became apparent from Jon's questions. First, the number of shit jobs received from either Ernie or Frank decreased markedly, and an incredible amount of information was picked up. How much of that information would be retained was another matter.

Some of the information Ernie provided turned out to be immediately valuable. An example was one tidbit of information discovered when Ernie explained the design, loading and protection of the powder room. Although Jon was originally uninterested in anything related with the powder room, that rapidly changed. Inside the powder magazine and also in the powder filling room there were pallets on the floor. Underneath the pallets, between the top of the pallet and the deck planking was a thick layer of charcoal. This charcoal originally absorbed moisture to keep the gunpowder dry. Since they were never going to have additional powder on board, Jon didn't hesitate to use some of this charcoal for cooking their meals. This saved valuable time collecting firewood for cooking the noon meals.

Based on one question, and several dozen follow-up questions, Jon gained a vast amount of insight about ships, never before considered. Ernie also became an important ally.

Although well on the way toward accumulating knowledge required for the master's examination, a shortfall still existed. Jon still needed to capture all of the information that Ernie was providing. Otherwise he'd lose the ability to further study and remember it.

While everything appeared to be going well with Ernie, the same could not be said of his dealings with Frank. Jon's first impression of Frank Mason when arriving aboard the Mermaid was that Frank was a puffed up rooster. He had adjusted this evaluation when Frank had looked after his money belt during the storm in the Atlantic. Since being with Frank and Ernie, his opinion of Frank had deteriorated. His current opinion of Frank was that of a lazy, puffed up rooster. The problem was that Frank was both competent and technically his superior. The discipline of the Royal Navy didn't allow much leeway so Jon found himself having to show respect to someone he didn't like. How does one work effectively with someone he doesn't like?

Each afternoon and evening, Jon spent working on his navigation lessons using the books he had acquired or taking notes from Ernie's discussions. Over time, he read each book he had. What's more, he understood the majority of what was read. There was some concern about certain points in the books, which did not make sense to him. Dickerson and Mr. Flynn had also indicated that the examiners asked confusing questions and demanded an immediate response. Lack of experience in this area would work against him.

"Frank, you know a lot about sail handling. Mr. Flynn told me that during the examination, an examiner would describe a situation and I would have to respond on how to safely handle or manoeuvre the ship to avoid catastrophe. Given your experience, could you come up with some tricky situations and play the examiner?"

"What kind of situations?" asked Frank, before he shovelled some more food in his mouth.

"To be honest, I'm not sure," replied Jon. "The situations would be ones where the ship was in jeopardy, like on a lee shore in a storm, in close proximity to other vessels, or when there is a problem with the vessel."

"Okay, I could do that, but I don't want to hear you crying when you don't get it right," replied Frank.

Unsure as to what he had just gotten himself into, Jon nodded. Every night thereafter, Frank invented a different scenario, an almost impossible scenario, out of which Jon was required to navigate. Jon rarely gave the correct response -- or at least the correct response in Frank's opinion.

The scenarios had a positive impact, which Jon was quick to understand. These exercises helped train Jon to visualise the problem and prepare a possible solution. There was also a secondary benefit. Frank ceased targeting him with the shit jobs. That didn't mean that these tasks stopped completely, but they were shared equally. Frank instead got his kicks nightly by creating impossible mental exercises.

Jon's overall opinion of Frank did not alter all that much, but he had found a way to live with him. In essence, it was possible to respect a man, or at least that individual's abilities, and not like the man.

The days went by and things progressed. At the end of October, they received orders that the Mermaid would be moved across harbour and have her masts removed. A crew of men from the holding ship arrived. Frank organized them. One group pumped ship under the direction of Ernie Freemount. The second stripped off all remaining standing rigging under Jon's direction.

The ship was towed off with some effort and shifted across harbour. A smaller crew was engaged the next day and the foremast removed. The day after that, the main and mizzen masts were removed. The masts could be reused on another vessel at some point in the future. The remaining hulk was to be scrapped, as it was not considered viable for repair.

The three of them stayed aboard for another two weeks. There was even less to do than previously, so to stay busy the focus shifted totally to the study for the master's examination.

After he expressed an interest in Ernie's work, Ernie had taken a shine to Jon. At every opportunity Ernie made an attempt to impart new knowledge to Jon. Some of these things Jon was unlikely ever to use. Some were important enough to include in notes. As they neared parting, Ernie proposed something different -- something that would be useful to Jon, but unrelated to the master's examination.

Some wood was salvaged from the Mermaid with additional wood scrounged from the naval dockyards. Instruction on woodworking commenced with the intent of constructing a sea chest. Surprisingly, Jon became fully engaged in the preparation of the chest. Not only could he use a good sea chest, but also the ability to construct it was a beneficial skill to have.

"All finished?" asked Ernie. He was smiling at Jon's pride and enthusiasm even after spending hours sanding the chest.

"The only thing I'm wondering about is whether to carve my initials in it."

"I won't do that, and you're not finished either," replied Ernie as he examined the sea chest.

Jon was confused. He could see no further work that the chest needed, especially as Ernie advised against carving his initials on it.

"You're wondering what else needs to be done?" asked Ernie.

"Ernie, the sea chest is finished. It looks good; it's well sanded and it won't splinter. What's left to do?"

"Let me ask you a question," said Ernie. "If you are normally quartered in the cockpit, where do you think your sea chest goes when we're at quarters?"

"I've only ever had my ditty bag, and that has never been moved. When I was foreward of the mast, all of our kit was moved to somewhere in the orlop. I remember carrying other sea chests down to the orlop when clearing for action, but I believe those sea chests were from the commissioned officer's wardroom." Jon was wondering where all of this was leading.

"Some of the sea chests from the cockpit are used by the surgeon as a platform. The men call it the cutting table," said Ernie quietly. "If you stay in the cockpit, your sea chest will at some point in time likely end up as part of the cutting table. You need to protect it."

"How?"

"First we apply one or two coats of linseed oil. This fills the wood pores with oil and provides deep protection. If a knife or saw slips, the linseed oil will help protect the wood from stains. After the linseed oil dries, a surface protecting coat of varnish is used. This will repel moisture and blood. Understand?" asked Ernie.

Jon simply nodded absentmindedly while still visualizing some poor unfortunate having his arm or leg amputated.

"Blood splashes are as common on a cockpit sea chest as water stains," continued Ernie. "That's also the reason I suggest that you not engrave anything on the chest."

When the sea chest was complete it was a nice looking functional chest. They had even been able to scrounge metal handles and a metal hasp for it. The only thing missing was a lock. Jon placed all of his books in the box and all of his extra kit. He kept his clothes in his ditty bag. The chest was large, but it could be hoisted on his shoulders and carried for a short distance. Jon sewed a rope strap on to his ditty bag, so he could carry it on his back and across his shoulders. The top of the ditty bag would also cushion the chest on his shoulder so it would rest more comfortably.

In the third week of November, all three of them were ordered to report to the administration offices at the naval dockyard. Their time on the Mermaid had come to an end. Each of them was paid off, and discharged from the Mermaid's books. Jon shook hands and parted ways with Ernie and Frank.

All of them were "on the beach" now, responsible to find their own ship.

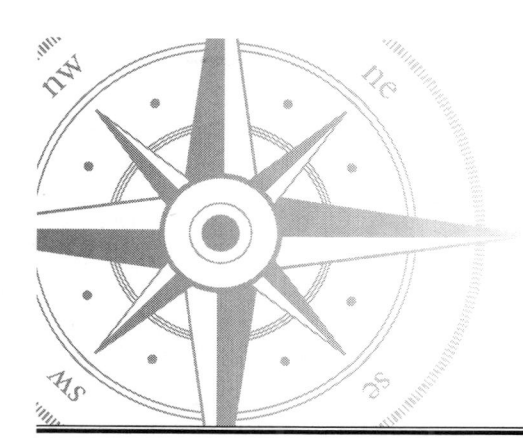

CHAPTER 35

Standing outside the port administration offices, Jon realized his greatest wish since being pressed had been achieved. He was out of the navy. He was a free man!

That freedom might be short-lived if he stuck around the Portsmouth area. Remaining as a sailor in a navy town, the possibility of being pressed at any time was dramatically higher. Only the jacket with the white piping might provide protection. A press gang would not likely shanghai a senior man from another ship.

Consequently, Jon's initial concern was directed toward personal security. Being pressed at this point would eliminate any chance of taking the master's examination. As he was carrying a considerable sum in vouchers, he also needed to consider protection from robbery. Any port had a certain unsavoury element and Portsmouth was no different. Getting out of Portsmouth would likely reduce both threats.

That posed the immediate question of where to go.

In reality there were only two places Jon considered at all. The first was home north of Rye. There was an obligation to let the Swift family know he was safe, and to ensure that his absence had not harmed them. The second place was London. He had an obligation to Mr. Flynn and Captain Montague to write the master's exam, since they had provided both the opportunity and time to study. London was where that exam would be written.

Added to the debate between the two locations was the question of funds. In order to convert the vouchers into cash, they had to be redeemed at the Admiralty in London. A small portion of the funds he carried was rightfully owed to the Swift family. Without redemption of the vouchers, there was no way the payment to the Swift family could be discharged. The decision was obvious -- London first.

With all of this in mind, Jon turned around and headed back into the port administration offices. He found a different clerk in the office.

"Morning. My name's Smith. I'm a master's mate off the Mermaid. I have orders from my master to go to London and write the Trinity House master's examination at the Navy Board. I'm wondering how I go about getting to London?"

"Let me ask," said the clerk and left Jon standing at the counter.

After some time the clerk reappeared. "We don't seem to have any records of any orders sending you to attend any examination at the Navy Board. In fact, according to our records, you were just discharged when the Mermaid was paid-off."

"So where does that leave me?"

"Since you are no longer in the navy, I'd say a free man," smiled the clerk.

"I mean, how am I supposed to get to London and write the exam? I'm carrying documents prepared by my master for the examiners." Jon lifted an envelope and displayed it to the clerk.

"As I see it, there are three ways. There is a coach for London that leaves here every second day. That costs over a pound. You could walk I suppose. The only other option is to take a ship up the channel. I don't know what that will cost you. As far as the navy is concerned, you're on your own," said the clerk before turning and walking away.

An irked Jon left the navy yards. He didn't have a pound to take a coach, or the extra money it would cost for food and accommodation. All his funds were tied up in the vouchers. Walking was out of the question, especially with the sea chest. That only left the sea option.

A beeline was made for the taverns near the commercial port. The tavern proprietors generally knew of ships leaving, or the taverns were filled with sailors that did. That was the best place to search for a merchantman heading toward London.

Dropping the sea chest and ditty bag in the first tavern, Jon started his inquiries. The names of a couple of ships heading up the coast were soon determined. It was necessary to lug the chest and ditty bag along the wharf, as they could not be left in any waterfront tavern with the expectation of finding the contents intact upon return. The first ship that was approached turned out to be a dead end. Jon was told to "bugger off" before even reaching the gangplank. Obviously, this was not a happy ship.

The second mentioned ship, the Lucy, was a small brig that looked old and worn. Approaching her, he hailed the deck watch. Jon stated his business. The man on the deck watch went and fetched the captain. Captain Moore was a heavily bearded and gruff-natured, short, old man of at least sixty-five years of age. This age was older than average for a sea captain.

"I understand you want to join our merry crew?" asked Captain Moore.

"To be honest captain, I am looking to work my passage to London. I am heading there to write my master's examination," replied Jon

"You? You're not old enough to steer a jolly boat, let alone navigate a ship," quipped Captain Moore.

Jon smiled. He was used to such comments, and took them good naturedly.

"Well I might have challenges with a jolly boat, but I did steer a long boat with an untrained crew through French-held islands at night to land an assault force at Louisbourg. I have navigated one of His Majesty's ships across the Atlantic, under the guidance of the master of course. Just the same, I'm not looking for a master's position. I was a good topman before

I became a master's mate. I reckon I can hold my own as a topman on your ship."

Captain Moore stared at Jon for a long while. Jon stared back.

"I can always use a good topman. I can feed ya, and you can work your way to London, but I won't pay you. If that is acceptable, then welcome aboard. If it is not, then get the hell off my ship," said Captain Moore.

"Where can I stow my gear, sir?" replied Jon.

The Lucy sailed the next morning on the tide. Wearing his old slops, Jon was resting easy in the tops. Although just a topman, subject to the orders of the senior topman, it was obvious that little supervision was required. The sequence of sail handling on this little brig was simple. With fewer men in the tops there was more to do, but it was not the same atmosphere as in one of His Majesty's ships. Jon fell into an easy familiarity with his co-workers.

The Lucy plodded along the coast from port to port looking for cargo. Finally, with sufficient cargo in her hold, she headed for the Thames estuary. At Sheerness, a Thames pilot boarded for the trip up river.

As they were making their way up river, Captain Moore called for Jon. Approaching the captain on the quarterdeck, it was possible to overhear the captain speaking to the pilot. Their subject was none other than Jon Swift.

"This is the man I was telling you about. Swift claims that he is heading to London to write the master's certification exam," stated the captain to the pilot.

"Swift reporting as ordered," said Jon as he knuckled his forehead.

"Swift, this is our pilot, Captain Price-Cooper," said Captain Moore.

"Sir," Jon nodded.

"Tell me Mister Swift, how is it, someone as young as you is in a position to write the master's exam?" questioned the pilot.

"Well sir, what I'm hoping for, is to secure a place as a master's mate. I realize I need a few years experience before I could ever hope to become a master, but as a master's mate I would be in a position to learn. I was a master's mate on my last ship. She was paid off. I now find myself competing against older more experienced men for the same position on other ships. With a master's certificate under my belt, I would have a better chance of getting that position than someone with more experience that did not have the qualification."

Captain Price-Cooper looked at Captain Moore. Neither said anything, and Jon could not discern what they were silently communicating.

"Excuse me sirs. Do either of you know anything about the Trinity House examination for master?"

Unfortunately, neither of them could help.

CHAPTER 36

London. Having never been here before, Jon was amazed at the size and bustle about the place.

The Lucy was anchored in the Thames waiting for a position at the wharf to unload their goods. It was part way through the afternoon watch. Jon was eagerly seeking a way to shore so he could sort out his business. He was this close and yet still so far away.

Taking advantage of the delay in finding a berthing space, Captain Moore headed ashore to speak to buyers of his cargo and to potential shippers. After requesting permission, Jon hitched a ride in the gig as it headed to shore.

Once on shore, Jon pestered people seeking the location of the Admiralty and Navy Board where the examinations were to take place. Eventually both were located, but it was dark by that time. Disappointed that the exchange of vouchers had to be put off for another day, he trudged back toward the docks. It was difficult just finding the way back to the Lucy through the maze of streets. In fact he never made it all the way. As he passed one of the wharf side taverns, one of the Lucy's crew beckoned him in. Stopping for a wet was provident, as it resulted in a free lift back to the ship. The cost of the beer was also less than the cost of a boat back to the ship. It was a fine ending to a frustrating day.

The next morning the Lucy docked and started to off-load the cargo. After dinner, Jon anxiously requested permission to leave the ship. His sudden departure was not accepted kindly by some of the crew, as it looked like he was shirking work. Jon was concerned that Captain Moore didn't see it the same way. He still needed a place to sleep, and the Lucy was the cheapest accommodation to be found. Jon's pressing concern was to resolve money and examination concerns. The Admiralty was his first stop to exchange the payment vouchers for cash.

The payment process took some time, but was worth it. Having over eighty pounds in one's possession far exceeded having vouchers which couldn't be exchanged for goods. Prudently some of the money was concealed in the jacket liner with the remainder stuffed into the money belt. Access and availability of both knives were checked prior to starting back to the Lucy. The delay in payment precluded his traveling to the Navy Board that day.

Luckily, there were still numerous people on the streets on the way back to the Lucy. At the docks a number of sailors were present, apparently heading to their ships. Jon ensured he remained in close proximity to these other travellers. A lone individual would be easy prey on the London streets. He arrived back at the ship unharmed, but with a heightened alertness and sense of caution.

The next morning they finished the unloading before he requested and obtained permission to leave for the Navy Board. It was still a pressing issue for him. He needed to know one way or another if he would be allowed to write the master's examination. He was nervous walking around with the amount of cash he was carrying. If he lost it …

At the Navy Board he spoke to multiple clerks before finding anyone with information. The examination was scheduled to sit in another two days. He submitted the papers that Mr. Flynn had given him prior to his departure from the Mermaid. The clerks were unhelpful with his questions. He was told to report back in two days time to find out if he would undertake the examination.

A discouraged Jon returned to the docks. It seemed it required an act of God to get a straight answer from the Navy Board. As he walked to the dock space where the Lucy had tied up, there was no sign of her. Disappointment turned to near panic. His kit was gone, not to mention a place to sleep and eat.

A couple of hours of frantic searching resulted in locating the Lucy anchored downstream. When he finally got to the ship, they informed him that since they were not ready to load cargo, the port authorities had requested they move so another ship could use the dock space. That explanation really didn't ease his mind that much.

Jon needed to resolve his accommodation concerns. With funds in hand it was possible to take accommodations on shore, but the Lucy was preferred. It was certainly cheaper than any alternative, and Jon was cautious with money. There was also the question of security. The shipmates befriended on the Lucy provided both comradeship and a degree of security for his effects. One thing was certain, Jon didn't want to depart the ship again for any reason only to return to find the Lucy had sailed.

Jon headed up to officer's country, approaching the mate on the quarterdeck.

"Sir, I have just returned aboard. I found out that the examinations I need to take will not be held for another two days. Will the ship still be here? Or do I need to find accommodations ashore?"

The mate asked him to wait and departed down to the captain's quarters. He returned in a few minutes time.

"Swift, the captain says that it will be three or four days until he arranges a cargo. We might have to wait to get a docking space and then we have to load. If you wish to sail with us, you will need to sign on," explained the mate.

"Thank you sir, I will let you know," replied Jon and headed below.

With that response, Jon felt the accommodation and food concerns were resolved, at least until after he wrote the exam, assuming permission to write were granted. What wasn't clear was what to do if permission to write were not granted, or what to do after the exam, if permission were granted.

Two mornings later, Jon entered the Navy Board offices and approached the clerk. After inquiring about the Trinity House master's examination and confirming they still had his documentation, he went to a waiting room. There were a dozen men already waiting, the youngest of which was at least ten years older. The oldest appeared to be over forty. There was a significant amount of grey hair or prematurely grey hair in the room. Jon felt ill at ease.

A clerk entered the room just before nine o'clock.

"Gentlemen, let me explain how this works," said the clerk. "In about ten minutes there will be a written examination in an adjoining room. You will have three hours to answer the questions. You will not be allowed to take anything in the room with you."

"At the end of the three hours the examination papers will be collected," continued the clerk. "You will be free to leave. The written examinations will be marked starting this afternoon, and continuing until complete."

"Tomorrow morning, oral examinations will commence. Only those individuals who have successfully passed the written examination, will be permitted to undergo the oral examination. You are all asked to report back here tomorrow morning by nine. At that time, you will be asked to stay if you have passed the written examination. If not, you will be free to leave. If you are asked to stay, your oral examination might not take place for a day or so, depending on the number of men who need to be examined. You will report back here each morning until released. Is that understood?"

There were no comments, so the clerk assumed everyone understood the instructions.

The clerk ushered the men into another set of rooms for the examination. Each man selected and sat at an individual table. Each table had a number of charts, navigational tables, pencils, paper and rulers. Each man received a series of written questions. For each question, the answer was to be printed, and the calculations used to achieve that answer listed beneath.

Jon started the questions. They were not easy, but he had answered several similar questions under Mr. Flynn's tutelage. After three hours the examination ended. Just barely completing all the questions, Jon beckoned the clerk and submitted the papers. It felt eerie being the last man out of the room.

For the entire journey back to the Lucy, Jon mentally replayed the examination questions over and over. Upon reaching the Lucy's gangplank, he believed sufficient questions had been answered correctly to be asked to the oral examination the next day.

It was just a matter of waiting until tomorrow to see.

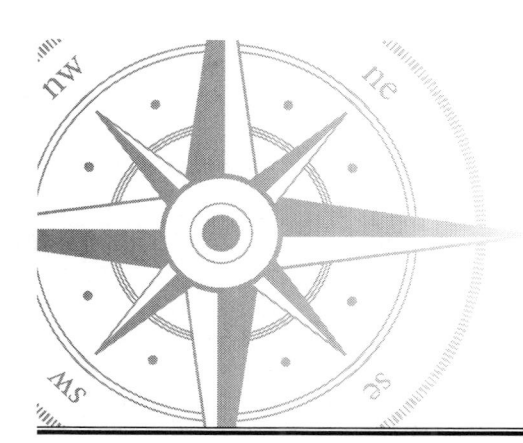

CHAPTER 37

At nine o'clock, as per instructions, Jon reported to the Navy Board offices.

The receiving clerk provided no verbal response; he just pointed to a waiting room. Several men, but less than half of those who had sat at the written examination, were present.

Jon sat silently, fidgeting from time to time. Although patience was a skill learned when poaching, his ability to apply that skill in the present circumstance was lacking. Lack of information further aggravated the situation. Foremost of the questions that needed answering was whether he had passed the written examination. None of the clerks would answer that question. If the response was negative, then sitting in the waiting room was a complete waste of time.

Repeated questions to the clerks over the course of the morning were met with stony faced responses. This lack of response only heightened his anxiety. His imagination was working overtime. Did he pass? Why was it taking so much time to tell him? By the noon hour, nerves were getting the better of him, convincing him that he had not passed the written examination.

At the dinner hour, hunger took over. He hoped that by getting something to eat his nerves would calm down. Heading into the street to find a cart vendor, he spotted the clerk who collected the written examination papers the previous day. The clerk queued up in line at one of the vendors. Jon increased his pace to ensure a position in line next to the clerk.

"Excuse me. You're the clerk that presided over the master's examination yesterday. I was wondering if I was to be called for the oral examination, or if I failed. Can you tell me?"

"What's your name, sir?" responded the clerk. He was still somewhat startled by Jon's attempt to gain his attention, but polite to a possible superior.

"Swift"

"So you're Swift. You're the mystery man," replied the clerk.

"What do you mean -- mystery man?"

"You passed the exam; however, we have no records about you," stated the clerk.

Instantly Jon realized what had happened. All his paperwork was for Jon Smith. He had signed everything in the examination as Jon Swift.

"Thank you, you're the first person that's given me a straight answer since I set foot in the Navy Board." Jon was smiling. What the clerk thought, Jon didn't care. He was just happy he passed.

Jon followed the clerk back to the Navy Board building after each had a quick bite to eat. The clerk ushered him over to the desk of an obviously more senior clerk.

"Excuse me sir, I have found Swift," said the junior clerk.

The senior clerk looked up. He wore spectacles, which had slid half way down his hawk-like nose.

"Swift is it? Just who are you Mr. Swift? We have no records of you, nor did you present any records yesterday before the examination. How did you manage to get in and write it?" asked the senior clerk.

"Sir, I presented all my records to the clerk prior to writing. I was ushered into a room and allowed to write the examination. I realize what happened. The records I presented were made out in the name the navy gave me, not my real name."

"The name the navy gave you?" parroted the senior clerk.

"Yes sir. You see I was taken by a press gang. I was hit over the head pretty hard. Since no one knew my name, and I wasn't conscious for over a week, the navy assigned me the name of Jon Smith. No one asked me my real name. As a result, all my papers are for Jon Smith. My real name is Jon Swift. I signed the examination with my real name."

"Ummmph. You'll be allowed to take the oral examination," said the senior clerk. "If you pass that, then I will take the time to sort out this name business."

"Henry, take him to the examination hall," said the senior clerk to the other clerk.

Jon was led to a chair in the hall beside the door to a room. Here again he waited for some time. Finally an older man whom Jon recognized from the day before exited through the door.

"If you're the next candidate for the oral examination, they want you in there," the man stated before moving on down the hall.

Jon entered the room, closed the door behind him and turned. In front of him were five men seated behind a long table. There was a chair in the middle, positioned directly in front of them.

"Report," said the man sitting in the middle chair.

"Sir, my name is Swift, Jon Swift. All my papers are listed as Jon Smith," said Jon. "I was master's mate on HMS Mermaid under the master Mr. Flynn."

"You say your name is Swift, but you also say that your documents are listed as Smith. Which is it? Are you here to represent someone else?" asked one of the examination board members seated to Jon's left.

"No sir, I am here to represent only myself," responded Jon. "I was taken by a press gang. I was hit over the head pretty hard. Since no one knew my name, and I wasn't conscious for over a week, the navy assigned me the name of Jon Smith. No one asked me my real name. As a result, all my papers are for Jon Smith. My real name is Jon Swift. I signed the written examination with my real name."

The man in the middle seat turned his head and quipped to the other man, "George, I don't believe it's the first time any of us have heard of a man using a false name in the navy? Eh?"

George looked at the man in the middle seat, "No, I don't suppose so. My concern is that if this man passes the exam, the certificate isn't given to another man not qualified to assume the position."

"Just so."

For the next two hours Jon was subjected to a series of questions by individual members of the board. Some of the questions were straightforward, and similar to questions asked by either Chad Dickerson or Mr. Flynn. Some of the others were similar to those asked by Frank Mason. Thanks to his experience with Frank, Jon was able to respond faster and with a better rationale for a particular course or sail configuration than would have been the case. After the session ended, Jon was shell-shocked. They told him to report back to the clerk in two days time to get the results of his examination and reclaim his documents.

Jon sat down outside the Navy Board building totally drained. Mentally reliving the oral examination was like repeatedly re-entering a nightmare -- not a great idea. Even after all the study, and all the questions that he had completed, there had been insufficient preparation. If the questions asked both by Frank Mason and Mr. Flynn hadn't been as difficult as they were, he would have been badly disgraced. As it was, he had no idea whether he passed or not.

In two days time the answer would be forthcoming. Whether it was success or failure, one thing was certain. He needed a decision about what to do next.

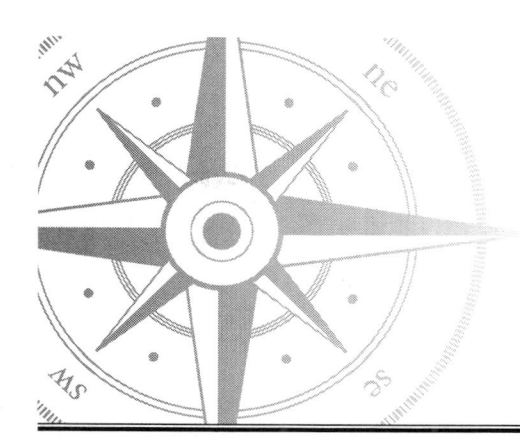

CHAPTER 38

Darkness was descending before he knew it.
It was a cold December night. Alone, in a strange area of London, holding more money than the average man made in four years was not exactly a healthy situation to be in. He needed a safe refuge, such as the Lucy. It was time to be moving.

The route back to the Lucy was well known. Jon had already travelled it several times getting to and from the Admiralty and Navy Board. The immediate area around the Admiralty was upscale and considered safe. Footpads generally avoided the area. Pedestrians in this area were likely to be naval officers who were armed and knowledgeable in combat. Easier pickings were available elsewhere. Closer to the wharves a person at night needed to be much more cautious. Regardless of the distance to travel, it would be wise to pay close attention to the surroundings and any noise.

As time went on and closer to the wharves the number of pedestrians on the street dropped. Either people had supper on their minds or they knew it was not safe to be on the streets in the waterfront neighbourhood. The odd person out and about shied away when they observed a stranger.

Jon sought comfort with an old reliable friend. Unconsciously reaching in his jacket to find the throwing knife, a quick wiggle ensured it could be readily drawn. Although not practical in a knife fight because it wasn't heavy enough, if thrown correctly, it would account for one attacker. Its owner was just the person that could throw it properly. In a fight, any knife was better than no knife.

In the dock area Jon adopted a slower pace and kept close to the side of buildings. When approaching an alley, different tactics applied. Rather than be surprised from the shadows that always haunted alleys, Jon moved out further into the street until the alley was well passed. All movements were slow, prudent and observant of everything in the immediate surroundings.

The river was visible in the middle distance when it happened. Three men were lurking back in the shadows near the entrance of a dockside tavern, waiting for their next victim. Before they realized a victim was present, Jon had started to back up. Unfortunately, that didn't last. One of the three nudged another, pointed at Jon, and all three of them started rapidly moving forward.

Caution thrown aside, Jon turned and ran back the way he had just come. Having previously passed an alley and a street he decided to cut down an alley because it was the closer of the two. The alley appeared to head down to the next street that ran parallel to the street he was on. By using it, he figured it would be possible to get around the three. It was a mistake -- the alley was a dead end.

As soon as he realized this mistake, Jon turned and started to head back out of the alley. To his bad luck, the three huffing men filled the entrance. Jon was cornered in a dead end alley. The only way out was through the three would-be robbers. These men were obviously locals, because they had all followed him into the alley knowing there was no other exit.

Jon assessed his chances and didn't like what he saw. As the robbers slowly approached there was no choice but to edge backwards. They were taking their time, as there was no hope of escape. Despite being scared, one thing popped into his mind. Don't lose your temper. Stay calm and think your way through this. His greatest enemy on the Mermaid, Lieutenant Rylett had taught him that lesson.

Fear tends to focus the mind for some. Preparing for the inevitable battle his first thought was to cut down the odds. Using the throwing knife to take one of the men down was a good idea. Its use, however, would render him weapon less. Not good, but if some other weapon was found, acceptable. He quickly scanned the alley. The scan had to be quick as it was never advisable to take your eyes off your opponent for any length of time. Lying against an old barrel was a piece of one-inch plank about eight feet long. By itself, in the present state it was impractical. That was rapidly changed by grabbing it, leaning it against the side of the nearest building and kicking the plank to split it in two. The shorter three-foot piece he grasped in his left hand. In his right hand, he drew and held his knife in a position for thrusting.

Jon waited, inadvertently ceding the initiative to the robbers.

The alley wasn't wide. Only two men could stand side by side. A more careful examination of the attackers was possible. The one on Jon's left was wearing a heavy coat and holding a short blade in a thrusting stance. The one on the right was a big man also holding a blade. The man in back was smaller and wearing lighter clothes. He had his clothes undone at the throat, showing a V at the neck. He didn't appear to be armed, or at least hadn't drawn any weapon.

With the drawn blades, their intent was obvious.

It was time to cut down the odds and seize the initiative.

Reversing the grip on the throwing knife, with the point in his hand, Jon focused on the third man. He would be the first target.

The front two approached to within ten feet of Jon. The third fellow remained five feet behind them, opting to supervise. Jon shifted his focus momentarily to the eyes of the front two. They both appeared to be watching and considering the piece of wood in Jon's left hand.

The piece of lumber was vicious looking. It was approximately three feet long, an inch thick and six inches in width. The sawn end which Jon held was relatively smooth. The end pointed toward the attackers was splintered, with a long splinter on one corner. As a bat, it was far from ideal. Its width would require a two-handed hold and would slow it down. As a jabbing instrument, it was superb.

Jon started to make jabbing motions. Capturing the attention of the two forward attackers, he re-focused on the V neckline of the third man, cocked his arm, and flung the knife.

The other two were focusing on Jon and watching the piece of wood. They didn't appear to notice the knife pass between them. There was virtually no sound of a strike -- just a 'thiic' sound. The man in the rear grabbed his throat with both hands and started to collapse with a faint gurgling sound.

The other two decided it was time to attack. Once his right hand was free of his throwing knife, Jon was able to use both his hands to grasp the wood. When he did this, it looked like he was transferring the wood from his left to right hand. The onrushing men were momentarily confused and hesitated. Jon lunged with the wood at the right man, and then swept the wood back to the left as he recovered from the lunge. Effectively, the lunge stopped the right hand man's advance. The sweep hit the left hand man on the inside of his arm numbing his arm muscles and causing him to drop his knife.

To recover from the lunge, Jon drew back his left foot. He did a complete three hundred and sixty degree turn while taking a short step forward. Gripping the wood harder and sideways like a bat, he came out of the turn closer to his two opponents. The plank connected with the man to his left on the side of the head. That man collapsed and struck the ground unmoving.

The right hand man turned to beckon the rear man forward to the left. He didn't see the rear man, until he spotted a lump on the ground. This was a mistake, because his focus was on the lump and not on Jon. Jon hammered the piece of wood into the remaining man's extended arms. He dropped his knife. Jon closed with the man and jabbed the wood directly into the man's face. The wood splinter gouged the attacker's face badly. The resulting scream was short lived because Jon used the wood like a boarding axe. He chopped downward with the wood's narrow side onto the top of that last opponent's head with a crushing blow, silencing the attacker forever.

Jon eased his foot forward and nearly slipped on the knife dropped by the left hand attacker. He reached down and picked it up. It was a really cheap blade.

There was no noise in the alley, or in the street beyond that Jon could hear. The scream apparently didn't arouse any response. He approached the big man on the left and rolled him over using a foot. It was impossible to determine if the man was alive or dead. A pat down and check of the man's pockets came up empty. Stepping over to the right hand man he completed another pat down and pocket check. This one was dead for sure. Again, there was nothing in the pockets.

The third man was unquestionably dead. Jon pulled the throwing knife out of the man's throat wincing slightly at the sucking noise. After wiping the blade clean on the man's clothing, he carefully replaced it in the sheath inside his coat.

One of the cheap blades he kicked over and placed in the dead third man's hands. A pockets check divulged a number of coins. Apparently this was the leader of this little band of cutthroats. As the leader, the man had kept the entire evening's 'take', what little there was of it.

Jon dropped the piece of lumber, as there was no further need for it. After pocketing the few coins that had been found, he wiped his hands on the last man's clothes and considered what to do.

Technically he should seek out the authorities, although who the authorities were or where to find them was unknown. Jon seriously considered seeking the authorities, but dropped the idea. If the authorities were contacted, the incident reported, and if it were possible to lead them to this alley, then what? They would probably detain and interrogate him. They might even be suspicious that Jon had waylaid each of these men one at a time. Thinking out that scenario, he decided it might be better to avoid any potential hassles with the authorities.

The other option was just to leave them there and head back to the Lucy. That surely was the intention of the attackers after the robbery. They would have left him lying in that alley, either dead or seriously injured, for who knows how long before he was discovered. No remorse about walking away was warranted, in his opinion. That's what he decided to do.

Jon walked out of that alley and headed down to the docks to find a wherryman that would take him out to the Lucy. Dickering over the price for the trip to the ship, he realized there was barely enough money from the would-be robbers to pay for the ride.

All things considered, Jon wasn't the least bit troubled by leaving those men in the alley. His final thought as he was heading to the Lucy was that he had provided a service to society by ridding it of these parasites.

Better them than me.

CHAPTER 39

The morning posed a dilemma for Jon.

Jon had been ordered to report to the Navy Board at nine. At the same time, the Lucy had obtained a berth and was about to load cargo. It was impossible to be in both locations at the same time.

Finding out the results of the examination was a priority. Regardless of the results, there was still the question of what to do in the future. For the short term it might be possible to sign on with the Lucy for wages. There was still an obligation to Captain Moore and the Lucy for the provision of meals and accommodation while in London that was just as important.

Not seeing an easy resolution to this dilemma, Jon requested to see Captain Moore. After a brief discussion, Captain Moore suggested he attend the Navy Board and get that resolved. When he knew the outcome, it would be easier to decide what to do.

Jon arrived at the Navy Board late. The duty clerk was just as forthcoming as any of the previous clerks had been. With a point of the duty clerk's finger, Jon became re-acquainted with the waiting room. As the morning was frittered away, his impatience grew aggravated by the knowledge that the Lucy's crew were loading and expected help. It didn't help that no one approached him. He felt like a leper.

Finally, just before noon, a clerk approached and beckoned. Trailing the clerk, they ended up in front of the desk of the senior clerk he had met two days before. The senior clerk was in a foul mood, and this was quite apparent. Eventually the reason the clerk had his nose so far out of joint materialized.

Jon had passed the examination and was to receive a master's certificate. All previously submitted documentation had to be altered and re-done to reflect the correct name. This is what had taken all the time. Each annotation made by Mr Flynn, had to be re-signed by a master in the new logbook. This meant the clerk had to obtain the signature from one of the masters who had examined him two days earlier.

With that news, the impatience disappeared. Jubilation replaced it. It took longer than anticipated but he finally obtained all of his documents including the coveted master's certificate. Regardless of the verbal abuse received from them, he thanked both the senior clerk and the junior clerk as the packet was presented to him.

The packet of papers tucked under an arm, Jon literally skipped back to the Lucy. Enroute, to celebrate, he stopped at a shop and purchased a padlock for his sea chest.

The Lucy was still loading upon arrival. Hustling below he attended to some business before changing into slops to help load. With a padlock to secure the sea chest, he transferred the packet of documents, and most of his valuables. Only a few shillings and the key for the padlock remained in the money belt.

The remainder of the afternoon passed quickly. Having missed dinner, Jon spent some time trying to convince the cook to part with a few extras after the crew stood down from loading. It took the promise of some grog to liberate the appropriate rations.

Munching away, it was time to consider the future.

Signing on with Captain Moore, or any another merchant ship for that matter, it was likely the best position that could be achieved was as a topman. The best he could expect would amount to sixty five to seventy five shillings per month, depending upon the ship owners. As a second master on board one of His Majesty's vessels, income expectations would vary between sixty seven and seventy eight shillings per month, plus prize money. It was unlikely that a second master's position would be offered, but a master's mate position was assured because of his certificate. The pay could likely be approximately the same, depending upon how needy the captain.

Given the requirement to pay for extra food, extra clothing, etc., on board one of His Majesty's vessels, working on a merchantman was obviously a better choice. There was essentially the same risk for either option. Additionally, if pressed off a merchantman, presenting a master's certificate would either stop the press, or ensure a better position than other pressed men.

That was the sea option.

Since being pressed, Jon had traded successfully a number of times. Each trade had been enjoyable for various reasons. It was an area that could be explored.

As for farming, after watching his father labour for years and not get any further ahead, it was low on his priority of things to do. It was hard work with little reward. After speaking to colonials while at Louisbourg, he figured it would be better to farm in the colonies than in England. For one thing, the land, at least the land on the frontier, was free. All that was needed was money for setting up and draught animals. That he had. In England, you first had to purchase the property, then set up and acquire draft animals. The cost of that land was a problem.

Based on this limited reasoning, Jon thought the sea option was the best option to follow, all things considered. That option would have to wait until he saw his folks.

In the short term, Jon wondered if another deal could be negotiated with Captain Moore. While stowing the cargo, he had noticed that some of the cargo was marked for Rye. If he could work his way to Rye, the same as he had worked his way to London, he would stop and see his folks.

Once more, Jon approached Captain Moore.

"Excuse me, sir," said Jon as he knuckled his forehead to the mate who was on the quarterdeck.

"Yes Swift, what is it?"

"May I speak to the captain, sir? I would like to come to an agreement with respect to my passage," said Jon.

The mate disappeared and returned with Captain Moore.

"Well, I see you're here Swift. I warned you that you were a little young for a master's certificate. You'll need a lot more sea time before you try again," said a smug Captain Moore.

"You're right captain. I need a lot of experience before I master any vessel. That's not what I wanted to speak to you about. What I wished to speak to you about sir was shipping aboard until Rye. I noticed that some of the cargo was destined for Rye. I would like to get off there and visit my family. Would you be willing to offer me the same deal as before sir?"

"You'd not be signing on full time then?" asked Captain Moore.

"Maybe at some later date, sir. I have been absent from home for some time. I was pressed without my family knowing. I would like to at least see them and let them know I'm alive before I sail off again. When I decide to sail off again, I will be attempting to get an officer's position. If that fails then I can always sign on as an able seaman."

"Who's going to sign a young lad like you as an officer?" asked Moore.

"I have no idea, captain. I'll just show them my master's certificate to prove I have some capability and see what is offered."

"You're joshing me. You really passed the examination?" squeaked out Captain Moore.

"Aye, sir."

"I don't believe it. The standard must have sure dropped," said Captain Moore, shaking his head.

Jon stood still. He was going to have to get used to this. Captain Moore would probably not be the last to make similar comments.

"Sir, about Rye?" asked Jon again.

"Yes, yes, you can work your way to Rye. Same deal as before," said Captain Moore before turning and withdrawing to his cabin.

"Thank you sir," said Jon to the mate before withdrawing below to the crew's quarters. At least he got no lip from his fellow crewmates.

After another day of loading and stowing cargo, the Lucy set sail down river. They went first to Sheerness where the river pilot disembarked. They headed out to Ramsgate, dropped off a small amount of cargo, and proceeded to Dover. The majority of the cargo was off-loaded at Dover. New cargo was acquired, but before they loaded, all the Rye-bound cargo had to be shifted in the hold. They needed an extra day to accomplish this.

Finally, the Lucy set sail for Rye. It was the last leg of a journey that had taken Jon further mentally, as well as physically, than he had ever expected. It had changed his expectations greatly.

How would all of this affect the relationship with his family?

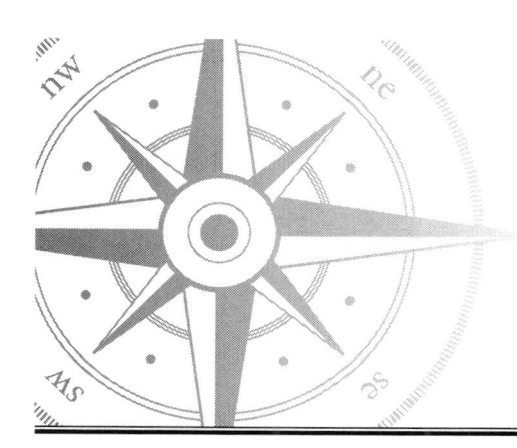

CHAPTER 40

The walk home was the longest journey that Jon had ever taken.

It started as the Lucy entered Rye harbour first thing in the morning. The Lucy had waited offshore as Captain Moore was not inclined to chance the harbour channel in the dark even with a pilot. A berthing space was generally always available at Rye, and this morning was no exception.

There was limited cargo to off load at Rye, so Jon had no reservations about leaving the ship prior to landing that cargo. By the time the Lucy had docked, Jon was ready to depart -- his kit was double checked and hauled to the entry port. Making his way to the quarterdeck, Jon made his manners with the mate and Captain Moore. He had said goodbye to each member of the crew the night before.

Without a rearward glance, Jon hoisted the sea chest on his shoulder, marched down the gangplank, and strode down the length of the wharf. The town had changed very little since he was last in Rye. That was over fifteen months ago. The open market area was nearly deserted. That was to be expected, as there were no crops to sell at this time of the year.

The Cross Bow tavern, which was the tavern where he had been pressed, was at the end of the market area. There were only a couple of people in the tavern at this time of the morning. The bartender was the same man that had been serving that infamous night. A young woman was present as well. There didn't appear to be any patrons. Given the time of the morning, that didn't come as a surprise.

Jon lowered his sea chest onto a table and dropped the ditty bag beside it. The bartender gave him a close examination as he approached.

"Mornin'," said Jon. "What's the chance of getting a pint?" Jon plunked down a shilling on the bar.

The bartender silently filled and slid a beer to Jon. He went to pick up the coin. Jon kept his hand over it.

"I got a twenty mile walk inland to see my family. I'd like to leave this sea chest here, until I can come back and fetch it. If you'll look after it, the entire shilling is yours," said Jon. The bartender nodded, but Jon didn't like the gleam in his eye.

Jon walked over to the sea chest and picked it up. He carried it over and set it on the bar. "Just so ye know, there's nothin' of value to you in it. Just sea books," said Jon. He opened the chest and showed the books to the bartender.

"When I return, if I find the chest gone or broken into, it's you that I'll come lookin' for, understand?"

To emphasize the point Jon quickly turned, drew the throwing knife and threw it across the room to land in the wood beside the door entrance. It was done without a second thought. It was sufficient to cow the bartender.

"Do we have an understanding?"

The bartender nodded, removing the padlocked sea chest from the bar and carrying it into a back room.

After draining his beer, Jon picked up his ditty bag, slung the strap over his shoulder and went to the door. Giving the bartender a long hard look, Jon extracted the throwing knife from the door mantle and returned it to its sheath inside his jacket.

With that, Jon headed out to the road toward home.

From the first step on that road out of Rye, Jon had difficulties determining what to say upon arriving home. What do you say to loved ones after being away for months? What do you say to them when you never even said goodbye? What do you say to your parents when you left a boy and return a man, physically, mentally and emotionally? What do you say when you left an innocent and return hardened and callous?

After twenty miles Jon was sore, both physically and mentally. Physically it was because of not walking that distance since being pressed. He had used different muscles in the navy. Although the leg muscles hurt, the feet, which were heavily calloused, were fine. That was probably because he had rarely worn shoes until becoming a master's mate.

Mentally it was a different story. After months of repressing any emotion, they were all coming to the surface. Just the thought of seeing his mother and father again caused his eyes to water. Despite having over twenty miles of walking to compose those initial words, so far none had come to mind that would suffice. No adequate words could possibly convey the wonders and situations he had experienced to his family.

Although it was cold, Jon was sweating. It was not only from the exertion of the walk. A short distance from the house he paused to gather his thoughts one last time. After thinking about it for a couple of minutes, he just shrugged his shoulders and walked on.

The farmyard appeared much the same as he last remembered; only the flowers had withered and died due to the season. There was smoke coming from the chimney. A warm feeling came over him.

Was it appropriate to stop and knock at the door, or just walk right in? His family had no idea he was coming. Considering the shock that might occur, he decided a more prudent approach was to knock.

A complete stranger answered the door.

"May I help you?" the stranger asked.

Jon was speechless for a few seconds. When he finally regained his voice, he said, "I was looking for the Swift family. I was led to believe that this was where they lived?"

"Not anymore," responded the stranger. The door slammed in his face.

The stranger's rudeness was both surprising and insulting. Folks in the area had always been hospitable, at least to the best of his recollection.

Still, this was the squire's property, which meant it could be rented to anyone. With a stranger occupying the property, Jon was at a momentary loss as to where to find the Swift family.

After thinking about it, Jon thought that someone at the local tavern would know. At the same time, a 'wet' would certainly be welcome after the walk.

Ten minutes later, he was standing in the tavern at the bar. There were no customers, even though it was approaching supper hour. The bartender was a stranger. Jon started to get an uneasy feeling about the place -- both the tavern and the parish.

"Pardon me. I was looking for the Swift family. Do you happen to know where I might find them?"

"And why would you be wantin' to see them?" asked the bartender.

Jon smiled at him. He was sorely tempted to punch the nosey bartender in the nose, but no good would come of it. This was the squire's territory. The last time the squire's men were upset, he had ended up pressed and nearly dead. It was more prudent to tread softly. Considering the number of new faces, either others hadn't or something else was going on.

Jon considered the response. If the folks weren't around somewhere, the bartender would have responded differently. Maybe the bartender provides information to the squire or squire's men.

The man was obviously a poor bartender. At this time of the season and this time of day there would normally have been some customers in here. The attitude displayed toward Jon would account for a lack of customers. The old timers that Jon remembered wouldn't put up with this kind of arrogance.

Rather than gaining a response, the bartender got Jon's back, followed by a closing door. Pausing at the entrance, a decision was needed as to who else might know the whereabouts of the Swift family. Jon snapped his fingers -- the pastor. The old pastor, Pastor Evans, knew everyone. The church and residence were only a few hundred yards away, so within a couple of minutes Jon was knocking on another door.

The door of the residence opened. "How may I help you my son?" asked the pastor.

The tall weedy individual that asked the question was a poorly dressed specimen of a man of the cloth. Jon got an immediate bad vibration from the man. It was possible it was from the man himself, or it was possibly because nothing had gone right since entering the squire's realm.

"Pastor, I'm a stranger to these parts. I was attempting to find the Swift family. Would you happen to know where I might find them?"

"The Swift family? They are now on a small farm over to the west of here about five miles. As desolate looking a farm as I have seen hereabout," said the pastor. His honest open answer surprised Jon. Perhaps he had been hasty in his judgment.

"I don't know the area, pastor. Can you give me directions?"

"Follow the road past the squire's residence for about five miles. I think someone said it used to be the old Cartwright place," stated the pastor. The pastor was inquisitive, and not willing to let things go. "And who might you be, to be so interested in the Swifts?"

That was the second time strangers had inquired about his business with the Swift family. There was something definitely wrong here.

"Thanks pastor, I appreciate your help." Jon refused to be drawn in to any discussion with strangers at this point, until he knew what was happening.

As Jon trudged along the road, the winter night descended. Quickening the pace to offset the cold penetrating his clothes, he heard horses cantering down the road towards him. Previously, only the squire had horses in this area, so it was probable these were likely the squire's men. Not trusting any of the squire's men, he quickly jumped to the side of the road and stayed out of sight. The horses went past, but in the darkness it was impossible to identify any of the four riders.

Either the directions provided by the pastor were wrong, or the pastor had never walked the distance. Jon estimated he had walked closer to eight miles than five. Adding to this discomfort was hunger. The last food consumed had been a piece of bread prior to departing the Lucy several hours before.

Some form of building was off to the right of the road. It was a single story and had a derelict look about it. There was no dog, nor livestock, present or they would have made some noise as Jon was passing. Jon paused, then backtracked, to give this place a look.

Even in the dark, the place was depressing. A shed to the side of the main building had collapsed. Its roof crossbeam had broken in the middle with roughly equal parts of roof meeting on the ground in the centre of the shed. This had not occurred recently. It implied that whoever owned or lived on the property either didn't care or was incapable of fixing it.

The main house tilted from the front to the back. While the front looked somewhat acceptable, the back was a different story. It was a wonder the building hadn't been condemned -- or possibly it had been. It apparently was still occupied however, as a low light was shining from a window near the side door.

Before disturbing the occupants, Jon decided to peek in the windows. By taking a position to the side of the window, it was possible to glance inside without frightening anyone inside. There was an old woman sitting with her back to him in a rocking chair by the fire. She appeared to be sewing. There might have been movement elsewhere in the room, but the windows were so distorted and misted that it was impossible to identify anything.

Someone inside spoke, and the old woman turned around to reply. Jon's jaw dropped. It was his mother. Time stood still. His mother had turned into an old woman.

Jon had no idea how long he stood there. He was numb -- whether it was from the cold or the shock of seeing his mother -- he was not sure. Finally stepping away from the window, he steeled himself, as the next few minutes were going to be harder than he had ever imagined.

Responding to Jon's knock at the door, a young man of nine and a half opened the door. Robbie didn't recognize the tall muscular man at the door. Robbie had grown so much, that Jon almost didn't recognize him.

Jon stepped forward into the room and pushed the door closed behind him to keep the heat in.

"Hey, wait a minute! You can't come in here. Get out!" shouted Robbie.

The entire household exploded in pandemonium. Mother Swift launched herself off the chair and charged forward to defend her son and household. Susan's head came popping out from the loft to see what was happening. Only his father was missing. Jon took in all of this, in a mere second, just as if he was in a boarding action.

"Hello mother," said Jon quietly. Rather than charging into him, Mother Swift staggered and fell into his arms.

Jon easily caught her and stood her on her feet. Her arms wrapped around him as his wrapped around her. Robbie stood dumbfounded. He had not even recognized his own brother. Susan came screaming down from the loft and joined the hug; then Robbie reluctantly joined in.

After some minutes, things calmed down. Mother Swift was openly crying. Jon walked her back over to the rocking chair and sat her down.

"Now mother, tell me the news. After I hear what has happened here, I will tell you my story."

"It started the day after you failed to come home," started Mother Swift. "Your father went looking for you. He walked all the way to Rye. He found Malcolm Cartwright dead and retrieved Malcolm's horse and wagon. According to the bartender at the tavern, the press from the navy appeared the night before. Several men were dragged away. Your father figured you were one of them. He brought Malcolm's body, horse and cart back home and helped bury him. The Cartwrights were forced off the property. They couldn't pay the rent without Malcolm, you see. We missed the money that you should have brought back home. Since there was one less mouth to feed, we had enough to pay the rent and look after us until this year's harvest. We missed having as much meat in the pot though." Mother Swift smiled at that.

"This year started well. We got the planting in. Robbie worked hard, and Susan helped in the fields. There was no school, as Pastor Evans left. The squire brought in this new pastor. Nobody likes him much. He preaches the squire's sermons and doesn't help the way Pastor Evans used to. The money in the squire just seemed to run out. Murphy sold the tavern, mainly to get his daughter away from the squire's men. Virtually no one goes to the tavern anymore. This new owner is detested," continued Mother Swift.

"Things went reasonably well until after the harvest. The harvest was good. The squire increased the rents. Most of the people didn't have enough to pay the rent. Many of our friends and neighbours were forced off the land they had worked for years. We had enough thanks to your father. He borrowed a cart and took our produce to Rye. He got a good price for the produce, so we used that money to pay off our debts at the store. He decided to take some additional produce to Rye again. This time, he was robbed on the way back. He was hit hard. He's lying in the back room. Jon he's not the same man. They did something to his head."

"When your father was lying broken, the squire's men came and forced us out of our place. They said we hadn't paid the rent, but we had. There was no way we could prove it though. We were forcibly moved into this hovel. The next thing I know is that one of the squire's men is hanging around Susan."

"Have you approached the squire?"

"No one has seen the squire for a year. According to the people at the big house, he's bedridden," replied Mother Swift.

"In other words, his henchmen are running things, and making sure of their own profit. By what I've seen on my way here tonight and from what you've been telling me, it looks like they're draining this place dry. I haven't seen one familiar face. I wonder what will happen once they ruin things here for everyone and the money runs out?" said a dejected Jon. "I guess I better see father."

"Brace yourself," said Mother Swift. "He's not the man that you remember."

Susan led Jon back to a small room at the back of the house carrying a small candle. It was cold in the room, but considering the number of blankets on the bed, Jon reasoned his father was likely warm enough. His father was asleep. His hair had been black. Now it was a salt and pepper colour. His father's face was grey in the low light and showed many more lines and wrinkles than Jon remembered. Not knowing what to do, he sat on a stool and watched his father for a few minutes. Memories flooded his mind. Father had been a strong, hard-working man with excellent farming knowledge. He was considered one of the best farmers in the parish. To see him in this condition was a major blow.

The chill of the room became noticeable, so a strategic retreat back out to the main room occurred. Robbie and Susan had retired up into the loft. Mother had found a blanket and left it on the table.

"Mother, I need to get some sleep. I'll talk to you in the morning. I need to think some things over."

Jon cleared a place to sleep near the fireplace. After all the walking he had done that day, falling asleep was not a problem.

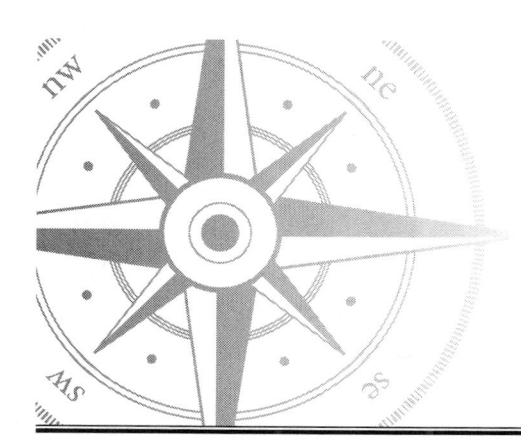

CHAPTER 41

Jon awoke the next morning in a strange place.

It was the first time Jon had slept on land in some time. It was also the first time sleeping on the ground since Louisbourg; most of the time sleep had been in a hammock. The result was stiff and sore muscles. Compounding the problem was the stiffness in leg and back muscles heavily exercised in the journey home the previous day.

Jon remembered many worse days, such as waking many mornings after boarding drill practice with the cutlass. Lieutenant Rylett had continually used Jon's body like a boxer uses a punching bag. The result was numerous colourful and painful bruises on virtually all parts of body except the face. Just as he couldn't show pain then, he needed to be strong now and show no weakness in front of the family. Now, more than ever, the family needed to see strength.

Like any young adult, Jon was hungry in the morning. The lack of food the previous day only exacerbated this hunger. After a year of eating ship's biscuit for breakfast, it was only natural to conduct a search for something that would substitute for 'bread'. Regardless of where he searched, little food could be found.

Mother Swift came back inside from the well with a bucket of water. She was in the process of cleaning Jon's father.

"Mother, where's all the food?"

"Look to the left of the fireplace," replied Mother Swift.

Jon searched to the left of the fireplace. He found a few apples, a sack of flour, some salt, cabbage, beets, carrots, and turnips. There was not enough to feed the family for more than a few days.

"Where is all the rest of the food?"

"That's all that's left," replied his mother. "We had enough for the entire year in the root cellar at the old place; but when we were evicted, we lost it all."

"What do you mean, lost it?"

"When they forced us out of the place, it was left for the new tenant. We argued about that, but they just ignored us," said Mother Swift, with a sad empty tone.

"That's not right."

"Not much we can do about it," said his mother. "What's done is done."

It was obvious to Jon that the Swift family was in worse shape than it had initially appeared. They needed more food if they were to survive. Jon knew this farm somewhat from the old days. It was a marginal prospect for producing enough income to support the family. Even if they were fortunate enough to survive, there was no guarantee that the squire's men would not re-appear and evict them again. It was obvious that living in this jurisdiction was foolish. Everything appeared to be stacked against them.

It was fortunate he had returned at this time before things had gotten any worse for the family. Being in a position to help would make all the difference. In fact, he was in a much greater position to help than if he had never left. The family just didn't know it.

As his mother shuffled off into the back room to tend to his father, Jon decided to speak to his sister Susan to find out more about what was happening. She had just appeared from the loft.

"Morning, Susan," said Jon. "I didn't get much of a chance to speak with you last night. Might we talk now?"

"Sure," replied Susan.

"What's been happening in your life since I've been gone? Why don't you start from the time I disappeared?"

"We were all shocked when you disappeared. Father went to Rye and returned with Mr. Cartwright's body. He told us that you had likely been taken by the press. Nothing much happened until the winter. After Christmas the pastor left," said Susan. "That finished any schooling for Robbie and me. It wasn't that great, but it was something at least. Other than that, things were alright until October when father was attacked. Since then things have gotten worse and worse."

"How so?"

"First there was father to care for. Father was always so strong. He always knew what to do. Since they brought him home, he has hardly moved from the bed. Mother has to wash him and clean up his messes. All that was bad enough, but then in November the squire's men came and evicted us from the farm," said Susan.

"I'd like to hear more about that."

"The day they came, it was early on a Thursday morning I think. There was this pounding on the door. Mother answered. Macmillan barged in. He said that we were evicted and had to be out by the end of the day," started Susan. "Mother objected. Macmillan waved this paper he said was signed by the squire. It was an eviction notice. They said we hadn't paid our rent. Since father was the only one that ever handled the rent and he couldn't speak, none of us could say for sure whether father had paid the rent or not. So out we went."

"I believe mother mentioned that they helped you move. If I remember correctly, they even provided men, a horse, and cart to move. They even moved you into this place. Is that right?"

"That's right," replied Susan.

"Before I left, there were a number of evictions. I never heard of the squire's men helping the people move. Usually, they were nowhere to be found. Everyone around was aware that the people were being evicted. In fact, just about everyone had known about it for a few days. This was the first I ever heard of an eviction without notice, and the squire's men helping. There is something else strange about it. If you had failed to pay the rent and that was the reason for the eviction, why would they move the family to another of the squire's properties? If you couldn't pay the rent on the first place, which had better land, how would you pay the rent on this property with its poorer land? Something just doesn't make sense."

Susan just shrugged her shoulders.

"Did anything else happen around that time?"

"Isn't that enough?" spat out Susan.

"Who were the men that came with Macmillan?"

"His regular cronies -- Abercrombie, Fitzgerald and Wells. Who else would do his dirty work for him?" said Susan disgustedly.

"Who is this Wells?"

"His name is Wells, but I call him weasel," said Susan. "He looks like a weasel, and acts like one as well. I guess he wasn't here when you left. He arrived sometime in the winter. He's no better than the other three."

Jon thought about the four riders who had passed him the night before. It had been wise to stay out of sight since he suspected they were the squire's men. Now that he knew about Wells, it confirmed his suspicions. The fourth rider had likely been Wells.

"Why do you say that he's no better than the rest of them?"

"He was one of the men that evicted us. That was bad enough, but ever since then he has been hanging around. He gives me the creeps," said Susan.

"How so?"

"He keeps trying to sweet talk me. Every time I'm alone he comes up to me and says something suggestive. I hate it," said Susan. Her tone and body language confused Jon. There was some degree of bitterness, but also a bit of revulsion mixed in.

"Has he done this recently?" asked Jon. This was something different, and perhaps more sinister.

"Only last week he was here," said Susan.

"How old is he? Do you know anything about him?"

"Why would I want to?" shot back Susan.

"Know your enemy. How can you counter his actions if you know nothing about how he will act in a given situation? Tell me everything you know about him."

"Well it's only since father was injured that I even saw him. I knew he was around sometime before that, but never around here. I heard some talk. He was after Pamela, you know the tavern keeper's daughter. They say that was one of the reasons that he sold and left - because of Pamela."

"Anyway, after father was injured, he started to show up wherever I was. If I walked into the hamlet, I was sure to bump into him on my way home. He was always forward -- arrogant actually," said Susan. "It got so that I never walked back home the same way I went into the hamlet. I had to cut across the fields. I never ventured far at night, just in case."

"You have described how he made you feel. You still haven't described the man." Jon was patiently attempting to extract useful information and so far he wasn't getting any.

Susan stuck her tongue out at Jon, just to show him her irritation with having to talk about a subject she'd rather forget.

"He's in his mid twenties, fairly good looking, and he can be charming at times. There is just this arrogant 'I'm better than you are' attitude that comes out all the time. He has a temper as well. I've seen him whip his horse when the poor thing shied. I don't know. It's just this 'I'm God's gift to women' approach he always seems to take around me that infuriates me," said Susan.

"There has to be more than that. You avoid him. You go so far as to cut across the fields to avoid him. There has to be more behind it."

"He's tried to kiss me," said Susan. Her face had turned beet-red as she discussed this.

"How far has he tried to go?"

"He has pawed me more than once," said Susan. "The last time I slapped him. That stopped him somewhat, but he was smiling afterwards."

"It sounds like he wants to have you. We can probably use that against him, but at this point I'm not sure how."

"I would rather die first," said Susan.

"I'll make sure that doesn't happen. You had better get on with your chores before mother gets upset."

After chasing Susan away to complete her chores, Jon just sat there considering things. He didn't realize how long he was sitting there, until his mother nudged him.

"You going to sit around all day, or are you going to help out around here?" asked Mother Swift.

"What do you need done?"

"We're low on wood. Find a dead tree, and chop it up for firewood. You'll find an axe around somewhere. Ask Robbie where it is," said his mother.

"Aye, aye, sir," said Jon mischievously, as he got up and headed toward the door.

The simple reply caught his mother's attention. She realized at that moment that her son was no longer innocent. He had not said one word about his absence. From his speech and clothes, he had been in a different world, one that she could not possibly imagine. As Jon closed the door behind him, Mother Swift sat down and thanked the Lord for her son's safe return.

As he was looking for the axe, Jon pondered the situation. The Swift family were hard pressed. Most of the food they had stored to feed them for the winter was gone. It was still likely in the root cellar at the old farm. They simply didn't have enough food to survive, especially now that there was an additional mouth to feed. The farm at which they currently resided had never produced crops as well as the farm from which they had been evicted. With his father unable to work, it was unlikely they could survive. They would be evicted from this farm later this year for failing to pay the rent, if they survived that long.

Things were about as bad as he had ever seen them. Without him, the Swift family had no hope at all.

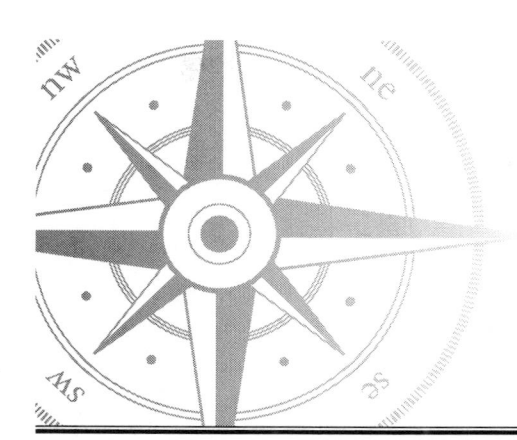

CHAPTER 42

The farm had been depressing in the dark. In the light it was much worse.

As Jon searched for the axe, he took a good look around. The collapsed shed in the back had been built for farm animals, but Jon guessed it hadn't housed any in a quarter of a century. It was doubtful that it had been used for anything else since it last held animals.

The farmhouse appeared to lean to the east. When it was built, it was probably a nice cottage. It was anything but at the present. The room at the rear where his father lay had been an add-on at some point. After years of no maintenance, the addition now looked like a hutch placed against the larger wall of the house to hide a problem and possibly to keep the wall from collapsing. The thatched roof showed signs of wear, and probably leaked.

Even the large vegetable garden, which was a fixture in every rural tenant farm, was a disappointment. At this time of the year, it should have been fallow and ready for planting next spring. It was overrun with weeds and other long since dead plants.

If the place had been his, he would be tempted to raze it to the ground and start again.

The weather matched his mood. It was overcast and threatening rain, or perhaps snow. Normally at this time of year the temperature hovered just above the freezing point. Overnight it had dropped and even the grass was frozen crisp. With little insulation in the walls, it was no wonder the house had been cold.

Jon finally located the axe. It was dull -- good for splitting wood, but not for cutting. He couldn't even find a whetstone to sharpen it.

Dejected, Jon set forth to the fields at the back of the property, accompanied by Robbie, to collect enough wood to keep them warm for the next few days. Even as he walked, the state of the farm continued to capture his attention. Fields had not been ploughed. Dead weeds were waist high in pasture fields. Why there were pasture fields when there were no animals on the place, was beyond comprehension. Even the fences, if they could be called fences, were nonexistent in places.

The good news was that there was plenty of dead wood. Jon and Robbie worked the remainder of the day felling a tree and chopping wood. Jon did all the chopping and sawing while Robbie carried armfuls of wood back to the house. Even Susan came out and helped carry wood.

While chopping, he considered ways to improve the Swift family's position. Legal action was out of the question. The squire was the court. The previous tenant on this farm had been Archie Cartwright. Jon had watched as the squire's men ambushed him poaching on the squire's property. They had shot him in the legs even though he was unarmed. If that weren't enough punishment, Cartwright had then been hauled into court. The squire sentenced him to ten years hard labour. Any action against the squire would result in the squire's sights focusing squarely on the Swift family. The consequences would be as harsh for the Swifts as they had been for Archie Cartwright's family.

That only left action of an illegal nature or leaving the squire's jurisdiction. His mother and father had been brought up in this area and had never travelled more than fifty miles away. Moving them to another place would be very hard on them. Even if that happened, without father being able to work and provide for them, they would be no further ahead.

Father's council would be welcomed, but according to mother, father couldn't speak, and it was unknown if he had full use of his faculties. Just the same, once he returned to the cottage, he would see father.

Despite the cold December wind, both Jon and Robbie worked up a sweat felling trees. By nightfall, three trees had been dropped. All the branches were trimmed off the trunks, but only a large saw would suffice for sawing the trunks. It would take another day or so to haul all the rest of the wood back to the house, but Robbie and Susan could do that.

Jon and Robbie washed up outside, and came into the house. There was a nice fire burning in the fireplace, which cast a toasty warm heat across the room. A frugal supper was laid out on the table. After working in the cold all day, the heat combined with the alleviation of hunger invited drowsiness. Robbie dropped off within minutes of finishing his meal. Jon was equally tired, but needed to see father.

As mother finished cleaning up after supper, Jon initiated a discussion.

"Mother, do you know why the family was evicted from the other farm?"

"No, it was only after your father was injured. It happened in early November. The squire's men just appeared at the door one morning and said we were evicted. They came right in and started loading some of our furniture on a cart and moved us that morning," explained his mother.

"Do you know if father paid the rent?"

"He told me that we were all looked after until the next year. That was before he took that second trip to Rye."

"What happened on that second trip?"

"I don't know for sure," said his mother. "Joe left early in the morning. Sometime after dark, some men -- Abe Hartwell and William Bushell -- you know them, came in with Joe. They had found Joe lying in the road near William's place. Joe had borrowed the horse and cart, so they took that back while I nursed Joe."

"He nearly died that night and a couple of times afterwards. Only by the grace of the Lord has he survived this long. When he finally came to he wasn't able to speak. His mind appears to be gone," sobbed Mother Swift. "Come on back. He was awake the last time I looked in on him."

Jon entered the cold small room to find his father propped up in bed. Jon picked up a stool and sat down beside the bed. He took his father's hand. Mother Swift set the candle down and left them alone.

"I'm back father. How are you doing?" asked Jon. He struggled to keep his voice even, but it wasn't easy. This man had been a tower of strength as Jon had grown up. To see him in such a condition hit Jon hard. There was no vocal response, but Jon felt a squeeze on his hand. Jon intuitively grasped the situation. His father's mind was working, but his motor skills, especially his voice, had been injured. Jon had seen similar cases in men on board ship after being struck in the head, but never as severe as this.

"Father, I know that your mind is working, just that you can't speak right now. I'm going to ask you some questions. Squeeze my hand once for yes and twice for no, alright?" said Jon. He felt a single squeeze.

"Do you know who it was that attacked and robbed you?" Jon received a single squeeze. "I thought so."

"Was it the squire's men?" A single squeeze occurred.

"Abercrombie?" A single squeeze occurred.

"Fitzgerald?" A single squeeze occurred.

"Macmillan?" Two squeezes occurred.

"This new man, Wells?" A single squeeze occurred.

"Any others?" Two squeezes occurred.

"You went to Rye to sell produce. How many pounds did you have when you were robbed?" asked Jon. He received eight squeezes in reply.

"Do you know why the family was evicted from the other farm?" He received three squeezes.

"I'm guessing that you're not sure, but you have suspicions?" One squeeze occurred.

"I'm thinking that these bastards are robbing the squire blind. I heard that he's bedridden and probably doesn't even know what's going on," murmured Jon. His father squeezed his hand once.

"When you went to Rye the first time, you came back and paid all your bills, like you normally do, right?" Again, he felt a single squeeze.

"You paid the rent, didn't you?" One squeeze occurred.

"They probably heard about your trip to Rye, and started watching you. So when you went the second time, they were prepared." His father attempted to nod, but was too weak. Instead, he squeezed Jon's hand.

"After they left you for dead on the road, they probably lined up some other tenant for the farm. Bad for them -- you didn't die. They still had to look after this new tenant. The good part for them was you couldn't speak; therefore, you couldn't make any waves with the squire," mused Jon. "I wonder if they stole your rent money, giving them justification for the eviction?" His father squeezed Jon's hand as hard as he could.

"You think so too?"

"I think we now know what we're dealing with. The question is how will we beat them?" asked Jon. "Any ideas, father?" Two squeezes occurred.

"Me neither, just yet."

"I'm going to leave you now father. I need some time to think things out. You concentrate on getting better."

The information his father passed on to him confirmed many of the things that Jon had deduced. The squire's men controlled the parish and were sucking it dry. The Swifts were just one of the victims. They had little left to cough up. Susan was perhaps the last asset of interest to them, or at least to one of them.

The family's situation was bad and needed immediate action. The first step had been today. They now had wood for heating. Tonight would be a second step. Jon would seek out some meat for the pot.

Since he was used to sleeping on a watch system, Jon rose after four hours, grabbed his father's old coat and headed out. He set some traps at the back of the farm and headed over to the squire's adjoining property. It was a good night. He took four rabbits. He gutted them, but didn't skin them. He buried the evidence, did some more scouting and headed home.

His skills were a little rusty. If he had to pit them against the squire's men, he would have to sharpen them.

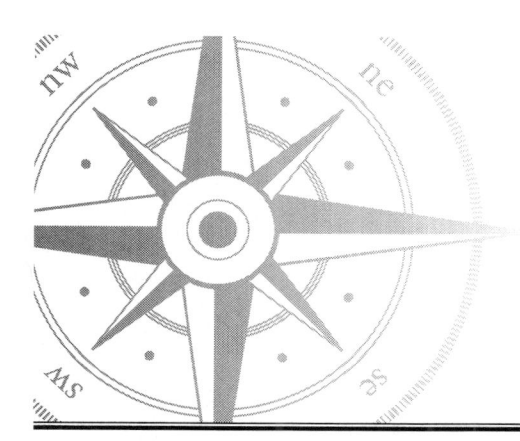

CHAPTER 43

Winter was generally a time when people hunker down and stay close to the fire.

In the Swift cottage, if the fire were to continue, they needed lots more wood. Hunkering down wasn't an option. Both Jon and Robbie chopped and carried wood back to the house all morning. Just after noon, rounding the back corner of the house with an armload of wood, Jon spotted a horse standing in the yard with reins dragging on the ground. Agitated voices could be heard from inside.

Susan was speaking. The words could not be heard properly, but the tone was defiant. Jon clearly heard Mother Swift saying, "Please leave!"

Jon quietly, carefully lowered the wood and backed around the corner of the house to remain out of sight. As the door opened, a man with a sly grin on his face exited. He was chuckling as he walked to his horse, mounted and cantered off. Jon waited until the rider was far down the road before venturing forth into the house.

"What was that all about?"

"That weasel Wells was just here. He was making advances toward Susan," replied his mother. Jon looked at his mother as she spoke and shifted his gaze to Susan.

"From what I overheard, you didn't seem too appreciative of his advances," said Jon. "What I don't understand was why he was chuckling and smiling when he left?"

"Because he thinks he can woo me for a cheap meal," spat Susan.

Jon looked closely at the visible interior of the house. The kitchen was readily visible. It was obvious to anyone looking that the larder was bare. A good meal would be welcome in Wells' opinion. It was likely he thought it was just a matter of time before Susan succumbed to his advances.

A seed had just been planted in Jon's mind.

There was still work to do, so Jon continued with the physical aspect of it. Mentally he was contemplating his current situation, and that of the family.

Jon was missing a plan. There was no clear insight on how to extract the family from their current predicament. Any starting point was not obvious. To exacerbate the situation further, even the direction to take was obscure. It was enough to drive a person around the bend.

Jon decided to focus on immediate problems. Food for the Swift family would run out in another week. It was winter so they needed more wood to heat the cottage and cook food. Without good food and appropriate heat, any potential recovery father might make would be delayed or completely lost. If father didn't recover, then everything would change for the family. To survive they needed income, and father had been the source of family income.

Jon had sufficient funds to ensure the family's survival, but was very reluctant to use those funds. Any money spent obtaining food now would be forfeited; then in a year or so, they could be in the same position as they were now. If the Swift family purchased food, especially in this parish, the squire's men would know about it in short order. They would come investigating. What would happen after that was unknown.

Despite several attempts to forget how the family came to be in their present predicament and to concentrate on how to get out of it, he continually found his thoughts drifting to the squire's men. He blamed them for everything. His thoughts took a turn for the worse as he contemplated revenge. Thankfully, logic prevailed. Revenge would not resolve the Swifts' current problems.

With difficulty, Jon focused all thought towards resolving the food shortfall. The Swifts' had had enough food for the year prior to their eviction from the previous farm. If they were able to recover that food, their most immediate problem would be solved. That food left behind was rightfully theirs, but a means to obtain it needed to be determined.

The current tenant wasn't going to give up the food or anything else that was left behind without a fight. That would bring in the squire's men. There was also the problem of transporting the food. That problem could be resolved with the aid of neighbours.

Having a full larder would give them peace of mind. It would also put paid to that weasel Wells' attempts to get to Susan with the offer of a meal.

Wells .... Susan ... meal ... food ... Hummmm?

A seed of a thought in the back of his mind started to blossom; however, it must be thought through.

The squire's men controlled the parish. To attempt anything in the parish without them knowing would be challenging. Why not let them know? Why not involve them? It would then be legal and not cause any backlash. Get the squire's men to deliver the food. There would be no fight from the tenant, and they could deliver it.

Jon started to think about the scenario. Wells would return to make the same offer to Susan. The more food consumed between now and then, the more desperate Susan would become. At least that would likely be Wells' thinking. A hungry Susan could be easily persuaded to leave the protection of the family.

What would happen then?

Wells might feed her, or he just might force himself on her without providing any meal. Jon's impression was the weasel would be so cheap as to forgo any meal.

Wells would not like anyone around when any attempt to ravish Susan occurred -- hence he would be alone. It would be important to impart his dominance, or station in life, on Susan. Riding a horse to fetch her would convey that position, and allow him to move her some distance away compared to walking. Susan would sit on the horse behind him. It would be necessary to ride with her arms around him increasing Wells' boldness. Because of what he was planning to do to her, he wouldn't likely have any weapons. If Susan got hold of them, her resistance would increase and he might incur some injury. Reliance on his physical strength to overcome Susan would be enough. Concentrating on Susan and his impeding attack on her, it was unlikely Wells' mind would be focused on the immediate surroundings. He would be open for attack.

Jon considered the implications of attacking Wells as he completed chores that afternoon. By supper he had decided upon a plan, but to implement that plan he was going to need some help.

"Susan, could I talk to you alone?" Jon did not want the others to overhear their discussion, so they stepped outside.

"Susan, do you know what will happen if Wells gets his hands on you alone?" asked Jon. This was something that was not discussed, and certainly not with your brother. Susan was therefore very hesitant to speak.

"I'll tell you what will happen," said Jon after a few moments of silence. "First he will remove your clothes. If you resist, he will beat you and rip them off. Once you are naked, he will fondle you, and force himself into you. He is stronger than you, even though you will have the strength of desperation. You will be hurt; you will be shamed. He will laugh at you. After he is finished, he will have two options. He might kill you. I doubt that will happen. He will likely just leave you lying there, pull up his pants, laugh, hop on his horse and ride off. You might become with child as a result. Being the type of man that Wells is, he will boast of his exploits to one and all. You will have no reputation left. No other man will want you for a wife. On the contrary, lots of men will think you are easy and try to take you the same as Wells did. It won't matter what you think of men, the result will be the same. Do you understand all of this?"

Susan looked at her brother. First, she was shocked at what he had said; then as she started to understand the seriousness, she bowed her head in resignation.

"So what am I to do?" she whimpered.

"Do you know that Wells was one of the men that attacked father and left him to die on that road?" Susan's head snapped up.

"No one knows who did that," she said.

"Father does. He recognized him. He let me know." Susan just stared at him with her mouth slight agape.

"Do you realize what this Wells is doing to our family? First he robbed father of money this family desperately needed. Second, he clubbed father and left him for dead. Then he was one of the men who illegally threw us off our old farm, stealing our food for the winter in the process. Now he is intent on spoiling you. After he accomplishes this, without food, the family will starve. Without hope of growing enough crops this summer on this miserable farm, we will be evicted. With no shelter, no food, and no way of gaining sufficient income we won't survive. Wells is attempting to kill all of us. Do you understand this?" Jon had taken Susan by the arms and was shaking her lightly.

Susan looked searchingly into Jon's eyes. She saw he was serious. She just nodded her acceptance of what Jon said.

"We can prevent any more damage from happening, but you are going to have to do something that you will not like. You are going to have to do it convincingly, and you can never breathe a word to anyone ever. Are you willing to do this?"

"What do you want me to do?" asked Susan. The timbre of her voice was low and sounded defeated.

"Wells is likely to show up in a day or two, to again make the offer of a nice meal."

"Tell me something that I didn't know!" shot back Susan. Jon smiled. He liked his sister's spirit.

"So when he comes, take him outside so the others can't hear you speak. Tell him that if he wants your affections, it's going to take more than a cheap meal. Tell him that you want all the food that should have rightly been brought over from the old farm. Tell him that everything that was not brought over needs to be brought over. When all that food is delivered here and placed in our cold room, then you will accompany him for a meal. You will have to make this very convincing. I know you have it in you."

"So what happens then?" asked a surprised Susan.

"Susan, you're turning into a good looking woman. If you like someone, you have a sweet disposition. When you are attempting to get something out of mother or father, you have a face of an angel. When you bat those brown eyes of yours, you can always get a reaction. Wells will be powerless against you. If you make the food a condition that must be met, Wells will move heaven and earth to meet them. Once the food is delivered here, you set the meeting for dinner, and the conquest he thinks is coming. Set it for a Saturday evening."

"Why a Saturday night?" asked Susan.

"If he asks, tell him it will be easier for you to slip away. The real reason is that a man like Wells will more than likely spend part of Saturday afternoon in the tavern telling all that will listen of his upcoming conquest of the evening. He will have a few drinks in preparation for this; then he will ride out here and fetch you. It would be preferable if you tell him to meet you at a rendezvous away from the house so that Mother or Robbie won't know what is going on. Mother will probably suspect, but they can't know anything about this, do you understand?"

"Yes, I can do this, but what happens when Wells comes to get me?" asked Susan.

"I'll be there. You won't. That's all you need to know."

Wells was going to have an accident.

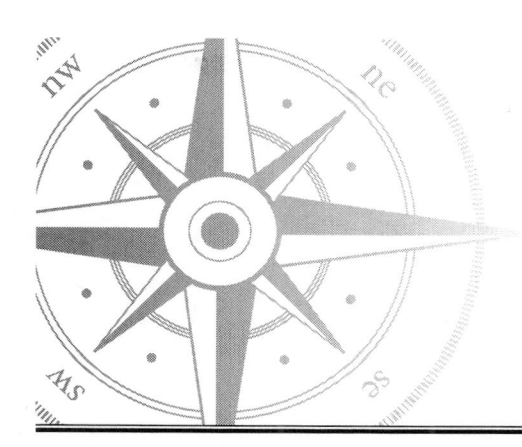

CHAPTER 44

How does one plan an accident?

By its very nature, an accident is something that should not have happened, but for some reason has. In the navy, Jon had learned that accidents rarely happen. There is almost always a reason for an accident, and in the case of the navy a search for the guilty -- the man who caused the accident. When Beck had fallen from the tops, it was not really an accident, although it seemed to be an accident. Beck had failed to ensure a grip with one of his two hands. He lost his balance and fell. He was the reason for the accident. In the search for the guilty, Jon had been targeted by both his superiors and, to some extent, by his subordinates.

If Wells' accident were to be seen as an accident, it would have to look like an accident and be believed to be an accident by his superiors, the squire's men, and all others in the community. If there were any inkling of murder, the squire's men would rip this community apart seeking the guilty. If the true guilty party were not found, the squire's men would finger someone for the deed. That unfortunate individual would be whisked through the courts. The squire's men ran the courts.

Not only did it have to look like an accident, there had to be no risk to Jon. What he needed was complete surprise in a setting that allowed no time for a fight, no opportunity for Wells to run or to defend himself.

To meet these conditions, Wells would have to be alone, with his guard down. Preferably, it would be dark, as recognition of danger would be harder, and fewer people were likely to be about. If possible Wells should be unarmed, as he would be taken more easily and thereby limit the possibility of injury to Jon. If possible, Wells should be on foot.

Jon recalled all the tactics he had acquired during boarding drill practice and in discussions with shipmates. Surprise counted heavily. Keeping your opponent off-guard, continuing to attack, so the other party couldn't attack you was important. Switching your tactics to keep your opponent guessing helped as well. Jon had sparred with numerous opponents bigger and stronger than he was. In each case, he was able to use the strengths of these individuals against themselves. He wondered how he could use Wells' strengths against him in this situation.

Wells biggest strength was his horse, and this was Jon's biggest concern. A man on foot is at a severe disadvantage when fighting a man on a horse. If he managed to unseat Wells and the horse broke away, there could be problems. No matter how long he pondered, no solution to this problem presented itself.

On a frosty Tuesday morning, Wells cantered into the farmyard. Everyone heard the horse. Jon ducked into the back room. Susan went to the door anticipating the knock. Wells' quickly stepped in. His eyes went to the kitchen where the lack of food was evident. He smiled as he greeted everyone in the house.

"Perhaps we should talk outside," suggested Susan.

A surprised Wells sucked in a lungful of air, turned and exited. Susan grabbed her father's jacket from the wall beside the door and followed him. Closing the door behind her, she took Wells' arm and steered him further from the house. When sufficiently far from the cottage to ensure their conversation couldn't be overheard, Susan let go of Wells' arm. He turned and looked at her expectantly. She said nothing.

"Susan, I came to ask you out for a nice supper," said Wells. His smirk could be readily seen from the window.

"It would appear that you want more than my presence for a meal Mr. Wells. I would venture that you are also seeking my affections," said Susan coyly. She batted her eyes and smiled at Wells. Wells' smirk turned into a smile, a smile that appeared genuine.

"Susan, a man who caught your affections would be fortunate indeed," replied Wells.

"I believe that I could be a very caring person toward anyone who caught my affections," said Susan as she batted her eyes. She was blatantly using every female trick she could think of to capture Wells. So far as she could tell as she watched Wells, it appeared to be working.

"Your affections toward me would be amply rewarded," stuttered Wells. To Susan it looked as if he was hooked. He now had to be reeled in and landed.

"I knew that I could count on your chivalry," cooed Susan. "Before you wine me and dine me; however, I would ask for a token of your affection to me. A woman couldn't be as affectionate to you as you would desire if she were in a constant state of hunger. A gentleman like you would provide for his lady -- say by delivering all of the food and contents that were left behind at our old farm. Once these items were delivered, then we could set the night for our enjoyable dining event."

Wells was momentarily taken back. Instead of a meal, Susan was asking for all the food and other items from the old farm delivered here. The trade-off she was offering was that she would be a willing companion afterward. He weighted the challenges in his mind. He could just take the food -- it wasn't the current tenant's property anyway. It was rightly the Swifts' food. There was an added upside. With Susan being a willing partner, he would avoid any possible legal troubles. There was also a possibility he could have her thereafter, any time he wanted without any repercussions.

It took a few seconds for Wells to make a decision.

"I believe that would be a small price for your affections," said Wells.

"Why thank you ever so much, Mr. Wells," said Susan coyly. She stepped forward and lightly ran her hand across Wells' face to leave Wells with the prospect of more to come. She turned and went back into the house.

Wells was truly besotted. He could see that his campaign of conquest was successful. There were only a few minor details to overcome, and he would be in carnal bliss. He quickly mounted and cantered off.

Jon had watched the entire display from the kitchen window. Watching the body language it was apparent Susan had been successful well before she re-entered the house.

Mother Swift was suspicious. She didn't like the way Susan had been acting, nor having her out of earshot when dealing with a snake like Wells. She accosted Susan the instant she closed the door. Susan looked at Jon, who put his finger to his lips to indicate she should say nothing.

"Mother it is nothing for you to be concerned about. I merely discussed with Mr. Wells whether we could get back any of the food left at the old farm," said Susan in response to her Mother's questioning.

"And what did that weasel say to that?" demanded Mother Swift.

"He said he would look into it. There was no agreement that it would happen," said Susan truthfully.

"Ummph," snorted Mother Swift.

The plan was in play. It remained to be seen if the food would appear. It was time to prepare for the next steps.

CHAPTER 45

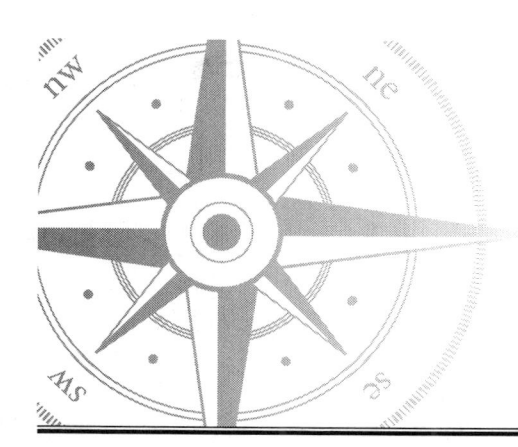

On Thursday afternoon a heavily loaded cart pulled into the farmyard. On it was stacked all of the food and possessions the Swifts' had been unable to retrieve from the old farm. There was enough food there for at least five months, and possibly longer depending on how frugal they were. Jon stayed out of sight as was the family agreement.

Robbie, Susan, and Mother Swift assisted in unloading and stowing the food in the old underground cold room. When complete, the cart departed. Wells had ridden in separately. He now waited impatiently by his horse. The fact that Wells hadn't helped unload confirmed Jon's opinion of the man.

Susan ambled over to Wells. Mother Swift and Robbie went back in the house. Jon stationed himself by the kitchen window as before.

"Why Mr. Wells, you have proved to be very chivalrous," said Susan. She was attempting to act appreciative to Wells.

"Susan, did you ever have any doubt?" Wells in turn was openly expectant. He had no idea of Susan's true feelings.

"Not for a moment," cooed Susan. "I realize this might seem very forward to you, but might you be available Saturday evening?"

"I will be available Saturday evening," replied Wells who now had an ear-to-ear grin on his face.

Susan moved closer to Wells, and whispered, "My mother is suspicious. Can I meet you down the road? There is a stand of three oak trees there. I could slip away and be there for seven. I think if I left before that she would cause some problems."

As Susan was saying this she had moved to Wells and was rubbing his arm. Wells appeared totally hooked.

"I'll see you at seven Saturday night down at the three oaks," whispered Wells. He winked at her, mounted his horse and walked out of the yard. When he hit the road, he sped off in a gallop.

Susan turned to the house with a look of disgust on her face.

Before she reached the door, Jon came out and grasped her arm. He steered her to the back of the house where they could not be overheard.

"Saturday night at seven, down the road at those three oaks," she said without hesitation.

Jon nodded. "I'll need some extra stuff from you; a bonnet and a skirt."

"What for?" asked Susan with a baffled look on her face.

"He's expecting a girl. He needs to see a girl."

"Why don't I just meet him, and explain?" said Susan.

"I don't want you anywhere near those oaks. In fact, I don't want you out of sight of mother and Robbie, and possibly even father the entire evening. Do you understand?" The hard, serious expression on Jon's face matched his tone. It caused Susan to step back. She had never seen her brother like this. There was something in his eyes.

"Alright."

The first portion of the plan had succeeded. That did not alleviate the jitters that Jon felt. He had never initiated a confrontation. He had acquitted himself well when engaged, but this was different. If anything went wrong, he would be in big trouble -- not only him, but potentially the entire family. He never had this much riding on one single action. His life, he was not worried about that. He was worried about the family. If he screwed up, what would happen to them?

Rather than sit and fidget at the table, he decided to get some fresh air. It was a dark night with some moonlight peeking between the clouds. While poaching, the value of reconnaissance had been hammered home. A look at the three oaks in the dark from every possible angle beforehand was critical and tonight was as good as any time.

Squatting on the road and looking at the three oaks, Jon attempted to imagine what Wells would see. If the night were moon lit, there would be a shadow on the forward edge of the tree. If it were cloudy or overcast, everything would be draped in shadow. If Wells were on his horse, what would he see? Anyone positioned in the shadows would appear only as an outline, a human form.

The distance from the shadows to the road was approximately fifteen feet. Jon attempted to cross that distance as fast as he could. He counted the time. After numerous tries, the fastest he could traverse the distance was a count of three. If he rushed Wells, and Wells remained on his horse, would the horse shy? Would he be able to pull Wells from the horse? Would the horse take off once Wells was pulled from it?

There were a lot of risks, but he was committed.

Despite considering the problem for a significant length of time, Jon was no further ahead than he had been prior to the reconnaissance. If truth be told, he was perhaps even further agitated.

Waiting had never been one of Jon's strengths. Even when poaching, he did it reluctantly. As Friday and Saturday dragged by, his nerves frayed. He spent as much time away from the house as possible. It was important that the rest of the family know nothing of what was going to happen. That included Susan.

Spending time walking both their farm and the adjacent farm was time well spent. Both farms had remained fallow for the better part of two years. The soil on these farms was about the same as on the Swift's previous farm. No work for the past two years meant the soil was primed for growth. The two farms totalled about two hundred acres with approximately one hundred and fifty being workable. Two men could easily work them, especially if they had draught animals. The only problem was buildings.

As he walked the farms, he checked the traps and found some additional surprises. There would be extra meat to accompany their meals. Already Jon could feel the difference since the returned food had found its way onto the Swift family table.

Saturday afternoon rolled around. The closer to the time the more impatient Jon became. It was a struggle not to show his impatience.

At six, Jon took a small bundle and left the cottage. In the bundle was the skirt and bonnet from Susan, canvas, some cord, and one other item. About half way to the three oaks, Jon paused. Taking the canvas from the small bundle, Jon wrapped canvas around each shoe. The canvas wrapping was well secured with the cord so it would not come off during rapid movement. This wrapping would also provide extra warmth for the feet while he waited for Wells to arrive. It also ensured that any tracks could not be recognized. It was a little poaching trick he had acquired.

Arriving at the three oaks, Jon fastened the bonnet on. He tucked the top of the skirt into his waist band as the skirt was too small to wear. The last item from the bundle was a piece of wood, fashioned similar to a belaying pin. This was tucked into the waistband as well. For backup there was the throwing knife. Unfortunately, a problem existed with the throwing knife. If used, the entire plan would have to change. A knife wound would not look like an accident.

Jon rehearsed each move multiple times to ensure it could be accomplished in the least amount of time with the least amount of effort. Now that the last phase of the plan had arrived, it was possible to relax a little. It was just a matter of waiting. He slid down against one of the oak trees and rested. Within a few minutes it would all be over. The only indication of restlessness was his movement from time to time to stay warm.

The cold air facilitated hearing the approaching horse long before it was visible. This afforded time to complete the final mental preparation for what was about to happen. The sounds changed, indicating the approaching horse had dropped from a canter to a walk. Time started to slow. Jon's heart raced.

"Susan, where are you?" From the slurred nature of the question, it appeared that Wells was totally intoxicated, or at least well on his way.

Jon cautiously stepped out from behind the trees, remaining in the shadows as long as possible to confuse Wells. He was also stooped to look much smaller than he was and closer to the size of his sister.

"I brought some extra clothes. Could you get down and help me?" Jon was whispering in as low a voice as possible. He was trying his best to imitate Susan's whisper. Even in the dark, Jon could see the grin on Wells' face.

Wells stepped down, and lost his balance. Only his grip on the reins kept him on his feet. As Wells struggled to gain his balance, and with his back turned toward the trees, Jon dashed the short distance between the two. This was an unexpected opportunity, which Jon didn't wish to waste.

Dashing forward, Jon pulled the wood baton from his waistband with his stronger right hand. He judged the timing and brought the wooden bat crashing down with all the force he could muster on Wells' head just above the left ear. Wells was dead before hitting the ground.

As Wells fell, Jon lunged to grab the horse's reins as the horse began to shy. The last thing he wanted at this point was to lose the horse. Having little experience dealing with horses, it was a challenge to gain control. It didn't help that the animal smelled blood and was skittish of it. Once the horse was under control, he knelt beside Wells.

A careful check of Well's pulse, or lack of pulse, confirmed what Jon had suspected.

There was no visible blood, but that didn't mean that there wasn't any. Jon immediately pulled the skirt off and tossed it aside back toward the oak trees. He grabbed Well's limp body and dragged it around to the left side of the horse. The horse's skittishness due to the smell of blood and the limp body continued. Jon struggled to control the horse, tugging at the reins. It didn't help that he had to keep a grip on those reins while manoeuvring Wells' body, lest the horse bolt.

Exasperated, he walked around the front of the horse and put his hands on the horse's muzzle. He spoke softly to the horse while concurrently stroking the muzzle. The horse seemed to settle. He grabbed Wells' left leg and jammed the boot and foot through the stirrup. It would look like a drunken Wells had fallen from the horse, and struck his head with his foot caught in the stirrup. If the fall had not killed him, then being dragged by the horse stirrup surely would.

Jon stopped to check Well's pockets. He found some coins, but not enough to worry about. He left the coins as they were. If he took them robbery would be suspected and he couldn't have that.

The thought hit him. There was not even enough money to pay for a dinner for one, let alone two. His guess had been right -- the bastard was too cheap to even provide the meal.

Jon checked everything twice. He tried to see everything as the squire's men would see it. Nothing could look out of place. Even if it looked correct, there were likely to be problems. When he was set, he slapped the horse on the rump. It trotted off toward home dragging Wells along.

Jon went to the oaks. He looked for signs that he had left. The grass had been crushed, but there were no distinct tracks or at least none that he could distinguish in the dark. He scuffed the area as best he could to eliminate anything else.

Backtracking out to the road, he retrieved the skirt he had tossed aside and took off the bonnet. He checked himself for blood. There was some. Where it came from he had no idea. Since there was some blood on him, there might be some on the road. He squatted and began as thorough a search as possible. He continually scuffed the road as best as possible to eliminate any trace of that blood. He rubbed some dirt on his clothes where blood had splashed. He continued to search until he was satisfied that there was no evidence.

Picking up everything, he walked back toward the house. Stopping well short of the house, he removed the canvas wrappings from each shoe. Silently he returned to the cottage.

After considerable time at the well washing his clothes, he decided there was little else that he could do.

He slipped back inside. Everyone was awake except his father. Jon took Susan aside and returned her bonnet and skirt in such a way that their mother didn't see the transfer. Very carefully, he whispered to her.

"If anyone asks, Wells was to come and get you tonight at seven. He was going to take you out. You were here the entire time waiting for him. Mother and Robbie can vouch for that. He never showed up. That's all true, and that's all you know. Do you understand?"

"Didn't he show up?" asked Susan.

"No. Do you understand what I just said to you?"

"I understand."

"Good, now go get some sleep."

Jon turned to the rest of the family.

"I'm going to head north tomorrow morning. I have a few things I need to check. I want to make sure that anyone who sees me is outside the squire's jurisdiction, so it doesn't get back to the squire or any of his men. I may be away a day or two, I'm not sure."

Jon very carefully checked the house for any item that would identify him as having been there. He didn't expect the house would be searched, but it was always best to take precautions. He gathered everything up, and placed everything in the ditty bag. He then placed the ditty bag beside him in case he had to move fast.

It was time to get out of the parish.

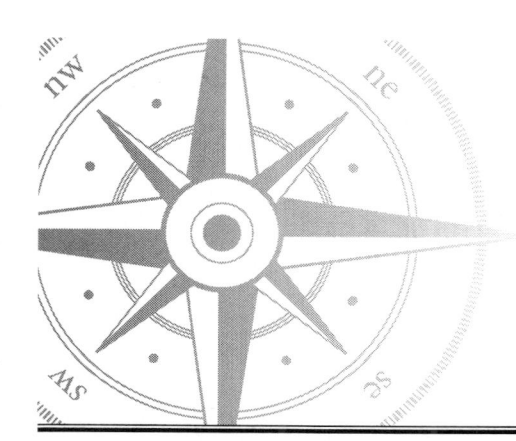

CHAPTER 46

A vicious pounding on the door in the early hours never results in good news.

The Swift household was rudely awaked just after dawn by an urgent pounding noise. Mother Swift answered, dressed only in nightclothes and robe. Surprisingly, it was Macmillan doing the pounding.

"Where is your daughter, woman?" demanded Macmillan. He impatiently pushed her aside and entered the cottage.

As Macmillan pushed his way past her, Mother Swift glanced at the rack beside the door. Jon's things were gone. It was just as well. There was no telling what might happen if the squire's men found him here or if they suspected that he was here.

"What do you want with her, especially at this hour on a Sunday morning?" demanded Mother Swift. This was her house so long as she lived here and she wouldn't have anyone ordering her around in her own house.

"Go get her and hold your tongue," ordered Macmillan. Fitzgerald and Abercrombie entered the house unbidden.

"Get out," shouted Mother Swift at Fitzgerald and Abercrombie. All of the squire's men ignored her.

Susan appeared at the edge of the loft. She had quickly dressed, as had Robbie. Abercrombie went into the backroom. Fitzgerald was looking around the place, for what Mother Swift did not know. Both Susan and Robbie came down from the loft. After they came down, Fitzgerald climbed up and looked through the loft.

"Just what right do you have to wander through my house?" demanded Mother Swift.

"It's not your house. It belongs to the squire. We are undertaking an inspection to determine if there's anything wrong," stated Macmillan.

"Nothing in the back -- just that vegetable she calls a husband," Abercrombie chortled.

Macmillan looked at Susan. "Girl, Wells said you were going out with him last night."

Susan looked at her mother, whose face showed her shock.

"That's right. He was supposed to collect me at seven. We were supposed to go out and have a meal together. I was waiting all evening. Mother and Robbie were here. He never showed up," stated Susan. She was dreading what her mother would say.

Macmillan caught the fact that Susan's mother was unaware of the meeting. There might be something here in the future. Macmillan shifted his focus to Robbie.

"Boy, who came last night?"

"Nobody," replied Robbie truthfully.

"Where's Wells? I notice that he's not with you, and he sure didn't show up as he said he would last night. So where is he?" asked Susan.

"He won't be showing up to fetch you. He's dead. We found him this morning. It appears he fell off his horse, got his foot caught in the stirrup, and was dragged back to the barn," snarled Macmillan. He watched Susan's face turn to shock as he described what happened. She even covered her mouth with her hands.

Macmillan had two thoughts as he observed this. The first was that Susan was either an extremely good actor, which he doubted, or had no knowledge of this 'accident'. The second thought he had was that maybe there was more between Susan and Wells than he had suspected.

Macmillan turned and said, "Let's go." The three of them departed.

As they exited the cottage Mother Swift turned on Susan. "You agreed to meet that weasel?"

Susan started to cry.

"Susan, tell me all about this meeting that you arranged with that weasel Wells," demanded Mother Swift.

Susan resumed crying.

"Are you out of your mind? You don't play with snakes and that man was a snake. What if he had taken advantage of you? Where would you be? Are you so naive to believe that nothing can happen to you? Just look at what happened to Pamela down at the tavern. Did you want the same thing to happen to you?" said Mother Swift.

Susan kept crying. Mother Swift shook her head.

"I guess there's no sense trying to go back to bed. Robbie, go out and fetch some wood for the stove. We'll have breakfast and go to church," said Mother Swift. "We need to say thanks to God, that you weren't harmed, and the squire's men left us alone."

"We should be saying thanks to God that he took Wells," said Robbie.

"That's blasphemy," said Mother Swift. "We'll have to pray for your forgiveness, young man."

"Maybe so, mother, but just the same, I'll be praying that he gets rid of the other three -- cause if anyone deserves it, they do," replied Robbie.

"That'll be enough of that, young man."

Mother Swift headed to the kitchen to commence preparing breakfast.

Instead of fetching wood, Robbie rushed to see his father so he could pass on the good news.

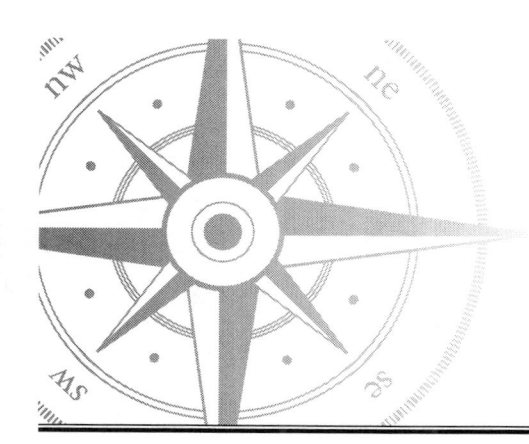

CHAPTER 47

It was the Christmas season -- a time for both prayer and celebration. The news of Wells' demise spurred that celebration across the entire community with the possible exception of the squire's residence.

The squire's men were still out and about, but the community attitude was different. Where before heads were averted in the presence of the squire's men, that no longer occurred. While men didn't look directly at the squire's men, the fear was gone. In fact, it could be said that the odd smile might have appeared, just so long as it was not seen by the squire's men.

It was a cold Saturday afternoon, a week after the Wells' incident that the door of the cottage opened and like a shadow Jon entered. It was starting to snow outside, and snow dropped to the floor as he removed his outer clothing. The family was preparing to sit for supper. Mother Swift wordlessly grabbed another bowl from the shelf and ladled some soup for her son.

"Thanks mother, I can surely use that," said Jon as he sat at the table. He maintained a distance from any other member of the family lest any body odour spoil dinner for the family. Even so, a nose wrinkled, because Jon had not had a bath in some time.

Hunger delayed any conversation. Using the soup bowl like a mug, Jon lifted it and tilted it back to his mouth. The contents drained out faster than a thirsty man drains a water bowl in the desert. A second helping was sought, but not available. Instead Jon claimed and consumed a carrot.

Jon's stomach still had not adjusted from the navy's meal schedule. At sea, they had a large meal at noon and biscuits for breakfast and supper. On land, there was a large breakfast in the morning before starting a day's work, and one at night after completing the day's work. Since leaving the sea, the feeling of hunger prevailed.

Jon glanced out the window and pursed his lips.

"No stalking tonight. Too risky. I guess I'll have to settle for a bath."

"You could certainly use one," snapped Susan.

"You check the traps, Robbie?"

"Got one rabbit on Tuesday. Nothing since," replied Robbie.

"How about a duck or goose for Christmas?"

"Do you think that's wise? They're on edge after Wells. You probably didn't hear about that. Wells got drunk and fell from his horse. He's dead," said Mother Swift.

Jon shrugged. "No great loss."

While the family finished supper, Jon carried in wood for the fire and buckets of water. The tub was setup and water set to boil. Mother Swift rigged a blanket so there was some privacy for the bather.

As he started to strip, Mother Swift spotted the scars on his side.

"What happened to you?" she asked.

Jon was so accustomed to the scars that he didn't realize at first what she was talking about. He frowned as he looked at her.

"The scars on your side?" prompted Mother Swift.

Jon looked down at the scars. "Oh, those. They're a result of a lesson I had one afternoon. I guess you could say the object of the lesson was to move faster in the future."

"What kind of place teaches that way?" asked Mother Swift.

"Survival school, mother."

"I don't understand."

"Simple mother, you graduate if you're still standing at the end of class."

Mother Swift shivered as she grasped what he was saying. What had her son been through?

Sunday morning brought church and an opportunity to learn what was happening in the community since Wells' accident. At breakfast, everyone was requested to keep his or her ears open.

Mother Swift completed her ritual inspection of Robbie and Susan before saying goodbye to Joe. It was the better part of a two hour walk to church. Their absence at church was an ideal time for Jon to speak to father without any ears listening in.

Joe's health was improving rapidly, most likely due to a better diet. He was sitting up in bed when Jon went in. That was a very encouraging sign.

"Father, I need to speak to you about Macmillan and the rest of the squire's men. You know all of them far better than I do. I need to understand how we're going to get redress for all the injustices that have been done to this family." His father nodded and sat up further so he could better view Jon. He grasped Jon's hand.

"Do you think the squire is an honest man?" His father squeezed his hand once to indicate yes.

"Do you think the squire knows everything that is going on?" His father squeezed his hand twice to indicate no.

"Do you think we can get redress from the squire if Macmillan doesn't interfere?" His father squeezed his hand three times to indicate maybe.

"You say maybe. Which is it -- you don't think you can speak to the squire without Macmillan interfering, or even if we are able to speak to the squire you're not sure we will get satisfaction?"

"Macmillan will interfere?" Jon felt one squeeze.

"You're not sure the squire would give satisfaction?" Jon again felt one squeeze.

"What you're saying is even if we get in to see the squire without Macmillan stopping us, it's unlikely we will get satisfaction." His father nodded.

"Damn, that's worse than I thought."

"Just out of curiosity, do you think we would have a better chance of getting satisfaction from the squire if we were somehow to prove to the squire that Macmillan is cheating him?" His father squeezed his hand once.

"How do we do that? Any ideas?" His father squeezed his hand twice.

"I have no idea what Macmillan does. Do you father?" Jon felt three squeezes.

"You have some idea, but are not exactly sure, is that it?" Jon felt one squeeze.

"Let me think. He is running the estate for the squire. The estate is just a big farm with tenants. So much of what he does would be the same as any farmer, only at a bigger scale." His father squeezed his hand once.

"What does any farmer do? He decides what crops to plant in each field. He buys the seed. He provides the labour to plant, weed and harvest those crops. He sells the crops. He ensures there are sufficient provisions on the table or in the house to feed and clothe the family. He handles all the money, pays the rent, and ensures any other costs are covered. Am I missing anything else father?" He felt two squeezes.

"For the estate, Macmillan would be doing all of that. He also assigns work to each man, handles the rents for tenants, and looks after the animals. He has to be running a log or ledger of some sort so that he knows who paid the rent, who owes for renting horses, how much work a man has done so he is properly paid, and other things like that. No one can keep all of that detail in his mind over time." His father squeezed his hand.

"That log would record all the money coming in and going out, wouldn't it?" mused Jon to himself. His father thought that he was speaking to him, so he squeezed Jon's hand once.

"On board ship, I saw more fights or bad will caused by money than for any other cause. If a man thinks he's being cheated, he'll get his back up. His temper rises and pretty soon he's fighting. It doesn't matter if fifteen minutes before the man he's fighting was his best friend. I bet that if the squire thinks Macmillan is cheating him, he'll get his back up and be fighting in minutes. What do you think father?" His father squeezed once.

"The question is, how can we prove there is a difference between the log or books and what actually happened?" said Jon to no one in particular.

Joe was looking hard at his son with pride in his eyes. The person seated on the stool to the side of the bed was a smart, thinking man, no longer a boy. Joe's only regret was that it was impossible to communicate this to his son.

At supper, Jon heard about the parish news that had been picked up while the Swift family was at church. As usual, if there was any 'dirt', Robbie was the cheerful bearer of it.

"Last week when we were at church, the news about Wells was just spreading. There wasn't that much said. This week you could see the difference in everyone," said Susan.

"What kind of difference?"

"Wells was hated -- I'm beginning to believe even more than Abercrombie and Fitzgerald. People are happy he's gone. I even overheard one woman comment that with Wells dead, Hell now had another well-deserving occupant," explained Susan.

"That's nothing," burst out Robbie. "They apparently buried Wells sometime during the week. Only the pastor and two gravediggers were present for the service, and they had to be if they wanted to get paid. None of the squire's men even bothered to show up."

"There was no mention of Wells in the service today, and there wasn't anyone from the squires' at the service either," remarked Susan.

"Before and after the service, all the people were talking about was Wells. They say that Macmillan hasn't been off the farm this week, and that Abercrombie and Fitzgerald only seem to be heading to the tavern. Just as well, as they seem to be the only patrons," said Robbie.

"Has there been any word on whether Wells will be replaced?"

"Haven't heard a word," replied Robbie. Susan shook her head. Mother Swift didn't participate in the discussions.

"Is there going to be any special service for Christmas?"

"Wednesday night on Christmas Eve," said Mother Swift quietly.

"I think it would be a good idea if we could take father to that service," said Jon. "Robbie could go over to Abe Hartwell's place and see if he and maybe William Bushell could borrow a wagon or cart to fetch father to the church. It would do everyone a world of good. They'll see that father is recovering, and it'll do father a world of good as well."

"Do you think he's strong enough?" asked Mother Swift. Jon nodded.

"What about you. Will you go?" asked Mother Swift.

"Too dangerous for me. For one thing, the new pastor might recognize me, and he'd make a beeline to the squire with that information if I have him pegged right."

"You do," said Robbie.

"Besides I have other plans for Christmas Eve." Jon winked at Robbie, although Robbie had no idea why.

Christmas Eve arrived. The temperature had warmed to slightly above freezing. Abe Hartwell and William Bushell arrived with a wagon and carried Joe out. The entire family, less a hidden Jon, departed for the church service.

A couple of hours after the family left, Jon slid out of the house and headed to the squire's marsh. Both his old slingshot, which had been reclaimed from Robbie, and several stones were in a pocket. Since returning home, he had practiced with the slingshot to regain the skill lost while at sea.

Although it was unlikely that any gamekeepers would be out on Christmas Eve, there was no sense in taking chances. A direct approach to the marsh was impossible because it would be too close to the squire's residence and inadvisable if concealment from the gamekeepers were to be achieved. The approach chosen was from the rear. It was a long walk, but rarely had any of the squire's gamekeepers appeared at the back of the marsh.

The stalk had been ongoing for over three hours before a couple of ducks were spotted. They were small, but better than nothing. In the expectation of finding better quarry in the form of a goose, Jon ignored the ducks.

The squire had domestic geese, but there were some wild ones still hidden in the marsh. Geese were always challenging to stalk. If roused they were noisy as hell. If roused, any hopes of a nice Christmas dinner would have to be abandoned.

After another hour of searching, Jon spotted two nice sized specimens. The only problem was that in order to recover them it would be necessary to wade through chest deep water. That's assuming it was possible to hit them in the first place. It was cold enough as it was. The thought of immersing himself in near freezing water was not overly appealing.

Quietly rubbing his hands to increase their warmth and dexterity, Jon manoeuvred into a better position for shooting. Finally, he let loose with a stone from the slingshot. There was no indication of where that shot went. What did happen was that the geese woke up and were searching around for danger. Carefully and ever so slowly he slipped another stone into the slingshot pouch. Slowly the slingshot was swung and the shot finally released. It was a solid hit, but not a kill shot. These geese were much tougher than expected. He needed a head shot for a quick kill, but that level of accuracy was not possible at this distance. The wounded goose started to make some noise -- not too loud, but in the silence of the night it sounded like it could be heard a mile away. Two stones were let loose as fast as possible at the wounded goose. Both hit, and finally, all the noise it was making stopped. The other goose was paddling close by, unsure what to do.

Jon decided to go all out and take the second goose. Recovery of the first goose would disturb the second one anyway, so why not have the meat.

Taking careful aim, a stone was let loose at the second goose resulting in a solid hit. The goose immediately started honking loudly. A second, third and fourth stone were fired as fast as possible. All the time the goose was literally honking its life out. Finally, on the fifth shot, the honking ceased.

With all that noise, it was critical to recover the bodies as fast as possible and get the hell out of the marsh before the gamekeepers showed up.

Jon stripped and waded into the marsh. As the water covered his body, he sucked in air in shock. The water was as cold as or possibly colder than the North Atlantic. Remembering the aftermath of that experience, there was added incentive to get out of the water as fast as possible.

Holding a knife in his mouth, Jon swam to the geese. Checking them, it was apparent they had both died. There was no need for the knife. Quickly grabbing them by their necks, he towed them as fast as possible back to where he had left his clothes. Tossing the geese ashore, Jon followed as fast as his shaking body could allow.

He dressed from the top down so that he could generate as much warmth for his core as possible. It didn't seem to help because he was still vibrating severely despite being fully clothed.

Two things were apparent. Jon needed immediate warmth, and he needed to get the hell off the squire's property. He chose to distance himself from the marsh rather than attempting to clean the birds.

Clumsily he worked his way out of the march, leaving a trail a blind man could follow. Once in the open fields, he picked up the pace until he was running. By the time two miles had been covered, he was feeling better. He was warm again; and no longer shaking, except for the heaving of his chest while sucking in air.

The path chosen during the run led away from the Swift cottage, thereby reducing the risk of discovery. At the current distance from the squire's homestead, it was also safe from the gamekeeper's prying eyes. It was an appropriate place to dress out the birds rather than doing it at home. It would mean less incriminating evidence at home. Rather than attempting to pluck the birds, he skinned and deposited them in a bag carried for that purpose. Without much enthusiasm, he dug a shallow hole to bury the feathers and discarded remains of the bird. He exerted even less effort camouflaging the evidence.

Most of the night was gone. It was time to get home. It was a long way back to the cottage, especially because of the necessity of avoiding any homes and roads. The sky was lightening to the east as he crossed a fence to the Swift property.

As it was Christmas morning, he slipped into the house first with the geese and laid them on the kitchen table. When up north, Jon had obtained some Christmas presents for the family. These presents were packaged in canvas and stashed in the collapsed shed. Retrieving them, he placed one on everyone's respective seat at the kitchen table. It was during this last venture outside that he smelled a rank odour. Casting about for the source of that odour, he realized it was him. He smelled of swamp.

He needed a bath, and to wash those clothes that he had been wearing. For the second time that night, his body was shocked by near freezing water, as he bathed directly at the well.

Cold, shivering, and exhausted Jon scampered back to the fire. Merry Christmas!

As normal, Mother Swift was the first one rising. As Jon was heading to bed, she was in the kitchen working away on the geese.

Jon slept for four hours and was shaken awake by Robbie, who was impatient to open his present. The smell of roasting geese immediately assaulted Jon's nostrils. It got his mouth watering. Jon dragged his butt over to the table and ran his fingers through his hair. That was normally as well as his hair was ever combed. Yawning repeatedly, he motioned for them to commence with the presents.

In mere seconds, the presents were open. For Mother Swift, there was a bible. Although Mother Swift couldn't read, Jon knew she had long coveted a bible. For Robbie there was a school reader, and some old discarded newspapers that Robbie could use to practise his reading. For Susan, Jon had found a nice tweed coat. She wouldn't have to use one of father's hand-me-downs again just to stay warm.

Compared to Christmas the previous year, there was some cause for celebration. Jon was back. This celebration was tempered by the injuries that Joe had suffered, and the fact that they had been evicted from the farm they had worked since before Jon was born.

When compared to their situation even one month previously, there was a greater cause to be thankful. They had a huge Christmas dinner and sufficient food to survive, hopefully until the next harvest. Joe was on the road to recovery and Susan for the time being was safe.

It didn't mean they were out of danger.

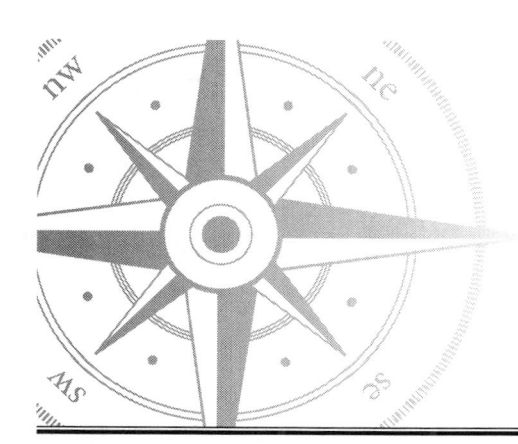

CHAPTER 48

Jon's poaching had been noticed.

Snagging the geese on Christmas Eve had been the opening salvo in a war of wits with the squire's gamekeepers. Since Christmas, there was evidence that Abercrombie, Fitzgerald, or both had been out checking the squires' home farm grounds.

As a matter of safety, the gamekeeper's routes, methods and timings were needed. Being surprised by a gamekeeper was something a poacher could ill afford.

Jon's absence most nights was perplexing to Mother Swift. By all appearances, he was stalking game, but unlike before, rarely returned with any meat for the pot. Perhaps it was the time of the year. Little game was about, and most of that was about during daylight when it was warmer.

In reality, Jon was improving his stalking skills, which he had neglected by necessity while in the navy. The difference, however, was that his quarry was human, as opposed to game for the pot.

Abercrombie and Fitzgerald were observed from just before dark until the wee hours of the morning. The two started most evenings in the tavern. They appeared to be, on most occasions, the only patrons. After departing the tavern, their actions differed by day.

On Sunday, the tavern was closed. The God fearing residents of the squire didn't tolerate the sale of spirits on the Sabbath. There was no indication that either of the gamekeepers ventured out on Sunday night. It was as if they believed that since no work was supposedly done on Sunday that also included poaching. It also could be that they weren't paid for Sunday work. Jon had no way of knowing, and he sure wasn't about to ask.

On Saturday night, the two of them were typically so drunk that they went back to their quarters and slept it off. They certainly weren't in any condition to carry, let alone use firearms most Saturday nights.

The remaining nights of the week, the two went patrolling.

It was winter, and he was cold while stalking Abercrombie and Fitzgerald. In two weeks of stalking, what he had learned was of limited value. He already knew that the two were dangerous, and unscrupulous. They would do whatever they felt like doing, including murder. If they caught Jon, there would be no second chance. Withstanding the cold for a few hours to observe Abercrombie and Fitzgerald seemed a small price to pay for additional self-preservation knowledge.

As he squatted hidden from view, Jon mulled over possibilities. Abercrombie and Fitzgerald never seemed to separate. That made things very difficult. The old divide and conquer rule couldn't be used. It would be very difficult to take both of them together. An attempt might be successful, but if he was injured or if word of his existence got back to Macmillan, he was finished. Likely the Swift family wouldn't be far behind.

The key was somehow to get Abercrombie and Fitzgerald to separate. Taking them one at a time would be easier and less risky. There was another aspect, just as important as getting them to separate. Whatever method was used to take them down, it needed to look like an accident. If it didn't look like an accident, then everyone would be on the lookout, and that would not bode well for anyone.

There were further concerns. The foremost of these was timing. Macmillan had already lost Wells. A replacement for Wells didn't appear to be forthcoming. It was possible there would be no real need until the spring. If Macmillan lost Abercrombie and Fitzgerald, the squire would hire other men to replace them. Unscrupulous men like Wells, or the other two, could be obtained easily in any big population centre. If Abercrombie and Fitzgerald were removed, then it stood to reason that their replacements would be forthcoming within two weeks to a month. Perhaps Macmillan would wait until spring, but that was unlikely, as Macmillan would need to keep his foot on the neck of the parish. Before taking any action against Abercrombie and Fitzgerald, Jon needed a plan to tackle Macmillan. Macmillan was the key as he was the link to the squire.

Of all the squire's men, Macmillan was the least known. Habits, weaknesses, traits -- none of these were known. When the navy sent him into Brest to spy, the concept of know your enemy had been explained. The fear experienced on that journey ensured that Jon thoroughly grasped the concept. The concept was just as valid in this context. Jon needed to gather intelligence on Macmillan before making any decisions.

It would be a challenge just obtaining such information. Jon could not show himself because it would alert the squire or the squire's men that there was a threat. That wasn't too great a problem as it was doubtful there were many people who knew anything about Macmillan. There was also ample opportunity to think of strategies to separate Macmillan from the squire while hiding in the underbrush stalking Abercrombie and Fitzgerald.

Through the first part of January, Abercrombie and Fitzgerald's pattern had not changed much. Jon needed to shake them up a bit. The fastest way to accomplish that task was to poach. Early one night he poached three rabbits and two ducks on the squire's land, leaving the entrails visible. Sure enough, Abercrombie and Fitzgerald spotted these entrails and began patrolling in earnest.

Their typical weeknight routine was to head to the tavern for supper and a drink, or just a drink. Around nine o'clock they would leave the tavern to patrol. Jon watched the nine o'clock routine carefully. Every three or four nights, Abercrombie and Fitzgerald would walk to the eastern end of the squire's property and start their patrol together. One would take the edge of the brush-line and the other would go further in to the edge of the marsh. They would then move in parallel toward the west. Any poacher in the woods would likely be caught between them. By beating westward, a fleeing man would be forced into the open fields at the western end of the woods. In the open any would-be poacher faced a high probability of being caught, shot or identified. It was a simple yet effective way to trap most poachers.

To keep them engaged in the patrols, Jon occasionally stalked some game just after last light. He left entrails visible so there was no doubt that poaching was still occurring. Well before the nine o'clock start of the patrol, Jon had vacated the patrol area and was generally observing the tavern.

These tactics were having an effect. Both men were increasingly frustrated they couldn't spot the perpetrator of these crimes. As the nights passed, this frustration increasingly focused on each other. Being close enough to listen, Jon could hear them snapping back and forth at each other. Earlier in the month, the conversation had been friendly banter. It was also probable that Macmillan was adding to their frustration by possibly nagging them, needling them, or blasting them for not stopping this poaching.

Timing and opportunity were everything. The conditions had to be right, such as a cold night with little moisture. At that time of year, the ground was hard, sometimes frozen on the surface. It was noisy, as everything crunched underfoot, even grass. Moisture had two possible negative impacts. In some cases, it softened the vegetation so it did not crunch. Generally, that was when it was warmer, say just above freezing. That was alright, and preferable if Jon was mobile. If he was in a static location and the gamekeepers were moving, then it was a disadvantage because it made hearing them more difficult. Another potential problem was that tracks were easier to make and to spot with added moisture on the ground. The ideal conditions for Jon's little enterprise would be a night that was sufficiently cold that after the nine o'clock patrol began the ground vegetation would be crunchy, but without any additional moisture.

The moon was another consideration. Since Jon was reasonably sure no other poachers were about, anyone else wandering around the squire's property was likely a gamekeeper. No moon was preferred, as he was less likely to be spotted. The lack of moon would impair his ability to see the gamekeepers just as much as it impaired their ability to see him. This had implications on position. It was imperative that Jon identify any gamekeeper before being spotted. This meant being hidden in the shadows while the gamekeeper remained in the open. To achieve this objective, the man working the tree line would be the first target. Jon could stay hidden back in the trees while the gamekeeper would be moving in the open along the edge of the trees.

Jon was counting on Abercrombie and Fitzgerald following their normal timing patterns. Specifically, on either the third or fourth night, they would start their patrol on the east side of the squire's property and split up. If they stayed together, it would be dicey.

It took until the first week of February for all the conditions to align. On a Thursday night, the trap was set. For the previous three nights, the eastern edge of the squire's property had been watched from a safe position. The patrol had not started on that side on anyone of those evenings. On the assumption that the patrol would start on the eastern side on the fourth evening, Jon moved into position.

The position selected was approximately three hundred yards in from the eastern property boundary. Working along the tree line, Jon selected a small evergreen for concealment. By tucking under the branches, his position was totally hidden from sight. The position also provided good vision in an arc facing the forward edge of the brush line and open field. One of the gamekeepers had been observed walking along this tree line on numerous previous patrols.

The moon was obscured by heavy moisture laden clouds. It was, therefore very dark. Sound and shadows would be the only way to track the game wardens.

Comfortably established in this concealed position, Jon prepared the slingshot. Several smooth stones were readily available in the right pocket, although if more than one was needed it would be trouble. He removed one stone, gently felt it for roundness, and then placed it in the pocket of the sling. The stone was let loose to ensure the slingshot wouldn't get caught in the branches. The stone flew without problems. Another stone was placed in the slingshot. All was set. It was now just a matter of patience and waiting.

Every ten minutes or so Jon very slowly and carefully shifted position. This greatly alleviated the possibility of muscle cramping, and helped circulation to an extent.

As time ticked by, worry set in. It seemed that Abercrombie and Fitzgerald were well behind time. Had they started the patrol on the other end of the squire's property? If so, the planned exit route wouldn't work. It would be necessary to head west across the squire's entire property. With the noise that movement would create because of the crunchy footing, the danger would greatly increase.

Jon started mentally playing out different scenarios, all of which ended badly. He tried to get control of his mind before it spooked him so badly he made a mistake.

A noise to the right caught him off-guard. It snapped his mind into focus. Realizing his hands were very cold, he started to rapidly squeeze and flex them in an attempt to warm them. It would be too costly to fumble a shot because of cold hands.

A further noise, much closer increased his alertness. The night was very still and quiet, like the lull before a storm. Perhaps a storm will occur, mused Jon. The skies had certainly looked menacing earlier on.

Another prolonged noise surprised him, primarily because of the duration. The noise was coming from the right toward the eastern edge of the squire's property. Alertness was as heightened as possible. Something or someone was moving. Whatever was moving was large and slow. The noise was approaching and seemed measured.

The noise stopped just outside Jon's right arc of vision. Extremely slowly, his hand searched for and picked up the slingshot. A gentle squeeze confirmed the stone was present and ready for release.

Waiting...waiting....every second seemed a minute, every minute seemed an hour. Still there was no motion or sound. Then he heard a loud belch. More noise started from his right. Someone was moving.

A shadow appeared in Jon's right arc of vision. The shadow moved closer. It was a man and that man was only ten feet away. As the shadow moved, Jon slowly raised his arm and prepared the sling.

Despite being ready to fire, it was impossible to define the target properly. It was so dark, only a slight differentiation between the head and the body could be made. It was also too dark to see if there was a hat. If the shot hit a hat, it was unlikely to incapacitate the man. The man was carrying a loaded musket. If the man still had the ability to fire, at this range it was unlikely that he would miss. Even if he did miss, there was another gamekeeper that would be alerted and seeking a target.

The shadow swivelled its head. Jon could finally identify the outline of a face as it was pale compared to the remainder of the head. Jon aimed at the top centre of the circle as the face stared in his direction.

The sling whirled, launching the stone. A crack against bone was audible as the stone hit. The shadow collapsed.

Jon sprang forward, dropping his hand in which he still held the slingshot. He used his left hand to draw his fighting knife. He shoved the slingshot into his pocket as he covered the ten feet to the lying target. Grabbing the body, he savagely jerked the limp form around, preparing to thrust his knife. There was no need. The man was unconscious or dead -- it was impossible to tell. Regardless, there was no resistance.

Exerting control, both on breathing and emotions, now that the situation was under control, he could smell the odour of beer emanating from the man. That could explain why the man belched and possibly why they were late. It was still so dark, that it was impossible to identify the man. Was it Abercrombie or Fitzgerald? In reality, it didn't matter, as the other one was close and had to be disposed of, if Jon hoped to survive the night.

Some noise had been made when the dead man fell, and when Jon had launched out of the hiding spot to finish the assault. Those sounds were abnormal. If heard by the other gamekeeper, he would come to investigate. Jon needed to be prepared.

Jon was shivering. He wasn't sure if it was from the cold, or the shock of action. Unfortunately any movement to get warm was out of the question. Stillness was needed so any movement by the other gamekeeper could be heard.

Preparations needed to be completed before the arrival of the second gamekeeper. Jon recovered the unconscious man's musket, checked for a load, verified for prime, and set it aside. He secured all weapons. The knife went back in its sheath and a pocket was checked to ensure the presence of the slingshot. Finally, Jon knelt down and searched the hiding place on hands and knees to make sure nothing had been dropped or left behind. Once accomplished, Jon assumed a position in the shadows, cocked musket in hand, and waited.

It took some time, but Jon finally heard a noise. It was approaching from the southwest, inside the woods. The other gamekeeper had apparently been ahead and was now coming back. He was moving at an angle out from the woods to the tree line searching for his partner.

The other gamekeeper was smart enough not to call out. It was evident he had been drinking as well because his movement was noisier than Jon would have expected. The gamekeeper approached slowly, but far from stealthily. Jon waited motionless, crouched down again behind the same small evergreen.

As the noise got closer and closer, Jon raised the musket to his shoulder. He was relaxed, in a ready position with his finger over the trigger guard as he had been taught. Once he had a target, all he needed to do was raise the musket barrel, slide the index finger to the trigger, aim and fire.

In his peripheral vision, a shadow appeared to move. The shadow was approaching at an angle. Jon let him come, continuing to let the other gamekeeper approach until even a blind man couldn't miss. The index finger slid to the trigger and applied gentle pressure. The musket boomed and the approaching gamekeeper dropped; hit exceedingly hard. Jon crept over to check if the shot had been fatal.

The smell of beer on this man was very evident. After a close look, Jon positively identified the man as Fitzgerald. That meant the unconscious man to the rear was Abercrombie. A check of Fitzgerald for a pulse failed to find one.

Fitzgerald had fallen only twenty feet from Abercrombie. Jon considered the options. Abercrombie could be killed as well, or could be set up for the murder of Fitzgerald. There was no sympathy for Abercrombie. Abercrombie or Fitzgerald had nearly killed Jon the night the press gang took him. In fact, probably the only reason he was still alive was the arrival of the press gang. They had killed Malcolm Cartwright. They had tried to kill Joe Swift, and left him permanently injured.

Jon considered the possibilities that Abercrombie would get away scot-free by claiming it was an accident. Abercrombie's buddy and boss Macmillan effectively controlled the information presented to the squire. As the local magistrate, the squire controlled any legal actions. That would be in Abercrombie's favour. If Abercrombie lived, he would inform Macmillan that there was someone hunting them. Macmillan would hire however many men he thought necessary and rip the parish apart until he found the hunter. Jon could not afford that. If both of the men died in what could be considered an accident, there would be no legal repercussions for Jon, and Macmillan could speculate, but never know for sure.

The decision was obvious. Jon leaned over Fitzgerald and picked up the un-discharged musket. Carefully aiming, he fired a shot into Abercrombie's head, targeting the exact spot where the stone from the slingshot had struck. Just to be sure, he checked Abercrombie's pulse carefully. There was no mistake. The man was dead.

Now that the deed was done, there was no hurry. It was highly unlikely that Macmillan was out doing gamekeeper duties, and he was the only other man about whom Jon worried. Now it was just about setting up the scene so that when Abercrombie and Fitzgerald were found, it would be obvious that they accidently shot each other.

Jon spent considerable time placing the muskets. It had to look as if Abercrombie shot Fitzgerald coming out of the woods and Fitzgerald fired back while falling. He swept the area, including the hiding location, three times. The first time removed any extra tracks and anything that might not be considered either Abercrombie's or Fitzgerald's. The second time the area was brushed with an evergreen branch to further sanitize the site. The third time, he tossed some old leaves and broken twigs in the area to eradicate any possible remaining evidence. The frozen ground meant there was little worry about any tracks that might be left exiting the scene. Jon backtracked out the squire's property to the east and headed home.

There wasn't the slightest remorse. In the last two to three years, Abercrombie and Fitzgerald had taunted and harassed Jon. They had tried to rob him, nearly killed him and stolen over a year of his life. They had attacked and nearly killed his father during a robbery. Joe had been left incapacitated for months and would likely never speak again. They had preyed on the Swift family -- illegally evicting them from the farm they had worked all of Jon's life. They had shot Archie Cartwright and falsified evidence at his trial. They had killed his cousin Malcolm Cartwright. No, Jon thought, the world would be a better place without the likes of Abercrombie and Fitzgerald.

As Jon walked carefully back to the Swifts' cottage he thought about the situation. Three of his adversaries were now gone. The fourth one Jon knew would be the hardest to defeat. Macmillan was the mastermind behind all of this evil.

It was now about speed. He needed to take care of Macmillan before new men of the same ilk could be hired.

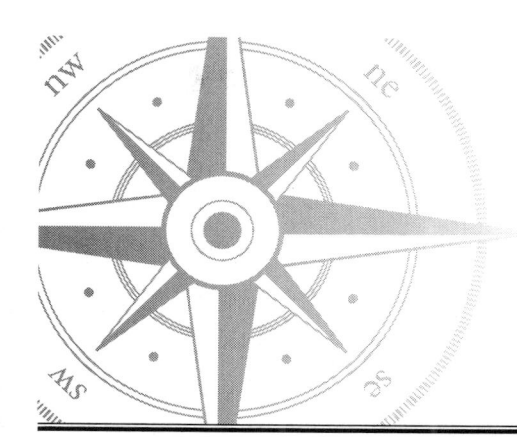

CHAPTER 49

Snow was falling heavily by the time Jon stepped back into the Swift cottage.

The same snow curtailed any movement within the parish for the entire day. At the Swift place, the only movement outdoors was to the woodpile, well or outhouse. Late Saturday afternoon saw a break in the weather and by the Sunday church services the entire community was out and about.

Joe and Jon were sitting by the kitchen table when the family returned from church. Robbie burst into the house full of energy and excitement.

"You'll never guess what happened," cried Robbie.

"The pastor's pants felt down during the service," said Jon straight faced.

Susan smiled. Joe made some type of noise somewhere between a cough and a sputter. It even appeared that Mother Swift might have had a flicker of a smile.

"No," cried Robbie. "Abercrombie and Fitzgerald are dead."

"Really?" asked Jon. "How and when did that happen?"

"All the men were talking about it. Apparently, they were all called out by the squire yesterday morning. A big search party was formed. They found the bodies in the woods on the back of the squire's home farm near the marsh late yesterday afternoon. Both men had been shot and the critters had got at the bodies. A couple of the men were sick when they saw the bodies," explained Robbie.

"You say they were both shot? Who around here has muskets except the squire?"

"According to Abe Hartwell they shot each other. Macmillan was furious according to Abe. He apparently called them a couple of drunken idiots."

"Why's that?"

"The way Abe described it, Abercrombie and Fitzgerald had drunk heavily before patrolling. According to the tavern barkeeper, their drinking had been a preventative measure to keep out the cold and was heavier than normal Thursday night when they left. Abe said a drunk with a loaded gun was a recipe for disaster. There was no moon Thursday night, and it was snowing. The visibility would have been very poor. Accidents happen, and that was the verdict of everyone that found the bodies," continued Robbie.

"If they identified a problem on Thursday night, why didn't they mount a search Friday?"

"Don't know. Maybe it was the weather," replied Robbie.

"If all the tenants were forced to join the search, how come no one came here to get father or you?"

"Guess they didn't think I could handle it and father's not strong enough yet," said Robbie. Jon turned to Joe who just shrugged.

"So what'd they say about all of this at the service?"

"Not a word at the service," said Susan. "Afterwards, there were lots of prayers of thanks given, I can assure you."

"Susan," scolded Mother Swift. "Don't speak ill of the dead."

"Why not Mother? If any man deserved to die, they did. After what they've done to this family, I would have gladly pulled the trigger that killed them," retorted Susan.

"Me too," said Robbie.

"It appears that you have been outvoted on that one mother," said Jon, effectively ceasing any further conversation along those lines.

With the loss of all his confederates, Jon figured that Macmillan was in a more exposed position than at any previous time. That exposed position might only be an illusion. Macmillan was a smart man, who had protection in the form of the squire. He could not be disposed of without serious consequences. Time was fast slipping away. Jon knew he had to act soon before Macmillan hired more disreputable men.

The first step of the strategy was to separate Macmillan from the squire somehow. Anyone looking at the squire's accounts would probably be able to determine something was amiss. Since Macmillan was responsible for the accounts, he would be blamed. The strategy was viable and would work. Unfortunately, Jon still had not determined a way to execute this strategy.

Robbie and Susan ventured into the hamlet the next morning to pick up sugar and salt from the store. Jon asked them to keep their ears open for anything they could about Macmillan, the squire, or affairs at the squire's homestead. They returned with limited information.

"According to the pastor, he has only seen the squire once in the last two months. The squire was sick in bed when he saw him," reported Susan.

"Ferguson, who works at the homestead, was in the store when I was there. He was talking to Mr. Jenkins. He said that since Abercrombie and Fitzgerald's accident, Macmillan hasn't even left the house, except to use the outhouse. Mr. Jenkins commented that there have been a lot of letters being sent by the squire in the last week," continued Robbie.

"You didn't hear where the letters were going, did you?"

"Nope," replied Robbie.

"Anything else?"

"Only the impression that not much is happening out at the squire's place right now. I mean, if Ferguson has the time to come to the hamlet in the day, and talk, then it can't be that busy, can it?" suggested Robbie.

"Good observation," said Jon while ruffling Robbie's hair. Robbie beamed.

Macmillan was protecting himself by staying close to the squire. He was writing letters, lots of additional letters. That meant that he was either recruiting more men, or getting ready to run.

Jon considered the impact of new men. It would take some time for them to identify everyone in the area. It would also take time for them to determine who could be intimidated, and who would need extra persuasion. Initially, they would be working for wages -- any true loyalty to Macmillan would take time to develop.

What would be the impact if Macmillan were leaving? First off, why would he run? Everything was working his way, although his grip was slipping at the present. To him that might only be a temporary setback. What if the money was running out?

Run...run...hmmmm! The word run triggered some images in Jon's mind. A slow smile appeared on Jon's face as he thought of a possibility. Where had he learned the expression 'run'? He learned all about it in His Majesty's navy.

The navy was always looking for men. Ships heading for the West Indies found it difficult to attract men, so a large number of pressed men headed that direction. As well, captains of short-handed vessels rarely asked many questions. If Jon could find a vessel fitting out for the West Indies, it would readily accept a 'volunteer' such as Macmillan. The more he thought about it, the better he liked it.

If Macmillan simply disappeared, the first things that would be checked were the records concerning money. If tenants such as the Swift family started claiming rents had been paid and the money didn't appear in those books, everyone would think that Macmillan had stolen the money and had taken off. There would be a warrant issued for him.

What would be better justice than to press Macmillan into a landsman position heading to the West Indies and yellow jack. Everyone would have power over him. It would be as good as gaol, maybe even better. Jon smiled at the thought.

There was a slight problem, before that happened. He had to find a way to get that 'volunteer' to the ship. That was easier said, than done.

Any ship being outfitted for foreign shores was likely at a large navy port. The closest was Portsmouth.

To get to Portsmouth, you either had to take the roads, or go by ship. To carry a shanghaied man through a number of villages and towns to get to Portsmouth was asking for trouble. It might also be possible for someone to trace them. If going by ship, it might be a direct passage, but the same problems might occur. He would either have to find a captain willing to go along with his endeavours or buy a small smack and make the trip himself. There was one further problem. That was how to deliver Macmillan to the ship in question without being pressed himself.

Jon decided to head to Rye to get information. He should also check on his sea chest while he was there. On a cold February morning he donned his naval jacket and tramped through the back fields until hitting the road to Rye. From the road, it was just a matter of walking another twenty odd miles.

There was very little difference in Rye since the previous short visit. At the waterfront, he searched flyers tacked up looking for seamen, but nothing of interest was discovered. That really did not come as a surprise as this was a small port. What he was looking for would be more likely found in Portsmouth or Sheerness. There were no ships in port that would meet his transport requirements.

Jon headed back to the Cross Bow tavern at the end of the market area. It was a little further than a couple of bars on the waterfront, but it still served a number of sailors. Just in case a press gang suddenly appeared, tucked in the money belt was his master's certificate.

The tavern was warm and inviting upon entry. It was also empty of customers, being before the supper hour. As Jon approached the bartender, he took out a shilling.

"You still got my sea chest?"

The bartender was surprised, as he had not recognized Jon.

He nodded, "Just as you left it."

Jon looked at him, "Thank you. Keep it for awhile longer."

He slid the shilling across the bar.

"Give me a ploughman's special and small beer."

Another shilling slid across the counter to pay for dinner. Seated on a bench, he killed time waiting for the normal seafaring crowd to arrive. It would be a long wait. Over the course of the supper hour and evening, he overheard a number of conversations, but learned nothing of interest.

After a few hours of achieving nothing, he was ready for bed. A hand slammed on his shoulder.

"How are you Jon?"

It was a crewmate from the Lucy. Jon couldn't remember his name at first.

"You still with the Lucy? I didn't see her when I was down at the waterfront earlier."

"Just got in before dark -- you know how much the captain likes to enter this harbour in the dark. The rest of the crew will probably be along shortly. So what have you been doing with yourself? You look a little down on your luck," said the other man good-naturedly.

"Went home to see the family. Found my father sick. He's getting better now, so I might be looking for a ship soon. Just checking things out at the moment," replied Jon. "What's going on at sea? I've been a little out of touch."

"Same old thing. We get a cargo someplace. Move it to another place. All the time, the ship's getting older and so am I," chuckled the other man.

"What's going on with the war? Seen any Frenchmen or any navy vessels nosin' about?" inquired Jon.

"Scarce seen either. I tend to keep my head down anywhere near Portsmouth," replied the other.

"Can't say as I blame you. I'd be especially careful if there were ships outfitting for overseas, as the captains don't ask too many questions about the source of their 'volunteers' if you know what I mean,"

"That's got me nervous. We're heading to Portsmouth in a couple of days. Last I heard there was a two-decker heading to the Indies mid-month," stated the other man.

"Surely, you got your papers to exempt you?"

"Sure, but like you say, those captains don't ask too many questions. So I stay nervous," replied the other.

The captain of the Lucy entered the bar with a number of other members of the crew about fifteen minutes later. Jon bought two beers and went over to speak with Captain Moore.

"Well if it isn't the young master," hooted Captain Moore. "A little down on your luck, are ye?"

Jon handed him a beer and shrugged his shoulders.

"How's life captain?"

"Well, it's good, but I've always got room for a good topman that works for real cheap wages," said Moore.

Jon looked at the captain, as if considering the proposition.

"When are you sailing captain, and where are you bound?"

"Day after tomorrow on the morning tide bound for Portsmouth. After that, depends on the cargo," replied Captain Moore. Jon eased back in his seat and smiled at Captain Moore.

"I feel another one of those special deals coming," smiled Captain Moore. Jon grinned.

"Let's put it this way captain. Johnson said there was a navy two-decker outfitting for the West Indies, sailing mid month. I have a special 'friend' that deserves to be on that ship. I would be willing to give you two weeks service if you would carry this friend and me over to Portsmouth. He will be leaving us there. Now my friend won't be working on the run to Portsmouth. He will need his rest, so I will need a place he can be accommodated so no one disturbs his sleep," said Jon quietly.

Captain Moore said, "Let me think it over."

Jon nodded and left to speak to the barkeeper. He needed some paper and someone to deliver a message by horse in the morning if this worked out. The barkeeper could handle both. The paper was supplied, and Jon sat in a corner and composed a message. It said:

"Mr. Macmillan.

You do not know me, but I have information about the series of incidents that have happened recently. I have reason to believe that someone I know wishes ill of you. I am prepared to provide you this information for a fee. I will be in the Cross Bow tavern in Rye between 7 and 9 tonight if you wish to obtain this information. Bring cash.
A friend"

Jon folded the paper up.

Captain Moore approached and asked, "Just what has your friend done to you that you are so good to him?"

Jon sat back and considered his response for a few seconds before speaking. "He arranged the killing of a man I knew. He ordered an attack on my father, which left him crippled for life, and nearly resulted in the death of my entire family. To get me out of the way, he was the one that arranged to have me pressed. I can't prove any of this in a court of law, so this is a way to even out the score so to speak."

Captain Moore looked at Jon and studied him for a period of time.

"I sure hope that you never think of me as the same type of friend," he said. "When do you expect to bring him aboard?"

"Tomorrow night after nine, if he shows."

"And if he doesn't show?" asked Captain Moore.

"My word is still good. I'll be with you when you sail." Captain Moore nodded.

"Do you have a place to berth tonight?"

"No sir."

"Then come back aboard with us tonight," said Captain Moore.

"Aye, aye sir, and thank you, sir."

Jon went up to the barkeeper. He handed him the message to deliver.

"How much for the paper, and to deliver it tomorrow?" asked Jon.

"Considering the distance, four shillings," stated the barkeep.

"Here's three additional shillings. Use the other one I gave you to look after my sea chest. I'll take the sea chest with me, now," responded Jon. The barkeep wasn't especially happy, but he would do it. One didn't cross a man like Jon.

Jon grabbed his sea chest and carried it down to the Lucy accompanied by other members of the crew. He found a spot, slung a hammock and was snoring away in minutes.

Either the plan worked, or he would be taking a cruise for nothing.

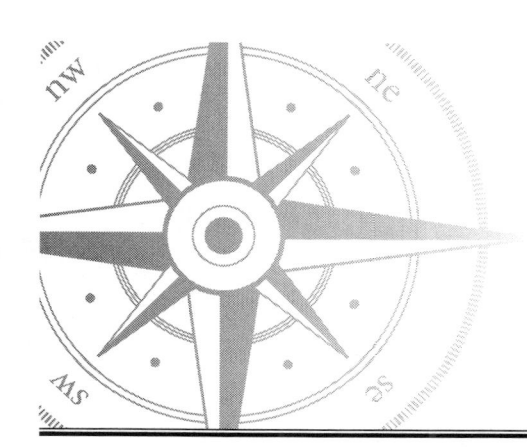

CHAPTER 50

It was refreshing waking on board a ship again. Jon had missed it.

The day was typical of any day spent in any port loading cargo. Yards were rigged for hoisting; cargo was lifted from the dock and lowered into the hold. Breaks were taken for water and dinner; otherwise loading continued until just before supper. Luckily Jon had appropriate clothing in the sea chest. After eating, Jon returned to the tavern to wait and see if Macmillan appeared.

Nothing happened until after eight o'clock when Macmillan and two big bruisers walked in. This was unexpected. Upon entry, Macmillan surveyed the entire tavern, apparently not recognizing anyone present, including Jon. In fact, while dressed in slops with a short beard, Jon was essentially invisible to Macmillan.

Jon had to think quickly. It was necessary to separate Macmillan from his protection if his plan was to succeed. The best way to distract a man in a bar was to get that man drunk.

Jon sauntered over to the bar, signalling Johnson and a couple more of his shipmates over at the same time.

"Barkeep, a mug of beer for each of my mates, the crew of the Lucy."

"That tall fellow that came in with these two big bruisers is after me," said Jon. "I need you fellows to keep those two bruisers occupied while I take care of business."

Jon signalled the barkeeper over.

"Give me four mugs. Fill each almost full with neat rum. Add some beer to the top so it tastes like beer. We're going to play a joke on these friends of mine," whispered Jon to the barkeeper.

The barkeeper poured all the mugs. The special ones he placed in front of Johnson.

The two bruisers were standing at the end of the bar watching the door. The crew of the Lucy waved them over.

"Come join us for a toast," said Johnson. He handed each of them one of the special mugs.

"To the Lucy, bottoms up," said Johnson.

Everyone, including the bruisers, emptied their respective mugs.

"Another round," said Jon.

The second round was for insurance. Each of the bruisers got another special mug.

"To a smooth sea, willing women, and a full purse," toasted Johnson. "Bottoms up."

Again everyone emptied his mug. Between the two toasts, the bruisers had consumed approximately forty ounces of neat rum in less than ten minutes. That should be enough to floor anyone in time. Jon had an empty mug on each occasion. He could not afford to be anything but fully alert.

It was unclear whether Macmillan was aware of what was happening to his escorts. He was sitting at a table watching the door carefully.

Jon gave the rum thirty minutes to become effective, before approaching Macmillan.

"Macmillan, outside alone if you want the information I have. I'll not have anyone see me talking to you in here," said Jon as he walked by Macmillan to the door.

Macmillan started for the door. He signalled to his two escorts. They both started to move toward the door as well. The crew of the Lucy were in a lively state and hated to see these two leave. They good-naturedly obstructed their egress. As a result, Macmillan walked out into the dark alone.

Alone he might be, but un-armed he was not. Exiting the door, Macmillan drew a pistol. It was good, but not enough. Jon had anticipated something, so once out of the tavern he had moved off a distance in the dark. Being further in the dark Jon would have a momentary advantage as Macmillan's eyes adjusted from light to dark. It was enough.

A stone flew through the darkness from a slingshot, striking Macmillan in the head near the temple on the left side. Macmillan stumbled and hit the ground. Calmly and deliberately approaching Macmillan, Jon lifted a belaying pin, courtesy of the Lucy. A solid tap in the head was rendered just in case Macmillan was conscious and considering any resistance. The blow was satisfying, but far lighter than Macmillan deserved considering all the harm he had inflicted.

Jon recovered Macmillan's pistol and shoved it into the waistband in the small of Jon's back. With some effort, he lifted Macmillan up and over the shoulder in a fireman's carry. Jon proceeded to carry his drunken 'friend' back to the Lucy, singing like a drunk along the way. It wasn't difficult to act like a drunk as Macmillan was a heavy load to carry and Jon staggered under the weight from time to time.

Once aboard ship, Jon carried Macmillan down to a cabin that had been specially set aside. Macmillan was stripped of everything, dressed in an old pair of slops, had his hands tied, and was secured to the floor. A bandana put around the mouth eliminated as much noise as possible should Macmillan regain consciousness.

Macmillan had twenty pounds in cash with him. That thankfully covered the cost for the drinks and then some. To top it off, Jon had acquired a nice pistol. Macmillan's clothes and jacket were nice. With some tailoring to alter the fit and appearance, lest they be recognized as Macmillan's, they would be a welcome addition to a limited wardrobe. All of these items were stowed in the sea chest.

The tide was early, so it was the morning watch when Jon rolled out of the hammock and went to work. A cursory check on Macmillan ensured he was still 'sleeping' and secure. The Lucy put to sea.

Next thing on the agenda was a visit with the navy at Portsmouth.

CHAPTER 51

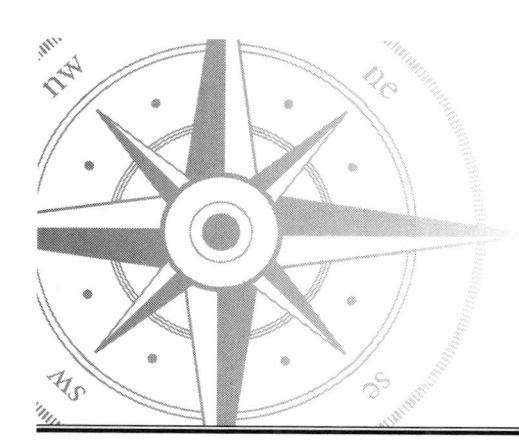

The Lucy entered Portsmouth harbour without any fanfare. She was just another merchantman. As they were moving up the harbour, a close examination of the navy yards failed to identify the Mermaid. Apparently, she had been already broken up. That was sad as she had been a good ship.

The Lucy was fortunate enough to find an empty berthing space and docked. A port official immediately came aboard to check the manifest and cargo. Apprehensive that Macmillan would make a commotion while the official was onboard, a pre-emptive tap on the head resolved any concerns.

The official had other concerns.

"Captain, I strongly suggest that your crew remain aboard, as the press is out and about in town," said the official.

Jon approached the official.

"Excuse me, sir. What ship is currently outfitting for the West Indies? I want to know which one to especially avoid," asked Jon.

The official turned and pointed out a two-decker. "The Lichfield is the one to avoid, unless you're looking for sunnier climates." He chuckled.

"From what the captain says, we'll be here two or three days. Any hope that she'll sail before then?"

"She's supposed to sail in five days, if she can get enough crew. That's why I'd be cautious if I were you," replied the official.

"Many thanks, sir," said Jon. He knuckled his forehead to the official, turned and went back to work.

The crew spent the remainder of the day unloading cargo. At supper, the strategy to transfer Macmillan was discussed amongst the crew.

"Just hand him over to the press," said Johnson.

"So long as he is on land, he has the capability of talking his way out of this mess, and pointing a finger in our direction," said Jon. "If he's on board ship, they will keep him locked up until they sail, just so he can't jump ship. Once they're at sea, they'll release him. He can't run then."

"Won't he be screamin' his head off about us on board that ship?" asked Forester.

"Probably will, until they tell him to shut up," said Jon. "We have to make sure they disregard any story he might tell."

"How are you going to do that?" asked Forester.

"Good question. Any ideas?" asked Jon.

"Any seaman worth his salt hates a thief. From what you told us, this man's a big thief. Tell them the man stole from his messmates. Tell them that he got drunk one night and mentioned that a warrant has been issued for him. For that matter, tell him. It might scare him and cause him to keep his mouth shut," said Johnson.

"Reasonable," murmured Jon.

"So how you going to deliver him?" asked Forester.

"I'm going to ask the captain if I can use the gig tonight. Hopefully, he'll say yes. Tonight, after dark, I'm going to row over to the Lichfield and call up the watch. Ask them to haul him up. Then I'm going to row like hell away from there, just in case," said Jon.

"Got more guts than I do," said Johnson.

"Looking at your stomach, I don't think so," said Jon with a chuckle. That comment evoked chuckles all around.

Jon excused himself and went looking for Captain Moore. He found him in his cabin.

"Excuse me, sir."

"What is it Swift?"

"I was wondering if I could borrow the gig to deliver a certain package tonight, sir."

"What happens if I don't get my boat back?" asked Captain Moore.

"I venture you would find it drifting in the harbour somewhere, and me as a new crew member of the Lichfield, sir."

"You do like to take chances, don't you?" said Captain Moore. "Alright, you may borrow the boat. I want that 'package' as you call him, off this ship."

"Aye, aye, sir," said Jon and he departed.

That night, the crew lowered the gig. Quietly, a bundled, unconscious Macmillan was lowered down to Jon. Slowly and easily, Jon rowed out to the Lichfield, conserving every possible ounce of strength. It might be necessary to row for his life if the guard boat appeared.

As Jon approached the Lichfield someone hailed, "Boat in the water approaching us, steer off."

"Ahoy Lichfield, I have a volunteer on board for you," shouted Jon.

"Come ahead," replied a different voice.

Jon continued to close with the Lichfield.

"Come aboard with your package," shouted the new voice. Jon suspected it was the officer of the watch.

Jon chuckled loudly, "Thank you for your offer sir, but all you need to do is lower a rope and hoist this miserable bugger up."

Jon heard the order to rig a line for hoisting. Jon kept his eyes moving, checking for the guard boat. He kept a close watch of the bulwark also lest someone drop a shot through the bottom of the gig. A line was tossed down. He edged the gig forward; snagged the rope, and quickly backed away from the Lichfield's side. A bowline snaked under Macmillan's arms.

"Hoist away."

"What's the story on this one?" called down the officer of the watch.

"His name is Denis Jackson, or at least that's what he was calling himself in Sheerness where he signed on as a landsman. No skills as a sailor. Got drunk in Dover and let it slip that there's a warrant issued for him under the name Macmillan. That's probably his real name. He's a useless, lying, thieving bastard. He was caught stealing from the ditty bags of some of the crew. The captain thought that some better discipline might straighten him out. He was pretty well fed up with him. Hope you can straighten him out," said Jon as he edged away.

"Oh, you can rest assured of that," replied the officer of the watch.

Once Macmillan was clear of the gig, Jon turned and pulled with all he had. He was right about the guard boat. They must have had a boat in the water on the other side of the Lichfield. It was fully crewed, and they were rowing for all of their might as they came around the bow of the Lichfield.

Jon had a lead, but with every stroke his lead was reduced. Doubting he could out-row the guard boat for very long, the desperate search for an alternative location to land commenced. Within a minute, any thoughts of reaching the Lucy before being overtaken were quashed as the guard boat surged forward and narrowed the gap. The gig was aimed at the nearest docked ship. He would climb aboard her, run across her and down onto the dock. From there he would attempt to get to the Lucy. It meant abandoning the gig, but that was better than ending up on the Lichfield.

Jon barely made it to the nearest ship ahead of the guard boat. Scrambling up the side of the ship, just feet ahead of a sailor reaching up from the guard boat, he rolled over the bulwark and yelled.

"Press party, repel boarders larboard."

Pandemonium erupted on the merchantman as the deck watch of the merchantman grabbed belaying pins and whatever was handy. As they spotted the sailors climbing over the bulwark from the guard boat, they launched into a furious attack. Despite the merchantman's efforts, some of the press gang managed to reach the deck. As the free-for-all occurred on deck, Jon ran down the gangway. Hitting the wharf, no time was lost as he sprinted toward the Lucy. Chest heaving and sucking air while navigating the gangway onto the Lucy, he was nearly overcome with relief on making the ship.

The fight on the other ship was loud. Other merchant ships were now coming alive, ready to repel boarders. The Lucy's crew were no different. After Jon caught his breath, he reported to the captain.

"Sir, I abandoned the gig to the larboard of that docked vessel, where all the action is occurring. Once the action settles down, I will retrieve the gig if it is still there," huffed Jon.

"Was it worth it?" asked Captain Moore.

Jon looked at him, "I sure as hell hope so, sir."

Jon and most of those crewmen remaining on board the Lucy gathered at the bulwark and watched the fight over at the other ship. It took awhile but the crewmen of the other ship finally gained the upper hand over the press gang.

The press gang retreated, bruised and battered, back to their longboat. Some of their comrades who had not fared well in the recent brawl on the docked ship were unceremoniously dumped over the side. The surviving members of the longboat fished out their buddies and hauled them back into the boat. They then started the short-handed pull back to the Lichfield.

Jon waited for about an hour after the commotion had died down. He casually walked over to the docked vessel and called, "Permission to come aboard"

"State your business here," was the response from the watch.

"Sir, I'm just attempting to recover our gig which went adrift. It has drifted over to your larboard side."

There was a moment's hesitation while the ships' watch confirmed there was a gig on their larboard side.

"Come aboard."

Jon walked up to the gangway and knuckled his forehead to the officer of the watch waiting for him.

"Thank you sir. If I may, I'll drop over the side and row the gig back to our ship. That was quite a fracas you folks had. Was it a press gang? I've never heard of them boarding a ship like that in harbour."

The officer of the watch was ready to dump on someone, but this appeared to be just an innocent seaman sent to fetch an adrift boat.

"Just go get your boat, and tell your mates to pay closer attention when they secure their boats," he said.

"Aye, aye, sir" said Jon. He wasted no time moving to the larboard side and scrambling down to the boat. In case there was a guard boat still lurking in the darkness, he rowed the gig as fast as possible back to the Lucy where the crew were waiting. Hooking on the tackle, Jon stayed catching his breath in the boat, as it was hoisted aboard.

Jon wasn't finished for the night. Since the entire harbour was on edge, he was detailed to an extra strong harbour watch.

Macmillan had been delivered, but that didn't mean it was over just yet. There was always a possibility Macmillan might talk his way out of the cruise to the West Indies. A watch on the Lichfield was needed. As well, there was still a contract to fulfill with Captain Moore.

The Lucy remained in Portsmouth while Captain Moore attempted to attract some additional business. The next two days were spent loading cargo. All the while, numerous eyes kept a vigil on the Lichfield. Those eyes watched to see if Macmillan had either escaped or been allowed his freedom. They were also watching to ensure that no further press gangs paid a visit to the Lucy. During the entire vigil, there was no indication that Macmillan had gained his freedom.

So long as the Lichfield was in harbour, the crew of the Lucy were nervous. Additional delays occurred to keep the Lucy in port until after the Lichfield sailed.

As the Lichfield hoisted her anchor and departed, there were sighs of relief throughout the harbour.

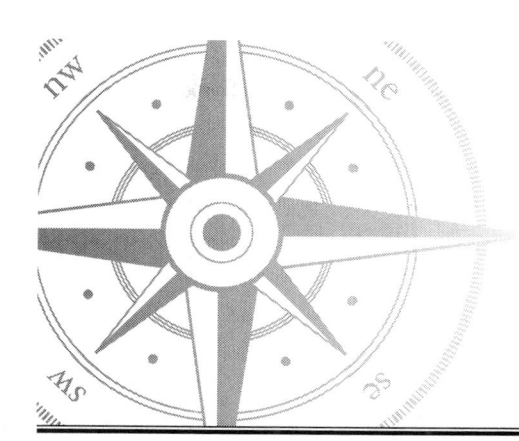

CHAPTER 52

Almost three weeks later the Lucy sailed into Rye harbour.

The Lucy had headed west down the south coast stopping at port after port to discharge or load cargo all the way to Falmouth. Departing that harbour, she headed east toward Dover, stopping at several ports en-route, including Rye.

Once the cargo was unloaded, Jon made his way to the quarterdeck.

"Captain, with your permission, I'll take my leave. I'd like to thank you for all of your assistance," He extended his hand to the captain.

"Not so fast young master. First there's a matter of compensation," stated the captain.

Jon said nothing. He was aware of ship's discipline, only too well. Discourtesy to the captain was a punishable offence in the merchant fleet as well as the navy. Captain Moore observed his puzzled looked and started laughing.

"Swift, you and I agreed to two weeks free work for providing a service to you and your so-called 'friend'. You have worked three and a half weeks on board this vessel; therefore, I owe you a week and a half pay as a topman," said Captain Moore.

"If you say so captain. I consider us even," responded a relieved Jon.

"Are you that rich, that you don't need money?" asked Captain Moore.

"Captain, I surely am not rich, but I don't take money from friends that help me. Besides, you never know -- maybe I'll have need of your services again. I consider us even captain, and thank you. I appreciate all you have done for me," stated a sombre Jon.

They shook hands and Jon left the quarterdeck. He shook hands with most of the crew on his way to the gangway.

After grabbing his sea chest, Jon walked off into Rye. As before, he stopped at the Cross Bow Tavern to negotiate leaving his sea chest. A quick change from slops into farm clothes and he was heading home.

After his unexplained absence for a month, Jon wondered what he would find when he got home.

It was well after midnight when Jon arrived back at the Swift cottage. Badly needing a drink after the long walk, he made a stop at the well to quench that thirst. There were no lights in the cottage, so there was a reasonable expectation that everyone was asleep. He was, therefore, startled when opening the door he found a man standing there ready to pounce.

"Whoa father, it's me, Jon."

His father relaxed, relieved that he didn't have to fight. Jon looked at him in the dim light. He had only been gone a month, but the difference in his father was remarkable. He had regained much of his strength. He apparently still could not speak properly, but there was muted vocal acknowledgement. For the first time in years, Jon walked over to his father and hugged him. There was a release of emotion that he had not experienced before. His father felt it as well. Silent tears ran down each face.

"Are you well Father?" He received a long squeeze on his arm.

"I've been at sea for four weeks. What has been happening around here? Is there anything I need to know?" This time he received a short single squeeze on the arm.

"Really? Well, I suppose it will have to wait until tomorrow morning. I have just walked from the ship in Rye, and I'm tired. I need some sleep. We'll talk in the morning, father."

Jon found a warm spot near the fire and lay down. Dragging a blanket over himself, he immediately dropped into a sound asleep.

He woke late to the sounds of his mother making breakfast. Ambling over to the kitchen table, he received a big hug from his mother. "I was so worried when you didn't come back again. I wondered if we would ever see you again."

"Some former shipmates needed a hand mother. I pitched in to help them. It was only supposed to take two weeks, but ended up at almost four weeks before we returned to Rye. I didn't have time to come back to tell you. I'm sorry, but there was nothing I could do at the time," explained Jon. "So what's been happening around here? Father indicated something was happening, but I was too tired to try and find out last night."

"Macmillan is gone. He hired two big fellows and went to Rye with them. They came back, but he didn't. The squire's barrister came down from London some time after Macmillan left. Apparently he went through the squire's records and found lots of questionable things. There's a warrant out for Macmillan. He apparently knew somehow and skipped out before the authorities could get him."

"So now that he is gone, what's happening?"

"Nobody knows anything. The barrister is in charge at the present, but what he's doing, no one knows," replied his mother.

"What about the squire? Is he well? Is he able to manage his holdings?"

"That I don't know," stated Mother Swift.

"Well, I think it is important for us to go over to see this barrister, and lodge a complaint about the ill treatment the Swift family has received. There should be some form of compensation for all of our troubles. I think I'll walk over with father later this morning to see either the squire or this barrister fellow."

"Do you think that's wise?"

"Mother, they nearly killed me, and stole a year of my life; they nearly killed father, and left him permanently injured; they stole from us, illegally evicted us off the farm we had worked for my entire lifetime, and harassed us. If there is no justice after all of that, then the law in this country is worthless," growled Jon.

His father came in from outside.

"Father, we should go over to the squire's to see either the squire or the barrister. We have been ill done by, and redress is needed."

His father nodded.

A famished Jon wolfed down a quick breakfast.

He needed to prepare himself for battle, because a battle was likely before getting anything from the squire.

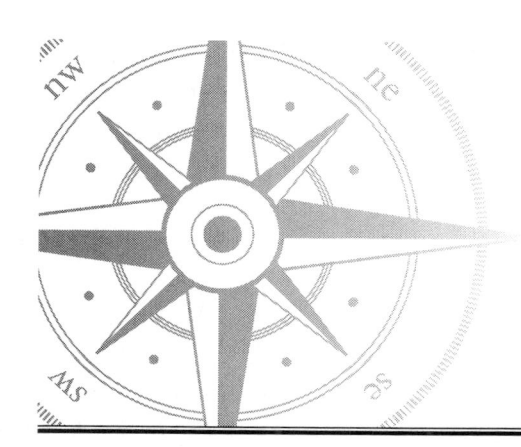

CHAPTER 53

Jon and Joe arrived at a near deserted home farm. Nothing was moving. Jon had never seen the home farm this quiet. It was unnerving.

When they knocked at the door of the main house, the deserted atmosphere was reinforced. It took some time before a short bespectacled man with thinning hair answered the door.

"Good morning sir. My name is Jon Swift, and this is my father Joe Swift. My father is a tenant of the squire's. We would like to have a word with the squire about the ill treatment we have been receiving from his manager and men."

"What ill treatment are you talking about?" asked the man.

"Sir, that would be for the squire's ears, or I guess his barrister's ears as well."

"I am the squire's barrister. My name is Peabody."

"Mr. Peabody, I have been assaulted. My father has been robbed, beaten and left for dead on the road. We were illegally evicted from the farm on which we had worked since before I was born, after having paid the yearly rent. We have been repeatedly harassed, with threats to my mother and my sister. The reason I am speaking on behalf of my father, is that after months of recovery, he still cannot speak properly. I believe sir, that we have reasonable grievances."

"You had better come in. I have let most of the staff go, because I do not know who was at fault, or who was trustworthy. Since the problems that I have discovered were done over a period of time, I believe blame can be assigned to most of those that worked here. So Mr. Swift, what are your expectations with regard to your alleged ill-treatment?" asked Mr. Peabody.

"Rest assured Mr. Peabody, the ill treatment is not alleged, it actually happened. I also believe that it can be proven in a court of law. To answer your question directly, we would like compensation; although I have not been able to discuss with my family what form this compensation might take. Mr. Peabody, the squire has known my father for years. Is the squire available to discuss this matter?"

Mr. Peabody was apparently about to say no, but he hesitated. "Wait a minute, and I'll see."

Excusing himself, he returned a few minutes later pushing a wheelchair. It was the first wheelchair that Jon had ever seen. He was both amazed at the wheelchair and concurrently stunned to see how much the squire had aged since he last saw him almost two years previously.

The squire's voice was weak.

"Joe Swift, how are you?"

Joe stood in the presence of the squire. He approached the squire and took his hand.

"My father cannot speak yet. In October when returning from selling some produce in Rye, he was attacked by three men. He has identified them as Abercrombie, Fitzgerald and Wells. They robbed him and clubbed him repeatedly over the head. He has only just regained the ability to walk in the last month."

"I'm sorry to hear that Joe. You understand that I cannot be held accountable for the actions of men that worked for me when they were obviously acting on their own. Besides, as you well know, those men are dead and therefore cannot defend themselves," said the squire.

Jon let that pass. He had expected nothing less from the squire. It wasn't important at this point as those men had already paid for their transgression.

"Squire, my father paid the rent to you in September, as he usually does. In November, your men showed up at our doorstep, entered the house and tossed some of our furniture onto a cart. They forcibly removed the family and dumped them in the place Archie Cartwright used to rent. Another tenant was in our old farm within twenty-four hours. He is using most of our furniture, eating the food we had grown and stored to keep us through the winter. That act, you were definitely accountable for sir, as it was your property, which we had legally rented, as we had for the past several years."

Jon was getting a bit hot under the collar. Joe placed his hand on Jon's arm and applied some pressure.

Mr. Peabody flipped open the books for the farm. "I can see no record of you paying your rent. The eviction was justified under such circumstances."

"Over the past twenty years, sir, how many times have you issued a receipt to my father for his rent? I can tell you. Never once! My father is not able to read, so a receipt would have been useless to him. His word was his bond. You have always accepted that. Are you or your barrister now going to tell me that without paper to back him up, my father is lying?"

Jon's voice had risen markedly.

"Let me also point out that when this 'eviction' took place, my family was moved from the farm we had rented and worked for years onto another of the squire's properties -- the place previously worked by Archie Cartwright. That is also the squire's property. If we had not paid the rent, then why were we still allowed to remain on the squire's property? That doesn't make sense," said Jon. "And why did the squire's men do the eviction and move? They never have before. The sheriff always did the eviction. Why were we also deprived of our furniture and effects, along with the food in the cold storage?"

"No, no," said the squire to Peabody. "In all the years I have known this man, he has never once lied to me. He has been late on his rent in some bad years, but he always told me and asked if I might extend him. He always paid."

"It would appear that this is just another case of Macmillan forging the books and making off with the money," said Mr. Peabody.

Jon thought about that statement. He considered it because he knew where Macmillan had headed. Something didn't strike him correctly. He put that in the back of his head. He tried to focus on the purpose of this meeting, to gain compensation from the squire.

Mr. Peabody brought the conversation back to the question of compensation. "So again, I ask the question. What are you looking for in the form of compensation?"

"Squire, Mr. Peabody, our family cannot make a go of it on the old Cartwright place as tenants. We could make a go of it, if we had clear title on the land. That's about the only way. My father can still farm, and he is one of the best farmers in this district. Despite his ability, even he cannot raise enough crops on that land to pay rent and support the family. The house itself is little better than a hovel. In all fairness, free title to the old Cartwright place would settle accounts."

His father squeezed his arm a single time.

The surprised look on Peabody's face and the scowl on the squire's face indicated some discussion on their part. It came as no surprise when Peabody said, "If you will excuse us, the squire and I would like to discuss this privately. If you would make yourself comfortable and be patient, we will return shortly."

With that, Mr. Peabody wheeled the squire out of the room. Jon and Joe sat down. Both of them were looking at the contents of the room. Most things visible were well beyond their means. Jon saw a row of books. He got up and went over to investigate. Some were actually bound books, while others were no better than pamphlets. He saw some interesting titles in the pamphlets, such as Husbandry of Animals, whatever that meant and something about growing crops. In the bound books, he saw titles such as Aesop's Fables, A Treatise of Human Nature and The Works of Mr. Alexander Pope. Jon got so caught up in looking at the books that he didn't hear the squire and Mr. Peabody re-enter the room.

"Do you read?" asked Mr. Peabody.

Jon scratched his head and looked down at the floor before raising his eyes to meet Mr. Peabody's eyes. "Not as well as I would like, sir. I have found there is wisdom to be found in some books, while others provide little value. Unfortunately, you generally have to read them to find out which category you have."

"Just so," replied Peabody. He gave Jon a thoughtful look, which Jon could not interpret. "Now as to your proposition for redress of grievances, the squire and I have discussed the matter. While you claim to have grounds, they would have to be proven without doubt in a court of law. Rather than take that tedious route, the squire has a counter proposal. He will offer your family five pounds cash for the loss when you were moved. On top of that, we are prepared to offer you a position at the home farm as a labourer at a compensation of three pounds a month plus found."

As Peabody explained the terms, Jon crossed his arms and his eyes became very hard. "You can't be serious?" Jon considered the offer a slap in the face for someone that had achieved a master's certificate of competency.

"Mr. Swift, I assure you that your demands far exceed any typical compensation for grievance that any court would award," said Peabody.

That statement contradicted everything Jon believed. The cost of their losses exceeded five pounds, and he sure as hell could make more than three pounds a month in the navy. His caution fled.

"Let me explain how I see things. The squire is in a bad position. All the staff that were here were suspect -- rightly or wrongly, it does not matter. You could not be sure of them; hence you discharged everyone. You told us that when we first arrived. With no staff on the home farm, you are in even worse shape. There is no one to tend to the squire, feed the animals, or plant crops. If you sell the animals, you can't operate the farm, and those tenants who rely on the animals will not be able to grow sufficient crops, and will not be able to meet their rents. The entire property could be lost just because the taxes aren't paid."

"That's just the easy stuff to imagine. I'm betting that when you examined the ledgers, you discovered other problems. I'm betting that not all of these problems have surfaced, and there may be more surprises. Our grievance is one of those surprises, and these surprises will not go away. They are going to cost you, whether you like it or not. Either our grievance is resolved here, or we will take them to court. Not to a court here, but at a higher level in which the squire is a defendant only."

"At the present, the squire's reputation locally is as bad as it can get because of Macmillan. If there is court action, word will spread beyond to all parts of the country. If there is anything that I have learned, it is that bad reputation, lack of funds, and mounting costs just lead to a worse situation. You will need money, but you won't find anyone to lend it. You can't raise rents anymore because your previous estate manager bled the tenants. When they couldn't meet these obligations, they were evicted, and now you have questionable tenants on those properties. It is doubtful that you will collect the rents from many of them this year; yet, you will still have to pay the taxes on those properties. All this means that meeting your obligations will be increasingly difficult. You have now entered a circle where a problem in one area causes a problem in another area, which then creates another problem in another area. It goes on and on, and the surprises will keep on coming, and not go away."

"I'd be surprised if you haven't figured all of this out already, but just in case you haven't I'll make my position perfectly clear to you. Either you resolve my family's claims to our satisfaction, or I'll bring the entire estate down around your ears," said Jon.

The entire room was silent.

"I'll have no threats against me in my own house. Get yourselves off my property, and that includes all of my property. You're evicted. Now go! Leave! Get out of my sight," rattled a very agitated squire.

Jon was tempted to resolve the problem once and for all. His hand automatically drifted toward the throwing knife. His father viciously pulled his arm, and propelled him toward the door. His red-faced father positioned himself behind Jon and continued pushing him toward the door.

The second push was too much for Jon. He turned and grabbed his father's arms. Exhibiting the great strength acquired from moving two-ton guns, he lifted Joe out of the way. He faced the squire and Mr. Peabody, his hands flexing unconsciously at his side.

"Mr. Peabody, I'll leave you with one last thought. Macmillan was an evil man. Evil can never prevail where goodness resides. Evil only thrives were other evil is present. By his actions today, the squire showed you why Macmillan was able to thrive. I do not know you, sir, but ask yourself if you are going to support that evil? If your answer is yes, be prepared for the consequences."

"As for you squire…" Jon spit on the floor.

Joe was repeatedly shaking his head as he dragged Jon through the door. By the time they had descended the steps, much of the anger seemed to have dissipated.

"Sorry father, I never realized how big a bastard the squire is until this morning. I thought that he was just being manipulated by Macmillan. This morning I saw the true evil in the man. I lost my temper."

Still holding Jon's arm, Joe gave him a single long, strong squeeze. Jon didn't understand the squeeze. Either his father agreed with him, or it was his rebuke instead of strangling.

Regardless, the Swifts had just moved from the firing pan into the fire.

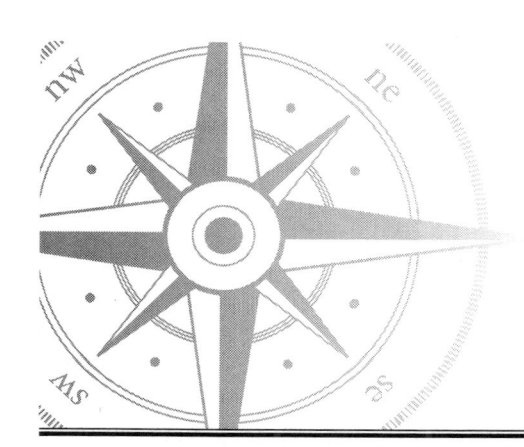

CHAPTER 54

When the news about the eviction broke in the Swift cottage, tears began to flow. Mother Swift was inconsolable. Susan and Robbie were stunned. Joe collapsed at the kitchen table with his head in his hands. No one had anything to say to Jon, but just the same, he knew that they all blamed him.

During the walk home, Jon fought to regain control over his temper. Everything he did since returning home had been for one goal -- to protect and to make a better life for the Swift family. All the risks taken, all the crimes committed, appeared to be in vain. If you had money, you made the rules. You could commit any number of crimes and retain power. If you didn't have money, someone with money could walk all over you with impunity.

That stuck in Jon's craw. That miserable bastard could sit in that wheelchair plotting and scheming to make himself richer regardless of the price others had to pay. The Swifts had suffered enough. It was time the suffering occurred on the other side.

The mood in the Swifts' cottage was oppressive. It was bad enough to be picked on by the squire and his cronies. To add the rest of the family to that list was too much. Jon had enough. He grabbed his jacket and left.

While leaving the farm, Jon remembered a quote that Liliput, the senior rating on the Mermaid's foremast, had once said in the mess -- Pride goeth before destruction and a haughty spirit before a fall. How true that was. He had let his pride and cockiness get in the way of looking after the family. Now they were in dire straits as a result.

It was totally up to Jon to find a place for the Swifts. His pride and temper was the reason they would shortly be evicted. There was an additional drawback -- Joe could not communicate with any prospective landlord.

Not having a clear objective, other than to get out of the cottage, he started drifting toward Rye. On his walk back to the farm from Rye he had noticed one property on the other side of parish line, with a sign indicating it was available. The property merited a look, which was at least something constructive to do.

Jon had briefly investigated properties before going after Wells. He had stopped because of father. He hadn't known before abducting Macmillan whether father would be strong enough to work a farm. Someone had to earn the money necessary to survive. If father hadn't improved, the Swifts would have to take a place in town.

Now with father at least fit enough to handle a plough, he could seek out a farm with a reasonable chance that it could be worked well enough to support the family. The problem was the availability of farms. There were no properties in the parish. Even if there were, being in the same jurisdiction where the squire had control could pose major problems.

After a good hour's walk, he came upon the place. The farm was small, about sixty acres, with only one building -- a two bedroom cottage. Jon entered the unoccupied cottage and started examining it. It had been hard used, although it was structurally sound and well laid out. With no outbuildings, except an outhouse, Jon wondered where the food for the year would be stored. He walked over to the well and tested the water, slaking his thirst in the process.

Jon spent the next hour walking the fields and fences. The fields were numerous and small, surrounded for the better part by rock fences. All the work on the farm had been by hand. Many of the fields were so small, they couldn't accommodate a horse and plough. The number of trees remaining on the farm could be counted using the fingers of both hands. That meant all the wood they'd need for cooking and heating would have to be obtained elsewhere. There were crown lands twenty miles away where all the wood needed was freely available. It would cost the rent of a team and wagon to fetch it. There was a reason the property was available. Any reasonable farmer couldn't make a go of it under even a normal rent.

Jon sat on a fence and contemplated options for the Swift family. Renting this property was out of the question. If it were purchased, it would be a fight for the first year. Most of the fences would have to be removed. The fields would have to be reworked, the house repaired and a root cellar built. Just moving the fences would take a man five to six months. There was only a month before planting. With the three of them working, they could get some fences removed. After that start, one man could do the ploughing using a rented team, while the other moved more fences. Robbie and the women would have to work an expanded garden. If a team were not available, they would continue moving rocks.

It would be hard work, but they should be able to harvest enough to pay the taxes, pay for all tools, repairs to the cottage, and possibly get the underground storage built. The expanded garden should be able to produce enough food for the family for the year. If they were lucky enough, perhaps they could put up a chicken coop and get some chickens for meat.

It would all depend upon the price of the farm. The average price of a farm in the area was one to two pounds an acre totally depending on the richness of the soil, condition of the buildings and the buyer's ability to negotiate. The soil on this farm was average, it had only one building and that needed repair. The layout of the fields was a distinct negative. It would be a hard negotiation.

Jon started down the road to Rye to find the owner. He managed to hop on a farmer's wagon, which eased the strain on his feet and cut considerable time from the walk.

Once in Rye, Jon started his investigation by acquiring and checking the local paper, such as it was. He found a number of properties advertised. Most were towards either Hastings or in the Romney Marshes. If this property didn't work out, they provided an alternative. He finally identified the one he was seeking. The contact listed was a person named Mr. Tittle at an address in Rye. Jon went searching for him.

It took a couple of hours, but Jon finally tracked down Mr. Tittle. They found a quiet spot to speak.

"Tell me about this farm you have available."

"It's a nice place. Sixty acres with a pretty little cottage, good well, and the fences are in reasonable condition. The place is empty at the moment. There was a tenant farmer in it last year. We had to get rid of him as he never met the rent."

"How much were you asking for the rent?"

"Ten pounds."

"If a man were interested in purchasing, what are you asking for the property?"

"One hundred pounds."

For a sixty acre property that's unoccupied, the price was excessive and way beyond what he was prepared to pay. Jon remained silent. The silence was a tactic he'd employed with success on a number of occasions when negotiating.

"Would you be interested in seeing the property? I warn you that it's an hour ride from here."

Mr. Tittle looked Jon over. Jon was wearing old well-worn farm clothes. He was somewhat dusty from the walk. With his beard, he looked exactly like any tenant farmer in the area, maybe one a little worse for wear.

"I can get a horse and cart to take us up and back," suggested Mr. Tittle.

'Seems like the man is motivated to sell. I wonder why?' thought Jon.

"Mr. Tittle, the going price for a farm with buildings, is about a pound an acre. You just quoted me a price of one hundred pounds for a property with only a cottage. At that price I'm not even interested in looking. In fact I'm not interested in any property over a pound an acre --less if the buildings need repair or the fields won't handle a team and plough."

"I'm willing to negotiate."

'Tittle is either going to waste my time or is very motivated,' thought Jon.

"If that's the case, why don't you get a team and we'll take a look.

They arrived on the farm an hour later. Jon took a fast look over the entire place. He approached Tittle who was sitting somewhat impatiently in the carriage. Jon rubbed his chin and tried to think how to start. He decided to say nothing.

"So are you interested?" asked Tittle.

Jon waited for a couple of minutes before responding. "I can tell you're not a farmer, sir. Any farmer would tell you that on a good farm, sixty acres of grain should make you twenty pounds in an average year, maybe twenty-five pounds if everything were perfect. That's what you apparently based your rent on. What you don't understand, and any good farmer will tell you, is that this is a poor farm. Not the land, the land is alright. It's because this farm is poorly laid out. Most of the fields are too small for a horse and plough. That means the farmer has to do everything by hand. One man can't plough, seed and harvest sixty acres by hand. At most, even in the best of years, a man could only expect to get maybe fifteen pounds from his labours, and that is being generous. Take away the cost of seed, getting wood, his food and clothes, and the average man would be really lucky to have seven or eight pounds at the end of everything. If he wasn't frugal and had more mouths to feed, he might not even make five."

"No sir, there's no farmer that I know that could make a go of it on this farm. I bet the tenant that you had was scraping the bottom of the barrel. No one in his right mind is going to rent this farm. So that leaves you with a property that will generate no income while slowly costing you money for taxes and upkeep. After looking at this property, anyone can see the upkeep is neglected."

Jon paused and looked at Tittle. He was not sure what Tittle was thinking. The impatience was gone for sure. The silence seemed to go on forever.

"So what'd ya think it's worth?"

"Nowhere near what you were asking. I told you that I wasn't prepared to pay more than a pound per acre."

"Sixty pounds. You just said that the land was good, and it has a good cottage on it," said Tittle.

"No way. This property is far from good. Just to get this property in that condition would take thirty to forty pounds at least."

"I'll go as low as fifty, but no further."

"Forty pounds. You'll lose ten pounds this year on taxes and deterioration of the property anyway."

"Fifty."

"Forty five. Take it or leave it."

After a period of silence, Tittle reluctantly grumbled, "Deal."

They shook hands, and proceeded back to Rye to complete the paperwork.

An exhausted and financially lightened Jon entered the Swift cottage shortly after midnight. It had been a long, hungry, and thirsty walk home.

As he sat drinking a mug of cool water, he realized work was about to get much harder.

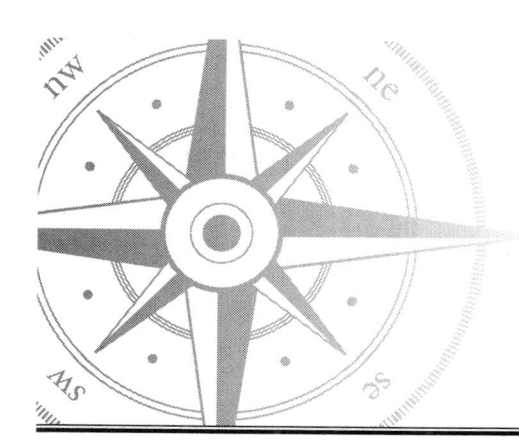

CHAPTER 55

Having the sheriff pound on your door first thing in the morning is never a good omen, even when you know it's coming. Joe opened the door with trepidation. Mother Swift was holding her breath.

"Joe Swift, I have an eviction notice with me ordering you to remove yourself and all of your possessions from this property." Mother Swift sucked in a mouthful of air and placed a hand over her mouth to stifle a wail.

Jon was sitting at the kitchen table munching on his late breakfast. Since Joe couldn't speak, Jon did.

"Excuse me sheriff, how much time do we have to comply with this order?"

"It's effective immediately."

"Seems mighty harsh and awfully queer to me, sheriff. How many evictions have you done in March, just before planting season and with no notice?"

"Well, you know -- I just do what I'm ordered to do. I know your family has been hard done by, but I still have to do my job. The paper says you got to leave."

"Sheriff, it's going to take us some time to pack, and we need to speak to our friends to see if we can get some help. If I give you our word that we will leave tomorrow without any trouble, will you give us another night here?"

"I don't think I can do that."

"Sheriff, let me speak to you outside for a moment." The sheriff was somewhat hesitant, but he finally relented. Stepping back a few paces, followed by Jon and Joe, he crossed his arms and waited for an explanation.

"Sheriff, you know as well as we do that this eviction is unheard of. It's never happened in all the time our family has been living here. It just shows everyone how far gone the squire is at the present. Any eviction has been after a few days' notice. There hasn't even been a day. How are we supposed to find someplace to go in that time and get organized to move? That being said, the squire still has the right to evict us, and you have your job to do. Everyone understands that. All we're asking is one more night."

The sheriff looked at Joe when he replied. "I'm sorry Joe. For some reason the squire's adamant that you get out of here. It has to be today. There's nothing that I can do."

"Can you at least do us one favour sheriff? Could you ride over to Abe Hartwell's and see if he could spare his team and wagon for us today? Robbie could go over with you."

"That I can do. Get Robbie."

After the sheriff rode off, with Robbie perched behind him, Joe took Jon by the shoulders. Mother Swift asked what Joe needed to know. "Where are we going to go?"

"I found a place on the other side of the parish line. It's a small place of sixty acres. The house is only two bedrooms and needs work, but it is in far better condition than this place. The soil is good, but it's going to take a lot of work to make a go of it. The good news is that we are out from under the squire."

"How are we going to pay for it?" Mother Swift was about one breath away from crying.

"Mother we don't have any other option, unless you want to be sleeping on the side of the road tonight. So let's get on with it and prepare everything for moving."

Somehow over the next few hours, the news of the Swift eviction spread around the parish. Abe Hartwell, who was a true friend of Joe's, arrived with his team and wagon. Other people dropped by to assist. When it was learned where they were heading, there were numerous comments, which further increased Mother Swift's fears.

By dark, everything had been transferred to the new property. There was no wood, not even enough to light a stove to cook supper, so Joe, Robbie and Abe went back to the old place and stripped every piece of wood they could find. They made arrangements with Abe to borrow the team the next day to forage for wood.

Sleeping arrangements were somewhat cramped. Susan took one of the bedrooms, while Robbie and Jon took the sitting room.

At first light the next morning, work began. It continued seven days a week all day and sometimes into darkness without interruption. Meals were before first light and after last light. It was brutal, strenuous and dispiriting, but it had to be done.

A month passed. Rain delayed planting for two weeks. The rain only slowed fence removal on the farm; it didn't stop it. The rain had other negative impacts on the Swifts, however, as the team they were counting on to plough their fields and prepare for planting was unavailable. It meant their crop was in danger, as it might be planted too late.

By the end of the second month, teams were still not available, so they continued removing fences. Robbie and the women spent hours preparing and planting the garden.

Finally, Abe Hartwell was able to spare his team, but not willing to risk his plough with all the rocks on the Swift property. Jon wasted a day going to Rye to purchase a plough. Once he managed to get it back to the farm, the ploughing began.

Ploughing was nearly as brutal as removing the rock fences. That was because numerous rocks were unearthed using the plough. These had to be carried by hand over to the fence line. Jon got that task while Joe ploughed.

Three months after moving to the place, the crops were in and all but two of the fields had been realigned. Whether they managed a good harvest was now in the hands of the Lord.

That didn't mean the work let up any. They continued removing the last of the fences, then started the unpleasant task of digging an underground cold storage. By the end of the summer the root cellar was finished and being filled rapidly with produce from the garden. The grain crop, which normally was harvested in August, was not ready until mid-September.

By the time of the harvest, the situation for the Swift family had changed. They were out of trouble. In fact, they would have an abundance of food for the next year, an improved home to live in, fields that could be readily ploughed, and that were well fenced. They started to lay in wood for the winter, and building a chicken coop.

Jon's situation had changed even more significantly. He had had his fill of picking rocks and ploughing fields. As an able seaman working the tops on a merchantman, he could make far more money than being a farm labourer. The work was far less demanding than what he had just completed over the past few months. As an officer on a merchantman, he could expect even better prospects than owning a small farm. If he had to choose between the two worlds, there was no contest. He would pick the sea every time. The risk was higher at sea, between the storms, the threat of being pressed, and the French. On land, however, it would only take one bad crop to place everything in jeopardy.

He needed to get back to sea, if for no other reason than to save his sanity.

As far as the squire was concerned, Jon hadn't entirely forgotten him. He still believed the Swifts were entitled to compensation for all the transgressions the squire had initiated against them. Just how he could go about achieving that compensation was unclear.

The lateness of their harvest hurt. The local grain market where they normally would sell their crop was flooded. The crops throughout the area had flourished, including their crops. That just increased the supply.

In the age-old battle between supply and demand, over-supply drove the prices down.

Jon hit upon a plan to take care of the family, help himself and make a little profit in the process. He had walked to Rye to check the grain prices at the farmers' market. While in the market, he noticed that ships' officers were buying grain. After some digging around, he was able to find out the market price in London. The ships were buying grain at depressed prices on the south coast and selling them in London or further north at full price. Even with the cost of carrying the cargo, they would still make a nice profit.

Jon's plan was simple. He would ship the Swifts entire harvest, less grain needed for next year's seed, to London to sell it. There was still cash in the money belt. With this money, he still needed to pay the yearly taxes, accumulated expenses, and provide a safety net for family emergencies. Whatever cash remained he would use to acquire more grain. That was the first part of the plan.

The second part of the plan was the transport of the grain. The Lucy would be engaged to carry the load. Jon would accompany the load and sell it in London. The money from the sale, less the amount owed to the Lucy, would be his. From London, he could decide his future direction.

Before leaving Rye, Jon left word at the Crossbow tavern that once the Lucy returned to port, Captain Moore should contact him.

Back home, Jon initiated the plan by contacting and negotiating with those farmers who still had grain to sell. The results of these negotiations were pleasantly surprising.

At the end of September, he received word that the Lucy was in Rye. Jon immediately dropped what he was doing and headed to the docks. It was near dark when he arrived at the ship. Permission to board was readily granted. Captain Moore was in his cabin, so Jon got right down to business.

"Captain Moore, I've got another proposition for you, if you're interested?"

"Am I going to like this one any more than the last one?" replied a wary Captain Moore.

"I'd say so. My family owns a farm north of here. We've collected approximately forty tonnes of grain, primarily wheat, but some rye and barley as well. There are eight hundred 120-lb. bags. There is no market here. I would like the Lucy to haul the grain to London and sell it there."

"That's a straightforward contract. Not like your usual propositions. What's the catch?"

"I go with the cargo at no cost. I can work as a topman again, if you like under our previous arrangement. When we get to London, you teach me your tricks selling the grain at the maximum profit."

"I don't see any problem in any of that. In fact it's so good that I'd be a fool not to take it. Any other captain would jump at it."

"If it works out the way I believe it will, there will be a possibility of repeating it after next year's harvest. I'll speak to my father about it."

"Even better. So when can I expect to load?"

"I can only move approximately eighty bags at a time. That means ten loads, and it will take approximately two and a half hours between each load because of the distance. It will take all day tomorrow and the next to fetch everything. With luck we should be able to catch the last of the evening tide on the second day."

"You'd best get cracking then."

Jon rushed down the gangway, and headed home as fast as possible. He first stopped at Abe Hartwell's place to ensure the availability of the team and wagon that he had previously arranged.

At five the next morning, they started out with the first load. Robbie went around informing all farmers who had sold grain to be prepared to load later in the morning. It was a long day. Before quitting, they managed to get six of the ten loads to Rye.

Over a late supper, Jon broke the news to the family.

"Father, I need to explain something to you and the rest of the family. When we moved here, I didn't sign on as a tenant. The fact is, I bought the place. I have already paid the taxes and settled up with Mr. Jenkins at the store. Everything that is currently on this property, with the exception of Abe Hartwell's team and wagon, is ours."

He had expected silence from his father. It was just as well, because the clamouring from the rest of the family would have drowned out anything that he could possibly have said, if father could speak. Jon raised his hands, palms out to plead for quiet.

"When I looked at this place, I knew, as did every other farmer in the area that a single man couldn't make a go of it on this farm. After redoing all the fences and enlarging the fields, a single man can now make a go of it. The repairs on the house, the garden, the root cellar, and soon the chicken coop will mean the family will be comfortable and may even prosper. You have more than enough food for the year, especially considering there will be one less mouth to feed. If you haven't guessed it, I'm leaving."

"Why?" asked Susan. She beat everyone else to the question.

"I came back for one reason. That was to make sure that you were alright, and to say a proper goodbye. I would have left home soon anyway. Being pressed just hastened that. I stayed because without me, I believe the family would have suffered. You are no longer in that position."

"When the last of the grain is loaded tomorrow night, I will sail with it. I'm leaving enough grain for next year's seed and ten pounds for father in case something happens and the family needs money. To my knowledge we have no other debts anywhere. You should be able to manage. It's the best I can do for you. The money I get from the grain I'll use to start somewhere else."

There were questions, none of which Jon could or would answer. Rapidly, each went their own respective way. For all the males that was bed, as it had been a long hard day.

The next day went reasonably smoothly. Before departing with the last load, Jon added all his kit to the wagon. The ditty bag and sea chest were full, almost overflowing. He said a tearful goodbye to Susan. She would be a woman, probably married before Jon saw her next -- assuming he ever saw her again. He gave Mother a short hug. He couldn't bring himself to go any further than that.

The three men climbed aboard and started the team. Jon watched the farm until it was lost to sight. He turned to Robbie and explained what he wanted them to do once he was gone.

At the docks, after the wagon was unloaded, Jon introduced Captain Moore to Joe and Robbie. Jon turned to say his farewells.

"Robbie, learn everything you can about farming and trade. Father is a good teacher. The farm will be yours one day. Make me proud of your accomplishment."

Jon then hugged his tearful little brother.

"Father, take care of yourself and the family. I doubt I will see you again, but who knows what the Lord has in store for me. You have been a good father. May the Lord protect you and the family! Goodbye."

Jon hugged his father, hoisted his kit to his shoulder, turned and went aboard.

The tide was turning, so the second Jon stepped aboard, Captain Moore rapped out the order to cast off. Jon immediately climbed the ratlines and slipped the gaskets off the sail, ready to let loose.

That was the last image the Swift family had of Jon.

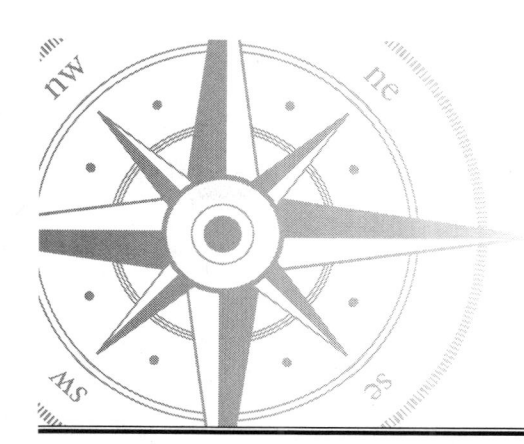

CHAPTER 56

As the Lucy hit the rollers in the English Channel, Jon glanced back at Rye. It was no longer possible to see Joe or Robbie. Jon's emotions were mixed. He was sad to leave the family, but at the same time greatly relieved to be at sea.

The one regret was not being able to finalize anything with the squire. Maybe it would happen later, maybe never. The squire was a sick man. Perhaps the old bastard would die before they got any compensation. Perhaps something should be done while in London. Maybe it would be best to let it drop.

As night descended and he adjusted to the watch routine, Jon felt a great burden removed from his shoulders. He had no money -- it was all invested in the grain carried in the hold. For the short term, at least until London, there was a place to sleep, meals, and work to keep him occupied. After London, assuming the grain sold well, enough money to start up somewhere should be available. Just where that should be was, as yet, undetermined.

Dawn broke with Jon in the tops. It was his watch, but even if it hadn't been, his navy training meant that he stood-to at dawn just in case any hostile or suspicious ships had closed during the night.

As the light increased, he observed the coast of France a few miles to starboard. Within the span of vision, only two sails were visible. One was aft and appeared to be heading in the opposite direction. The other was in front and looked to be closing.

An approaching vessel was always scrutinized with care. This one was no different. It appeared to be a schooner rig, but something about it didn't look right. The hair on Jon's neck rose.

"Deck there, possible French schooner coming for us on the starboard bow quarter. I don't like the looks of her," shouted Jon.

Captain Moore took no chances.

"Hard ta larboard," he immediately ordered. "Get those sails braced around."

The Lucy's crew scrambled to reset the sails. The Lucy wallowed to larboard and headed directly toward the English coast. Ramsgate was off in the distance, but to reach it, the Lucy would have to close with the schooner.

Within the Lucy, the atmosphere had rapidly changed from nonchalant to apprehensive. The Lucy was not a fast ship -- she was a tub with sails. Her sole purpose in life was to carry the maximum amount of cargo using the least amount of crew. The oncoming schooner was likely almost twice as fast. The crew nevertheless scrambled to set all available canvas.

The minutes ticked by. The Lucy closed Ramsgate. The schooner was closing even faster. Every man on board could clearly see the approaching menace.

The Lucy didn't have so much as a swivel gun on her. If this was a French privateer, there was little hope of resistance.

Jon came down from the tops, went below and grabbed the pistol from the sea chest. He checked the load and slipped a ship's powder horn over his shoulder. Extra balls and wads were placed loosely in the right pocket. On deck, he grabbed a boarding axe, and stuffed it into his belt.

A close examination of the approaching ship revealed her deck was lower than the Lucy's deck. That meant that boarders would have to climb up to board the Lucy. The Lucy had only twenty men on board. The approaching schooner's deck was swarming with men and they outnumbered the Lucy's crew two or three to one.

Off in the distance, Ramsgate was a refuge from the privateer, but a refuge the Lucy was unlikely to make. The guns sited there had a long reach. A closer look at the Frenchman's position in relation to the Lucy confirmed the Lucy would be intercepted just outside the range of those guns. What they needed were some delaying tactics so the Lucy could get within the range of the Ramsgate guns. Even once they sailed within cannon range, the Lucy wasn't necessarily safe. At the minimum, she would have to alter course so she did not screen the schooner from the vengeance of those guns.

One thing Jon knew for sure -- he was not going down without a fight, even if he died fighting.

As the ships continued to close, Jon walked over to Captain Moore.

"May I make a suggestion captain?" asked Jon. Captain Moore nodded.

"The wind is from the west. On this present course, the schooner will approach us on our leeward side, aiming at our bow. From the leeward side, their decks will be higher and ours will be canted down, reducing the height difference between the two ships and making it easier for them to board. They will grapple as they pass and count on the grapples to hold. Just before contact they will let their sails fly to slow down."

"If you were to alter course so that we were bows on, then change your course at the last minute to run down their lee side several things would happen," continued Jon. "Our decks would be higher, whereas theirs would be lower. That would make boarding much more difficult for them. Depending upon the timing, it would confuse them, as they will be massing for the boarding on their windward side. If we continued to swing to starboard, the gap between ships would be greater, so it would be harder for them to pull us together, and it would delay their boarding. If the Lucy caught enough wind, we could pull completely away with many of their grapples. Remember, they have to let their sails fly at the last minute. If we were able to pull away, then they might be caught in stays. All we would have to do is alter course back to larboard and head toward Ramsgate. We would be inside the Ramsgate arc of fire before the schooner could reach us again. They might try, so all we would have to do is alter course so the Lucy doesn't screen Ramsgate's cannons."

Captain Moore looked over towards the helmsman, "Put her bows on to the schooner."

Jon ran forward, shouting as he went, "Grab boarding axes. They'll try to grapple us on the larboard side. Cut as many lines on the grapples as you can, but keep low as they'll have muskets."

Jon continued all the way to the forecastle and lay down behind the bulwark. The two ships were closing fast. Jon readied his pistol, which was vastly more accurate than any sea pistol. It was now all about control and accuracy. Slow the breathing, adjust to the motion of the ship, steady the barrel, and track the target.

Jon looked behind him and saw the captain speaking to the helmsman. They were an open target. It would be a shame if they didn't survive.

As they closed the schooner, the Lucy started to turn to larboard. This initial turn to larboard startled the Lucy's crew. Suddenly, without any warning, they turned hard to starboard. The hard turn to starboard reassured them. The schooner, in contrast, was caught completely by surprise. The helmsman on the schooner had to swing hard to his starboard, the Lucy's larboard, to miss ramming the Lucy mid-ships.

Jon heard a shouted command in French. He had no idea what that command was, but it was shortly observed as a 'let fly" when the schooner sails were loosened.

Someone on the French schooner screamed a second command, and the grapples flew through the air.

Jon took careful aim and squeezed the pistol trigger. It was a long shot and he had to aim off. The ball struck the Frenchman's helmsman. It was only a wounding strike, but had the desired effect as the helmsman momentarily let go of the wheel. The schooner had her rudder hard over to starboard to miss the Lucy. As soon as the helmsman lost his grip on the wheel the rudder came back to amidships. The schooner bumped the side of the Lucy. The bump was hard enough for a number of Frenchmen to lose their balance and fall.

The grapples that were tossed were not as successful as the French captain would have liked. When the sails were let fly, because they were on the leeward side, the sails flew directly into the path of the grapples. That caused a number to miss. The grapple throwers had been on the windward side and had to re-position themselves on the leeward side, so they were off balance. The bump didn't help. Even if they were successful, and a number of them were, when the bump occurred they lost their footing. A man's normal reaction when he stumbles on a canting deck is to grab something by which he can assure himself that he is not going overboard. Since the grapples were pulling overboard, a number of these lines were released. The Lucy's crew managed to cut some, but not all of the other lines.

Because of the bump, there had been no accurate musket fire from the schooner. Jon had heard several muskets fire, but he could not determine where those shots had landed.

With both ships still moving, several men holding grapple lines in the schooner were pulled overboard by the momentum.

The Lucy continued forward. Both the courses on the main and foremast had been ripped as they brushed past the schooner. The sails were still drawing sufficient wind to keep the Lucy going. Once sufficiently past the schooner Captain Moore brought the Lucy back on a direct course toward Ramsgate.

Jon looked back at the schooner. She was stopped and appeared to be attempting to recover those men who had fallen overboard.

A cheering started on the Lucy, as the crew realized they had escaped. A shout from Captain Moore brought that cheering to an end. Men were assigned to retrieve the grapples and lines still being dragged along. Topmen were ordered aloft to trim the sails to squeeze that last bit of speed out so the Lucy could scoot into Ramsgate before the schooner returned.

As they approached the harbour entrance, Captain Moore ordered the courses dropped and sailed into the harbour on the topsails only.

After bringing the Lucy to anchor, the courses were lowered to the deck so that repairs could commence.

Captain Moore passed word that the Lucy would remain in Ramsgate until the schooner was long gone. An uninjured and greatly relieved crew thought that was a fine idea.

A few days later in London, the Lucy finally got a dockside position. By that time, Captain Moore had already been in contact with different buyers. As the first load was lowered onto the wharf, the buyers checked the contents. The bidding began and was over in a few moments. The winning buyer's wagons appeared, and the grain was loaded directly onto their wagons. By last light, the cargo was nearly all gone. Captain Moore had already lined up outward-bound cargo, so the next day would see the completion of unloading and commencement of loading.

For the next two days loading took place. At the end of the second day, Captain Moore summoned Jon to his cabin and handed him one hundred twenty pounds.

"Payment for the grain less transport costs. That's a lot of money to be carrying around. Do you want me to keep it locked up for you?" asked Captain Moore seriously.

"I'd appreciate it captain."

"So what do you intend to do now?"

"I'm not entirely sure. I'd like to stay at sea for the present. I am not inclined to re-join His Majesty's navy, so I'm thinking a merchantman. I'd like to get a job where I can use my Master's certificate, but my age is likely against me, so I'm at a loss," said Jon. "You have any suggestions or advice, captain?"

Captain Moore scratched his head. "I think you're right about your age. Look around at the ships docked or anchored here. I bet the youngest officer on any of those ships has at least ten years on you. I can't see any of the ship owners taking a chance on you, even if you do have the required skills. You proved that to me without a doubt off Ramsgate."

Jon allowed a smile to form on his face. That was as close as he would likely ever come to getting a thank you from Captain Moore.

Captain Moore continued, "So as I see it, you need to think about His Majesty's navy for a few years before anyone here will allow you the chance you seek."

"I don't think so," said Jon. "I have a knack for trading and that's not possible in the navy."

"The only other option I can think of is the Americas or the Indies," said Captain Moore. "I hear they are always looking for people in the Indies."

"Yes they are," said Jon. "I can tell you why. The yellow jack, or some other dam disease, claims a lot of men. I was transferred to a ship that had been struck with yellow jack. The compliment for that ship was supposed to be over three hundred men. When I got there, there were less than two hundred still able to move. I have to admit, though, you do have a point. Where there is a demand, there is likely opportunity."

"Why don't you ask around? There are ships from the Americas here. Maybe you could get some information from them?" said Captain Moore.

"Sounds reasonable."

"I'll ask around to see if there are any ships headed that direction that need a young master," chuckled Captain Moore. "By the way, we'll be sailing with the tide tomorrow morning."

"I'd appreciate that captain. If I don't find a ship here, I might hitch a ride out to Sheerness. Sooner or later there's bound to be a ship passing there to America."

After his conversation with Captain Moore, Jon headed to the waterfront taverns. The taverns were a good way of picking up information about ships and the traits of those ships. It didn't take too long to find out about a ship heading out in the next day or so to New York. She was called the Rockport, out of Rhode Island.

Jon found a couple members of the crew. After buying them drinks, he inquired if they had any vacancies for officers or seaman. They both mentioned there were always vacancies, but the owners were too cheap to hire anyone. After some more questions about the location of the ship and her crew, Jon left the tavern seeking the ship.

A brief word with the harbour watch and they allowed him on board to meet the captain.

Captain Roberts was very different from what Jon had expected. First, he was young, only in his early thirties. He was a tall, dark haired brute of a man. Jon estimated he was over six feet and very heavy. Jon's first impression was that the Rockport was unlikely to have any mutiny with this captain. Over the span of the next few minutes' conversation, Jon had reason to revise his initial assessment. Captain Roberts was very intelligent. His most noticeable flaw was his abruptness and grating personality. He would not be an easy man to get along with.

Jon signed on as an ordinary seaman. It was well below his station, but at least he was paid. The alternative would be to pay a fare as a passenger.

Back at the Lucy to fetch his kit, he said some sad farewells. Jon had shipped out on the Lucy three times. It was unlikely that he would ship out on her again.

His last stop was to collect his money from Captain Moore.

"Well sir, I'll be off. I'm not sure when I'll next see you, or if I'll be back this way. Let me say that it has been a pleasure, sir. I wish you and the Lucy the best of luck."

"Take care of yourself Jon. I wish you the best," replied Captain Moore, offering his hand. It was a significant goodbye, as Captain Moore had never used his first name in the past.

As Jon stowed his kit aboard the Rockport, he wondered what his destiny would be. For the next few weeks, it was a sea life, because in the morning he was sailing to New York.

AUTHOR'S NOTES

For those unfamiliar with 'starting', an explanation is in order. A 'starter' is a piece of rope 2-3 feet in length, generally with a knot at the end. Royal Navy petty officers carried this rope and used it as a means of motivation, or punishment, depending upon the individual wielding it. Getting 'started' happened when a petty officer flicked the rope, and snapped it into the back or buttocks of his victim. The initial intent was to 'start' the man moving faster, hence the name 'starter'. It was painful and often resulted in a bruise lasting a few days. Petty officers were supposedly the only individuals wielding a starter. It was beneath a gentleman, which both commissioned officers and midshipmen were believed to be, to carry a starter. Officers used the threat of 'starting' as a means of speeding a process (e.g., last man on deck will be 'started'). Needless to say, the men detested 'starting'.

Discipline in the Royal Navy was a critical necessity, especially when you consider a handful of officers controlled in some cases hundreds of men, a high majority of whom had been pressed against their will. Men were expected to be subservient. If a man looked directly into the eyes of his superior, it could be claimed as defiance and subject to punishment.

Before the fall of New France, all areas controlled by the French had French names. Once the French were defeated and these territories ceded to the British, the names of many places were altered. Ile Royale (Cape

Breton Island) and Ile Saint Jean (Prince Edward Island) are typical examples.

After the fall of Louisbourg in June 1745, the surrendered garrison and civilians were provided "unmolested" escort back to France as part of the Articles of Capitulation. They were loaded on English vessels and transported to Brest. The actual ship that escorted the French back to France was HMS Launceston. She and several transports carrying 1200 French 'refugees' sailed from Louisbourg on July 3rd, 1745. For the sake of this story, the Mermaid took her place.

The real HMS Mermaid did leave Louisbourg and ended up in England. She was assessed and decommissioned in the summer of 1746. Again, in the interests of the story, Mermaid's demise was accelerated by six months.

Readers with knowledge of the Royal Navy circa 1746 may question Swift's speed of promotion. To set that in perspective, in 1746, a pressed man usually was rated as a landsman for a year. After the first year, it was assumed that a man had learned enough to be elevated to the rank of ordinary seaman. Depending upon the individual's capabilities, in another two years he was generally upgraded to able seaman. To achieve the able seaman level he had to pass a test, usually administrated by the first lieutenant assisted by the boatswain or bosun. Obviously, if a man could pass the test, it mattered little how long he had taken to acquire the skills. Short-handed crews often saw qualified individuals accelerated through this process. Disease and battle casualties resulted in faster promotion of all ranks.

The manner in which seaman skills were acquired, was the main reason these time requirements had been introduced. At that time there were no formal courses or instruction for an individual prior to his acceptance on board His Majesty's vessels. It is estimated that up to fifty percent of all men on one of His Majesty's vessels were pressed. Typical training for a seaman was to pair him with a more experienced seaman and have the experienced man impart his knowledge to the other. Today, this is called on-the-job training or OJT. Many consider OJT as the best type of training. It certainly was well employed by the Royal Navy for decades. There are two major drawbacks to this type of training. The first is that it takes a much longer time to train an individual using this method. The second issue is that standards fluctuate. The source of your training is an indicator of your potential skill level. If you have a poor teacher, the resulting skills will be poor.

At more senior positions, the rate of promotion was slower. In any Royal Navy ship, Swift's logical promotion after able seaman would be to quartermaster, bosun's mate, or a similar position. The men on the wheel or helm were generally quartermasters. None of these positions required a man to read or write. At any higher position, a man required some ability to read or write because lists were involved. The captain of the ship rated a man for these positions based on the opinions of his first lieutenant and senior petty officers such as the bosun.

Teaching a man to read and write requires more formalized education, which most ships had limited capacity to undertake. The most formalized training on board His Majesty's ships was generally on larger ships. In fact, naval regulations even made provisions for a civilian officer teaching positions. The primary target for this instruction was the 'young gentlemen', later called midshipmen. There was no comparable training for the men.

A jump from able seaman to master's mate was very rare. A man who could read and write, and had the required skill, would be selected for a senior acting position before a man with skill who couldn't read or write.

Master's mates could attain their rank in a variety of ways. Most common was to be rated by the captain. This rating was only good as long as the captain retained command of the ship. A new captain could remove an existing master's mate, demote the man foreward, and replace him with a favourite. Although this occurred infrequently, it was still possible.

Another method of attaining the rank of master's mate was to be certified as a master. In this case, the individual had to pass a qualification examination administered by Trinity House. Generally, an individual who attempted this qualification needed three years of service, but that requirement could be waived. The qualification itself was difficult to attain. Additionally, it was no guarantee of a position as a master. Anyone attaining the certification could reasonably expect to gain a position as second master or master's mate on a ship-of-the-line before someone without the qualification.

When Swift was promoted aft to the rank of acting master's mate, he was ordered to be in the correct 'dress' for his next watch. During this period, there was no norm for uniforms for any rank. Regulations pertaining to naval uniforms came into effect in the summer of 1748. Each ship had rules as dictated by the captain. In general, officers were expected to dress like gentlemen. This meant they were required on most ships to wear a jacket, generally navy blue in colour with white or yellow piping or lapels to differentiate them from the men. Instead of wearing slops, they were expected to wear pants or more close fitting trousers as opposed to the looser clothing of the man foreward of the mast. A hat was always a part of the officer's uniform.

The position of midshipmen in the Royal Navy evolved considerably over time. In the late 1600's the position was a rating for an experienced seaman. The term is believed to be initially derived from where the rating was berthed "amidships". Beginning in 1661, boys aspiring to be naval officers were sent to sea by their families and paid as midshipmen. Beginning in 1677, the Royal Navy regulations for promotion to lieutenant indicated some service as a midshipman was required.

There were three categories of officers on one of His Majesty's vessels during the 1700's. The first group were officers responsible for ship maintenance. These included the master, boatswain, gunner, carpenter, sail-maker, master-at-arms and cook. Each of these was provided with a 'warrant' from the Navy Board. With the exception of the master, these 'warrant' officers, were considered senior 'petty' officers and had their own separate berthing area. The master was seen as a more senior officer than the petty officers, and was berthed in the officer's wardroom.

The second group of officers was civilian officers. These generally consisted of the purser, surgeon and chaplain (if the ship carried one). These were all berthed in the officer's wardroom.

The third group of officers were military officers -- the lieutenants and marine officers. Midshipmen were considered in this group, although inferior to the commissioned officers, as they held no commission. A different place was needed to berth these 'officers'. Hence the 'cockpit' evolved, at least on the larger ships.

In 1748, standardized uniforms for the Royal Navy were described in orders. The rank of midshipman and appropriate uniform dress was described in these orders. After that, the position continued to evolve so it was seen as an officer in training. By 1793, orders stipulated that a minimum of three years as a midshipman or master's mate and a total of six years at sea were required for promotion to lieutenant.

Although it would seem by this regulation that master's mates and midshipmen were equal, that was far from the truth. Master's mates generally were more experienced. They were also from the 'working class' as opposed to being 'gentlemen'. Class distinctions in the Royal Navy, as in all British society, were very important.

When a ship was paid off in the Royal Navy, the disposition of the serving crew was dependent upon the requirements of the service. If it were wartime, the bulk of the crew would be transferred to another vessel without any consideration to the individual. For a pressed man, it was like being pressed all over again. In some cases and with senior ratings especially, they were allowed to sign on to a different vessel at their current rank, depending upon the need for their services. If there were no need for the senior ratings, these individuals would be left 'on the beach' -- equivalent to getting laid-off today.

When a ship was laid up for long duration, the crew was generally paid off. Three key personnel remained with the ship. These were generally the gunner, the bosun and the carpenter. As the requirements onboard decreased, these positions were vacated, the carpenter usually being the last to leave. There are documented cases of a carpenter being with a ship from the time she was commissioned until she was decommissioned decades later.

The pay rate and pay process within the Royal Navy during this era and lasting well past the end of the Napoleonic wars was abysmal. The rates of pay were the same in 1790 as they had been since 1660. During the 1740's the rate of pay was approximately nine pounds per year for a landsman, and fourteen and a half pounds for an able seaman, before the amounts due to the purser were tabulated. An able seaman employed in the merchant marine could expect to earn forty-five pounds a year.

Men were not paid with any frequency. To see a ship six months or a year behind in pay was common. There were two reasons for this. The first and stated reason was to discourage desertion. Those in control of the navy believed that a man owed six months wages would be less inclined to desert. Statistics alone would disprove this theory. The second reason was the challenge of getting funds to the various ships. It took a month or more for a ship to sail to many of the duty stations. The Royal Navy didn't like having strong boxes with lots of cash on board. That would have been an incentive to mutiny or theft.

The normal pay process was to issue the man with a pay ticket or voucher instead of cash. This reduced the amount of cash to be transported; therefore it increased security. It did pose another problem. Virtually no merchant would accept the voucher at face value, if it was accepted at all. If they accepted it, it was at a discounted value. This led to the rise of money lenders. The average discount charged by these money lenders was between fifteen and twenty-five percent, but there are documented cases of as high as forty percent.

A typical man pressed into the navy as a landsman, therefore, was not paid for six months to a year after he was pressed. If it were a year, he would have earned nine pounds, less the cost of his slops, any luxuries, or other items acquired from the purser. The average man would receive between five and six pounds in vouchers. If he exchanged the voucher for cash, the total amount that he would likely receive was approximately four pounds.

The average general labourer or farm hand of the period had little or no skill, so pressed men used that position as a comparison for wages. The farm hand worked six days a week, normally dawn to dusk, as opposed to a landsman working seven days on shifts around the clock. The farm hand would often receive 'found' (food and lodging) as part of the job as did the sailor. Both would have to purchase their clothes and luxuries. Farm hand wages would average ten to twelve pounds annually before clothes and luxuries and eight to ten pounds after depending on how they spent their money. This was well over double what the average landsman received from the Royal Navy. The farm hand didn't have to put up with Royal Navy discipline and had much less risk (e.g., storms and battle injuries).

Pay and working conditions (e.g., lack of freedom, cruelty, etc.) were the main reasons for desertion from the Royal Navy.

Tenant farms of the era had the same challenges making ends meet as any tenant farmer in any era. The price of grain, which was a major cash crop, was roughly two pounds per five-bushel lot. This price fluctuated based on location, distance from market, the supply versus demand in the market and motivation of the buyers.

Very few tenant farmers had livestock other than chickens. There were multiple reasons for this. The first was the cost of the animals. A second is the amount of space required to maintain a cow or horse. That space is measured in acres, since pasture is necessary, as well as acreage for hay. For every acre needed for the livestock, it meant an acre less for cash crops. A third reason was that most tenant farmers had limited knowledge or no knowledge of animal husbandry -- they didn't need it, as they had no animals.

Normally someone in the area had horses or oxen to borrow or rent for ploughing or other uses. It was cheaper to rent for a day or two than to own and maintain for a year.

The cost of land in England circa 1746 ranged between one to two pounds per acre. Even marshland was sold as the owner had the right to hunt the property.

ABOUT THE AUTHOR

Alec Merrill served thirteen years as an officer in the Canadian Forces. He spent three years as the Chief of Emergency Services for Fisheries and Oceans Canada which includes the Canadian Coast Guard during events such as Hurricane Juan and Katrina. He has been a management consultant for over twenty years.

Made in the USA
Lexington, KY
08 February 2015